THE BRU

To Walker
fraw Uncle
Sandy & Aunt Gillian.
"NEW FREEDOM is
A NOBLE
THING"

THE BRUCE

THE HISTORY OF

ROBERT THE BRUCE
KING OF SCOTS

JOHN BARBOUR

TRANSLATED BY
GEORGE EYRE-TODD

MERCAT PRESS
EDINBURGH

First published by Gowans & Gray Limited, 1907
Reprinted in 1996 by Mercat Press
James Thin, 53 South Bridge, Edinburgh EH1 1YS

ISBN 1873644 582

Printed and bound by
The Cromwell Press Limited,
Broughton Gifford, Melksham,
Wiltshire

PREFACE

By reason of the archaic language in which it is written, Barbour's famous metrical history of *The Bruce* has long been a sealed book to all but expert students of ancient literature. It has now been translated for the first time in the hope that it may resume the popularity to which it is entitled by the splendid merits of its heroic tale.

John Barbour has long been looked upon as the father of Scottish poetry, and he occupies almost the same position in the literature of North Britain as the author of the *Canterbury Tales* does in that of the south. *The Bruce* is the earliest great poem we possess in the vernacular of the country. Other early Scottish poems, like "The Taill of Rauf Coilzear," "The Awntyrs of Arthure," "Sir Tristrem," and "The Pystyl of Swete Susan," were written in the more inflected language and in the alliterative and accented verse-forms of an earlier time. It was Barbour's *Bruce* which first defined and fixed the language of Scotland in the shape it was to keep as a literary vehicle for two hundred years, and it was Barbour's *Bruce* which definitely committed the poetry of Scotland to metre and rhyme, instead of the older alliteration and accent, as its distinguishing features. These were exactly the services which Chaucer rendered to the literature of Southern Britain at exactly the same time. And exactly as Chaucer's work remains the classic or standard of the English language before Shakespeare's day, so Barbour's remains the classic or standard of " Braid Scots" during the same period, to the Union of the Crowns.

Barbour and Chaucer were contemporaries, but
the Scottish "maker" was in no sense inspired
or stimulated by the work of the English poet.
Barbour, in fact, was considerably the elder, and
had finished his work before Chaucer had much
more than begun his. Barbour was born about
1316 or 1320, and he died in 1395, while Chaucer
was born in 1340, and died in 1400. And Barbour,
by his own statement, finished *The Bruce* in 1375,
when Chaucer had written little more than his
early translation of "The Romaunt of the Rose,"
the lament for his great patron's wife, "Blaunche
the Duchesse," and perhaps the first drafts of one
or two of his Tales. In 1357 and 1364 Barbour
had passports from Edward III. of England,
allowing him to journey to Oxford with certain
scholars and knights for purposes of study, and
he had similar permits in 1365 and 1368 allowing
him to travel with a suite through England to
France for purposes of scholarship. It has been
suggested that upon some of these occasions the
two poets may have met. But in 1357 Barbour
was a man of some forty years, and a great
church dignitary, Archdeacon of Aberdeen, while
Chaucer was a stripling of seventeen, a page in
the household of Elizabeth, wife of Lionel, Duke
of Clarence.

As a matter of fact, both poets derived their
inspiration from, and took for their first models,
the great romances of chivalry, which had been
introduced by the trouveres of Normandy, and just
then, in the fourteenth century, had reached their
greatest vogue and perfection. "The Romance of
Fierabras," which Barbour describes Robert the
Bruce as himself reciting to his companions while
they were two by two ferried across Loch Lomond,
was one of these productions; and again and again
the poet illustrates his poem with episodes from
others. It was from these romances that the
new fashion of metre and rhyme came into the
poetry of this country, and it was in their

octosyllabic measure and rhyming couplets that
Barbour wrote his great work. The poet's own
idea, indeed, was to write a romance, after the
fashion of the Arthurian, Charlemagnian, and
other romance cycles of his time, with the deeds of
the great Scottish king and his companions for its
subject. Thus near the beginning he announces,

> Lordingis, quha likis for till her,
> The Romanys now begynnys her.

In accordance with this poetic purpose his work
is written in a strain of noble sentiment which
befits well the high-hearted enthusiasm of that
heroic time. Many of its passages, too, as pure
poetry, can hold their own with anything in our
language of their vein. The famous panegyric
on Freedom, the portrait of James of Douglas,
and the description of Spring at Bruce's setting
forth from Arran, with many other passages,
remain classics of their kind.

But Barbour's purpose, after all, was not so
much poetic as historic. He was familiar, not
only with the Norman-French metrical romances,
and their translations in the vernacular, which
were the popular entertainment of his age, but
also with the historical rhyming chronicles which
were then in fashion. Robert of Gloucester and
Robert Manning, otherwise Robert of Brunne,
had both written their metrical chronicles of
British history in the earlier years of the century,
and Barbour himself, we know from Wyntoun,
followed the same example, and wrote a metrical
history of early Britain, founded, like theirs, on
the Brut of Wace, the Norman-French trouvere,
or perhaps on Wace's original, Geoffrey of Mon-
mouth, and describing the legendary descent and
deeds of the Scottish kings, from Brutus, great-
grandson of Æneas, to his own day. Clearly
the historic motive was strongest in Barbour's
mind. His opening lines declare his intention to
"say nocht bot suthfast thing." And as a result

we have a record, in eloquent and glowing phrase, which on all hands is admitted to be not only a noble masterpiece of poetic literature, but a trustworthy and minute account of the most thrilling and heroic period of Scottish history.

The general truth and accuracy of Barbour's narrative has never been questioned. Here and there the order of events is transposed. The great conspiracy of Lord Soulis, for instance, is made to come after the battle of Byland, instead of before it; Edward Bruce's assumption of kingship in Ireland is antedated by a few weeks; and the Earl of Arundel's expedition against Douglas is said to have been commanded by Sir Thomas of Richmond, who was only a knight in its ranks. These are but slight and trivial matters, detracting little from the general truth of the tale. It is true that Professor Skeat, in his notes to the latest edition of Barbour's poem, is inclined to treat as exaggerations some of the feats of personal prowess attributed to Bruce. And he and a still later critic, Mr. J. T. T. Brown, seem to consider the story of the Brooch of Lorne to be merely repeated in the later slaying of the three traitors in Carrick, and the three robbers at Cumnock. But such conclusions may be too hastily reached. The details of the three episodes mentioned are altogether different, and in no way improbable, and the king's single-handed slaughter of several assailants on these and other occasions becomes feasible enough when we remember that Bruce was not only of uncommon strength, but clad in complete mail, while his assailants were ill-armed peasants, or "naked ' men. There is the story, too, of Douglas setting forth with Bruce's heart for the Holy Land. This might have been looked upon as a mere embellishment in the style of the favourite romance literature of the period, and Mr. Brown indeed seeks to insist that it is a story taken by a later scribe from the romantic narrative of

Froissart, and embodied in Barbour's poem. But the whole event must have been well enough known to Barbour himself, who was a boy of twelve when it occurred; and if confirmation of the fact were needed for modern readers, it was supplied when the tomb of Bruce at Dunfermline was opened a hundred years ago, and the breast-bone of the royal skeleton was found sawn through.

Much more serious is another charge brought against Barbour's *bona fides*. In both of the extant manuscripts of the poem, the Robert Bruce who conquered at Bannockburn is made out to be the same person as the Robert Bruce who suffered indignity at the hands of Edward I. Several editors have argued that this travesty of truth was deliberately perpetrated by Barbour in order to cover up the fact that his hero had in reality been a knight at Edward's court, and had sworn homage to the English king; as if the indignity suffered by the grandfather justified the broken fealty of the grandson. Such a glaring figment, Sir Herbert Maxwell has said, is enough to render all that follows it, in the eyes of some people, of no historical importance. But Mr. J. T. T. Brown has happily shown that the whole mistake has arisen from a very slight corruption of the MSS. The passage in these MSS. runs,

> This lord the Brwyss *I spak of ayr*
> Saw all the kynryk swa forfayr,
> And swa trowblyt the folk saw he
> That he tharoff had gret pitte.

The same passage, quoted in *Wyntoun's Cronykil*, from an older and fuller MS. of *The Bruce*, altogether avoids the mistake:

> Quhen all this sawe the Brwss Robert
> *That bare the crowne swne eftirwart*
> Gret pytte off the folk he had
> Set few wordis tharoff he mad.

Barbour had the best of means for ascertaining
the events he described. In his youth he must
have known many of the personages who had
taken part in the great struggle, and again and
again he mentions his authority. In one case, the
exploit of Edward Bruce in Galloway, he even
names his informant:

> A knycht that then wes in his rowt, . . .
> Schyr Alane off Catkert by name
> Tauld me this taile as I sall tell.

The poet further was in close touch with the
court and its authentic sources of information,
while his clerical office brought him in his earlier
years into contact with the common people, their
songs, traditions, and impressions of the great
struggle which was only a matter of yesterday.
As a result Barbour's *Bruce* remains the chief
storehouse of information for the detail, character,
and circumstance which lend colour to the great
historic drama of the fourteenth century in Scot-
land. The accuracy of *The Bruce* was recognized by
Barbour's own contemporary, Andro of Wyntoun,
in his *Orygynale Cronykil of Scotland,* and a
century and a half later by the historian, Hector
Boece, both of whom excused their brevity in
dealing with the reign of King Robert by referring
their readers to Barbour.

The ascertained facts of Barbour's own life are
vouched for by no fewer than fifty-one entries
in contemporary documents. These entries the
editor of the latest edition of *The Bruce* has been
at the pains to extract and print verbatim in his
preface. They show the poet to have been not only
a churchman of high rank, but a man of affairs
of considerable note at the Scottish court, and
persona grata to the king. In the earliest of
them, the four permits to pass through England
above mentioned, the poet is already named Arch-
deacon of Aberdeen. He was named also in 1357
as one of the Scottish commissioners to arrange

at Edinburgh for the ransom of David II.,
then a prisoner in England, and it is possible
that his journey to England was in reality to
interview that king. But it is not till after the
accession of the first Stewart monarch that we
have a mention of his employment at court. In
1372 he was appointed clerk of audit to the house-
hold of Robert II. at Perth. In 1373, 1382, 1383,
and 1384 he was one of the auditors of exchequer,
and received various payments for his services.
In 1376 or 1377 he received from the king a gift of
ten pounds, probably in acknowledgment of the
first part of *The Bruce*, down to the battle of
Bannockburn, which was completed, according to
Barbour's own statement, in 1375. In 1378 he
received a perpetual pension of twenty shillings
sterling, which may have been a royal recognition
of the second part of the great poem. In the
entry, indeed, of the payment of the pension in
1428, the words are added, "qui compilavit librum
de gestis illustrissimi principis quondam domini
regis Roberti Bruys," which seems to connect the
pension with the work. In 1386 he received as
gifts from the king the sums of £5 and £6 13s. 4d.,
which may have marked the royal approval of
his second great work, *The Brut*. He had also a
crown wardship, and in 1388 King Robert granted
him a pension of £10, possibly in recognition
of the third great poem which, on Andro of Wyn-
toun's authority, is attributed to him, *The Stewartis
Orygenalle*. These facts are shown by entries in
the Exchequer Rolls of Scotland. Entries in the
Register of the Bishopric of Aberdeen show
Barbour to have taken an active part in the
affairs of the diocese, both temporal and spiritual,
and to other entries in the same record we are
indebted for knowledge of the fact that he
died on the 13th March, 1395. Even one of the
Archdeacon's petty lapses is on record, for in a
catalogue of the cathedral library the Register
contains the note that a missing book of decretals

had been lost "per magistrum Johannem Barbour."
There is evidence in the Register that the poet
took a real interest in the affairs of his own
prebend, the parish of Rayne in the Garioch.
His piety is shown by a deed dated there, in which
he assigned his pension of twenty shillings to the
cathedral chapter for the saying of a yearly mass
for the souls of himself, his parents, and all the
faithful dead.   And he appears to have died on
the scene of his proper labours, for a marble
memorial stone now on the inner wall of Aberdeen
Cathedral is said to have marked till a few
years ago his grave in the burying-ground
outside.

The text of Barbour's great poem has been
preserved in two manuscripts—one signed "J. de
R." and dated 1487, in the Library of St. John's
College, Cambridge, and another signed "Johannes
Ramsay," dated 1489, and bound up with a MS. of
The Wallace by the same hand, in the Advocates'
Library, Edinburgh.   There is also an edition of
The Bruce printed at Edinburgh by Andrew Hart
in 1616, which appears to have been taken from a
third and ampler MS. than either of the two
extant.   Of the more recent printed editions the
most important are Dr. Jamieson's of 1820, Cosmo
Innes's for the Spalding Club in 1856, Professor
Skeat's for the Early English Text Society in 1870,
and another by the same editor for the Scottish
Text Society in 1894.

Barbour's composition of *The Bruce* and other
poems has recently been made the subject of much
minute and interesting criticism.   Following the
criticisms of Köppel and Buss, Professor Skeat
rejects as by another hand some two thousand
lines in Lydgate's *Siege of Troy* in Cambridge
University Library, which were formerly believed
to be extracted from Barbour's lost poem, *The Brut*.
The reasons for rejection are certain "variations
in poetical expression, in small technical usages,
and in the rimes."   Against this criticism must be

noted the fact that the writer of the Lydgate MS. distinctly marks his quoted passages with the inscription, "Her endis Barbour and begynnis the Monk," and "Her endis the Monk ande bygynnis Barbour." The differences, too, between the style of the extracts and of *The Bruce* are balanced by the likenesses, and are not much greater than are to be found between the first and second parts of *The Bruce* itself.[1]

Mr. J. T. T. Brown, again, in his highly interesting volume, *The Wallace and The Bruce Restudied* (Bonn, 1900), declares for the fragments in the Lydgate MS. being Barbour's work, but holds against Professor Skeat, on the other hand, that Barbour's *Brut* and his *Stewartis Orygenalle* were one single work, referred to by Wyntoun under different names.

The point is indifferent here. Of more importance is the greater issue which forms the burden of Mr. Brown's treatise. His effort is to show that the "Johannes Ramsay" and "J. de R." who transcribed the MSS. of *The Bruce* were the same person, and that that person was otherwise "Sir John the Ross," or Ross Herald, mentioned in the Treasurer's Accounts as receiving twenty unicorns (£18 sterling) from James IV. in 1490, and in Dunbar's *Lament for the Makaris*, a few years later, as one of the notable poets of the time.

The conjecture is highly interesting, but Mr. Brown goes much farther. In order to provide a foundation for the poetic fame of Sir John the Ross he seeks to prove, first, that that personage was the substantial author of *The Wallace*, Henry

---

[1] A very striking falling off in style takes place in the poem after the description of Bannockburn. The subsequent narrative is marked by a looseness of treatment in recording facts, and an inadequacy in the description of great events, in singular contrast with the vigour, fulness, and general accuracy of the earlier books. Had the battle of Byland been described with the same detail and spirit as the battle of Bannockburn, it might have held almost as great a place in history.

the Minstrel merely furnishing the rough material
of the poem, and, second, that, in transcribing
Barbour's *Bruce*, he extensively improved and
embellished it. To prove his theory, Mr. Brown
cites numerous instances of striking similarity
between passages and expressions in *The Bruce*
and passages and expressions in works produced
after Barbour was in his grave.

This is not the place to enter upon the minute
details of so ingenious a thesis. It may only be
suggested that it is possible, in pursuit of a
theory, to set over-much value upon chance
likenesses of expression, and that in any case it
appears much more probable that later writers
borrowed expressions and ideas from a great and
famous poem like *The Bruce*, than that a late
transcriber set to work to make a minute and
marvellous mosaic out of Barbour's poem and
the works of a dozen other authors. This is the
view of Dr. Albert Hermann, whom Mr. J. T. T.
Brown quotes in a footnote.

Apart, however, from such criticism, there can
be no question of the transcendent merits of
Barbour's great epic. The work is full of passages
that are models of graphic force, natural descrip-
tion, and lofty moral apostrophe. Here and there
the pages are lit up with a flash of grim humour,
as when the Scots in Ireland on the verge of
starvation find their camp suddenly flooded, and
the poet declares that though O'Dymsy gave them
nothing to eat, he sent them plenty to drink.
And, for true tenderness and pathos, the story of
Bruce and the poor laundress, and the account
of the great king's death, must for ever remain
among the immortal things of our literature.

The translator cannot hope to have accomplished
his task to the complete satisfaction of every
admirer of the original work. In Barbour's case
the ordinary difficulties of translation are increased
by the fact that the language of Scotland in the
fourteenth century contained infinitely fewer

forms of expression than the language now in use, and the same epithet had perforce to do duty in a variety of ways and with a variety of meanings. But if the translation helps to render better known at the present day Barbour's matchless account of the adventures of the great Scottish king and his band of fighting heroes, with something of the atmosphere and temper of their time, the work will not have been undertaken in vain.

Professor Skeat's edition of *The Bruce*, published by the Scottish Text Society, has been almost exclusively followed in making the present translation. Apart from the admirably clear and carefully edited text, the translator desires to make the fullest acknowledgment to Professor Skeat's notes and glossaries for the elucidation of many obscure and difficult passages.

G. E.-T.

THE BRUCE

BOOK I

THE ENGLISH TYRANNY

STORIES are delightful to read, even if they be nought but fable. Therefore should stories that are true, if well told, have double pleasure for the hearer. The first pleasure is in the tale as a tale, and the second in the truth of it, that shews the happening right as it was. Thus truths wholesome for man's mind are made pleasant to his ear. Fain would I, therefore, set my will, if my wit suffice, to put in writing a true tale, that it endure henceforth in memory, that no length of time destroy it, nor cause it to be wholly forgotten. For stories of old time, as men read, picture to them the deeds of the stout folk that lived of yore right as if done before their eyes. And surely praise is fairly due to those who in their time were wise and strong, who spent their lives in great labours, and often, in hard stress of battle, won right great prize of chivalry and acquitted themselves of cowardice.

A

Such was King Robert of Scotland, brave of hand
and heart, and good Sir James of Douglas, so stout
a knight in his time that his achievement and
nobleness were renowned in far lands. Of them
I purpose to make this book. God grant that I
may so treat the matter, and bring it to an end,
that it say nought but truth.

When King Alexander, guide and leader of
Scotland, was dead,[1] the land lay desolate six
years and more, till the baronage at last came
together, and made diligence to choose a king—
one come of the ancestry of kings of the realm,
who should have most right to be their head.
But fierce envy made great dissension among
them. For some would have Baliol to be king
because he was come of the offspring of the eldest
sister; and others altogether denied that claim,
and said he should be king who was in as near
degree and come of the nearest male in a collateral
branch. They said succession to a kingdom was
not like that to lower fiefs, for there should
succeed no female while any male was to be found
of equal descent. They declared it was quite other-
wise than the method of lower inheritance, for
if this method were followed the next of kin,
whether man or woman, should succeed. For this

[1] Alexander III. fell over the crag at Kinghorn, March 16, 1286;
his granddaughter Margaret, the Maid of Norway, died October 7,
1290.

reason that party thought that without question the Lord of Annandale, Robert the Bruce, Earl of Carrick, should succeed to the kingdom.[1]

The Barons were thus at discord that could in no way be brought to settlement, till at last they all agreed that their whole argument should be sent in writing to Sir Edward, King of England, and he should swear that, without guile, he would decide the question which of these two should succeed to such an eminence: and let him reign that had the right!

This arrangement seemed to them the best, for at that time all was peace and quiet between Scotland and England, and they could not perceive the hurt looming towards them. Since the King of England had held such friendship and alliance with their king who was so noble, they trusted that he, as a good neighbour and friendly umpire, would judge in loyalty. But all otherwise went the game.

Ah! blind folk, full of all folly! Had ye bethought in your hearts the peril that might arise to you, ye had not wrought in that fashion—had ye taken heed how that king always, without rest, laboured to gain sovereignty, and by force to seize lands, like Wales and Ireland, bordering his own, that he put them to such bondage that their nobles

---

[1] Baliol was grandson of the eldest daughter of David, Earl of Huntingdon. Bruce was son of the second daughter.

must run on foot like rabble when he went to war! No man of Wales durst bestride a steed in battle, nor abide after nightfall in castle or walled town, lest he lose life or limb. In such bondage Edward held those that he overcame by his might. Ye might have seen he should seize by sleight what he could not by open force. Had ye taken heed what thraldom was, and had ye considered his custom, that grasped always, without giving again, ye should, without his decision, have chosen a king who might well and rightly have held the land. Wales might have been an example to you had ye foreseen. Wise men say he is happy who corrects himself by others' errors. For evil things may befall as well to-morrow as yesterday. But ye trusted in loyalty, like simple folk without guile, and knew not what should afterwards take place. In this wide world is none that shall for certain know things that are to befall; but God Almighty reserves to Himself the foreknowledge of the changes of all time.

In this manner were the barons agreed, and with their whole consent messengers were despatched to Edward, then warring against the Saracens in the Holy Land. And when he knew their embassy he made ready without delay, and left plans that he had made, and returned again to England. And presently he sent word to Scotland that they should meet together, and he would come

forthwith to do everything as they had written.
But he made sure, through their dispute, to find
a way, by craft and force, to seize the whole
sovereignty. And he said to Robert the Bruce,
" If thou and thy offspring for evermore wilt hold
of me in chief, I shall decide that thou be king."
"Sir," he answered, "as God will save me, I desire
not the kingdom, unless it fall to me by right;
and if God will that it do so, I shall hold it in
every way as freely as behoves a king, that is,
in freest royalty, as my ancestors did before me."
The other, enraged, swore that he should never
have it, and turned in wrath away. But Sir John
the Baliol assented to all his will, and through
that assent much evil afterwards befell. He was
king but a little space, and by great subtlety and
guile, for small reason or none, he was presently
arrested, and degraded from honour and dignity.
Whether this was wrong or right God Almighty
knows.

When the mighty King Edward had in this way
done his pleasure on John the Baliol, so soon con-
victed and undone, he forthwith went to Scotland,
and seized the whole country. So completely was
this done that both castle and town, from Wick
to the Mull of Galloway, were in his possession
and filled with Englishmen. Then he made Eng-
lishmen sheriffs and bailies and the other officers
of all kinds necessary for the government of a

country. These officers were so wholly cruel, wicked, and covetous, and so proud and disdainful, that Scotsmen could do nothing at any time to please them. The wives and daughters of the Scots they would often violate ruthlessly, and if any man were wroth thereat they lay in wait for him with greater harm, and soon found occasion to bring destruction upon him. And if any man had by him any thing of value, such as horse, or hound, that pleased their fancy, by right or wrong they would have it. And if any offered to gainsay them they would so deal that he should either lose land or life, or live in misery. For they doomed folk as they pleased, taking no heed to right or reason. Ah, how cruelly they doomed them! Good and gallant knights, for little or no cause, they hanged by the neck. Alas! that folk who had ever been free should, through their great misfortune and folly, be so wickedly treated as to have their foes for their judges. What greater wretchedness may man endure?

Ah! freedom is a noble thing. Freedom makes man to have zest in life, and gives him all comfort. He that lives free, lives at ease. A noble heart can have no ease, nor aught else to pleasure it, if freedom fail. For liberty to please oneself is desired above all things. Nor may he who has always been free well know the actual state, the suffering and wretchedness, that are coupled with foul thraldom. But if he had made trial of it, then should he know it all by heart, and should think freedom more to be prized than all the gold in the world. Thus evermore do untoward things make evident their opposites. He that is thrall has nought his own; all that he has is abandoned to his lord, whoever he be. He has not even so much freedom as to leave alone, or do, the desire of his heart. Clerks may question, when they fall into debate, whether, if a man bid his thrall do aught, and at the same time the thrall's wife come to him and demand her due, he should leave undone his lord's behest, and first pay his debt, and afterwards fulfil his lord's command, or leave his wife unpaid, and do what he is ordered. I leave the solution to them of more renown. But since they make such comparison between the duties of marriage and a lord's bidding to his thrall, ye may see verily, though none tell you, how hard a thing this thraldom is. For wise men know well that marriage is the strongest bond that any man can undertake. But thraldom is far worse than death. As long as a thrall lives it mars him, body and bones, while death troubles him but once. To put it shortly, none can tell the whole condition of a thrall.

In such manner and such bondage Scotsmen lived, both the poor and those of high rank. For of

the lords some were slain, and some hanged, and
some drawn, and some put fast in prison, without
reason or cause. And among others imprisoned
was Sir William, Lord of Douglas.[1] Of him they
made a martyr, for they slew him in prison, and
gave his fair lands to the Lord of Clifford. He
had a son, a little boy, then but a small page, but
afterwards of great prowess. His father's death he
so avenged that in England, I undertake to say,
there was none living that did not dread him.
For so many skulls he cleft that none alive can tell
the number. But wondrous hard things befell
him ere he was brought to his estate. No adven-
ture could dismay his heart, nor prevent his doing
the thing on which he was set. For he took
especial thought always to act advisedly. He
held that man of small account who should suffer
hurt from none; and he took thought to achieve
great things, and hard toils, and combats that
should double his fame. Wherefore, in all his
lifetime he was in great hardship and trouble.
Never would he yield to mischance, but would
drive the enterprise right to an end, and take
the fate God sent.

His name was James of Douglas, and when he
heard his father was so cruelly put in prison, and
that his whole lands were given to the Clifford,

---

[1] The elder Douglas had risen in arms with Wallace, but yielded
himself prisoner to Edward in 1297.

ONE POUND

SCOTTISH PARLIAMENT BUILDING

£1

The Royal Bank of Scotland plc

£1

SP1910075

The Royal Bank
of Scotland plc

PROMISE TO PAY THE BEARER ON DEMAND

ONE POUND
STERLING

AT THEIR HEAD OFFICE HERE IN EDINBURGH
BY ORDER OF THE BOARD
12TH MAY 1999

GROUP
CHIEF EXECUTIVE

Commemorating the
First Meeting of the

SCOTTISH
PARLIAMENT

£1

he indeed knew not what to do or say; for he had no means, nor was there any that knew him would do as much for him as see him sufficiently provided for. Then, utterly at his wit's end, he suddenly conceived the desire to voyage oversea, and stay in Paris for a time, and endure his misfortune where none knew him, till God sent him help. And as he thought, so he did. He set forth soon afterwards for Paris, and lived there very simply. Nevertheless he was glad and jolly, and gave himself to such thoughtlessness as youth demands, sometimes to ribald company. And that may ofttimes be of service, for knowledge of many conditions of life may be of use at times in many ways. So it befell Robert, the good Earl of Artois in his time; for frequently the feigning of ribald abandonment greatly served his purpose. And Cato tells us in his writings, "It is sometimes good sense to feign foolishness."

In Paris he dwelt nearly three years, and then came tidings oversea that his father was done to death. At that he was woeful and distraught, and thought he would return home, to see if he, through any effort, might regain his inheritance, and redeem his men out of their thraldom.

He came in haste to St. Andrews, where the Bishop received him most courteously and made him wear his knives, to carve before him at table, and clad him right honourably, and gave order

where he should lodge. There dwelt he a very
long time, and all men loved him for his nobleness,
for he was of most fair demeanour, wise, courteous,
and debonair. He was liberal and kind also, and
above all things loved loyalty.

The love of loyalty is a gracious thing. Through
loyalty men live righteously. With the virtue of
loyalty a man may come to be of high account,
and without it none, however strong or wise he
be, may win renown. For where it fails no bravery
can make a man so good as to be called simply a
good man.

Douglas in all his deeds was loyal, for he deigned
not to deal with treachery or falsehood. His heart
was set on high honour, and his demeanour such
that all who were near loved him. But he was not
so fair that we should speak greatly of his beauty.
In visage he was somewhat grey, and he had black
hair, I have heard tell. But his limbs were well
made, his bones great, and his shoulders broad.
His body was well formed and lithe, so they that
saw him have said to me. When he was blithe
he was lovable, and in company he was meek
and sweet; but whoever saw him in battle beheld
him of another countenance. In speech he lisped
somewhat, but that suited him right wondrous
well. To good Hector of Troy he might in many
things be likened. Hector had black hair, like him,
and limbs stark and right well made, and he

lisped also as Douglas did, and was compact of loyalty, and courteous and wise and strong. But in manhood and mighty strength I dare compare to Hector none that ever was in the world. Nevertheless the Scottish knight so wrought as to win great renown in his time.

Douglas dwelt at St. Andrews till it chanced that the proud King Edward came to Stirling with a great company to hold an assembly. Thither went many barons and among them the good Bishop William of Lamberton, taking with him this squire, James of Douglas.

The Bishop led him to the king, and said, "Sir, I bring you this child, who seeks to be your man, and prays you of your grace to receive here his homage and grant him his inheritance."

"What lands does he claim?" said the king.

"Sir, if it be your pleasure, he claims the lordship of Douglas, for his father was lord thereof."

The king then, extremely enraged, said, "Sir bishop, of a surety, if thou wouldest keep thy fealty make no such speech to me. His father was ever my cruel foe, and died for it in my prison. He was against my majesty, therefore am I entitled to be his heir. Let the boy go, get land where he may, for thereof assuredly he has none. The Clifford shall have his lands, for he has served me loyally always."

The bishop heard him answer thus, and durst

speak to him then no more, but went hastily from his presence, for he sorely dreaded his cruelty. The king did what he came to do, and went afterwards to England again with many a man of might.

Sirs, who care to hear, here now begins the romance of men that were in great distress, and experienced right great hardship ere they came to their desire; but afterwards, by God's grace and their great valour, despite their foes, one and all, they came to great estate and honour. Where God helps, what can withstand? In truth, their enemies were sometimes more than a thousand to one, but God Almighty, in His foresight, preserved the heroes to avenge the harm and the persecution done by that multitude of rascal folk to inoffensive, worthy people who could not help themselves. These heroes were like the Maccabees who, as the Bible says, with great bravery and valour fought many a stiff battle to deliver their country from evil bondage. They wrought so by their prowess that with few followers they won victory over mighty kings, and made their country free, for which their name should be praised.

This lord, the Bruce, of whom I spoke before,[1] saw all the kingdom so ruined and the folk so troubled

[1] Robert the Bruce, the hero of the poem, was really the grandson of Baliol's rival, who died in 1294. Barbour here, for epic purposes, uses a poetic licence.

that he was moved to great pity. But whatever
pity he felt he made no shew of it, till it chanced
that Sir John Comyn, as they came riding from
Stirling, said to him, "Sir, will ye not see how
this country is governed? They slay our folk
without cause, and hold the land without reason,
while ye should be its lord. If ye will trust me
ye shall cause yourself be made king. Provided
ye give me all the land now in your possession,
I shall be your helper. And if ye will not do
this, nor take such state upon you, let all my
land be yours, and let me take the state on me,
and bring the country out of bondage. For there
is neither man nor page in all this land that is
not fain to make himself free."

The Lord Bruce hearkened to what he said,
believing he spoke in honesty, and, since it pleased
his mind, he soon gave his assent, and said,
"Since ye so wish, I will blithely take the state
upon me, for I know the right is mine, and often
a just cause makes the feeble strong."

Thus the barons first came to agreement. And
that same night their bonds were written, and
oaths made, to secure what they had agreed upon.

But of all things, woe be to treason! For there
is neither duke nor baron nor earl nor prince nor
mighty king, though he be never so wise nor
strong, that can for ever be on guard against
treason. Was not all Troy with treason taken,

when ten years of the war were past. Many
thousands of those without had been slain by
the strong hand, as Dares tells, and Dictys,[1] who
knew all their state. Troy could not have been
taken by strength, but treason took the city by
deceit. And Alexander the Conqueror, who took
Babylon and the whole length and breadth of
the world in twelve years by his doughty deeds,
was afterwards, by great treason, destroyed with
poison in his own house,[2] dividing his land before
he died, and exciting great pity by his death.
Julius Cæsar, too, who by his bravery won Britain
and France, Africa, Arabia, Egypt, Syria, and all
Europe, and for his might and valour was first
made Roman Emperor, was afterwards stabbed to
death with daggers in his capital by those of his
secret council; and when he saw words might not
avail he closed his eyes with his hand, to die with
more honour. Also Arthur, who by his valiant
deeds, made Britain mistress and lady of twelve
kingdoms that he won, and further, as a noble,
gained in battle the freedom of all France, and
vanquished Lucius Iberius, then Emperor of Rome,
yet, notwithstanding all his great valour, was slain
through treason and wickedness, with other good

---

[1] Dictys of Gnossus and Dares the Phrygian, legendary authors of
accounts of the Fall of Troy.

[2] This was the account of Alexander's death given in the mediæval
romance.

men more than enough, by Modred his sister's son. Thereof "The Brut" bears witness.[1]

So this covenant-making fell out. For the Comyn rode to the King of England, and told the whole happening, though not, I trow, the whole truth of it. But he gave him the bond, which soon shewed the offence. For this afterwards, since he could offer no excuse for his deed, he suffered death.

When the king saw the bond he was enraged beyond measure, and swore that he should take vengeance on Bruce, who presumed to contend or rise or conspire in such ways against him. And Sir John Comyn, he said, should be rewarded highly for his loyalty; and Comyn humbly thanked him. Then Edward thought to have the rule of all Scotland without gainsaying, if once Bruce were brought to death.

But the fool's expectation often fails, and wise men's aims come not always to the ending they look for. Only God knows truly what shall befall. By His proper plan the matter fell out as I shall afterwards tell.

---

[1] Barbour is said to have written another great poem called "The Brut," but he is here probably quoting from Layamon's "Brut," which was derived from the French "Romans de Brut" of Wace, which again was borrowed from the Latin "History" of Geoffrey of Monmouth. From the same material, in Elizabethan times, Sir Thomas Malory derived his "Morte d'Arthur," and from this at a later day came Tennyson's "Idylls of the King."

Comyn took his leave and went home. And the king thereafter hastily called a parliament, and summoned thither the barons of his realm. And he sent to the Lord Bruce, bidding him come to that gathering. And he, having no knowledge of the treason or falsehood, rode to the king without more delay, and took lodging in London the first day of their meeting. Afterwards, on the morrow, he went to court.

The king sat in parliament, and there before his privy council he called the Lord Bruce, and shewed him the bond. The Bruce was in utmost peril of his life, but Almighty God, who would not that he died so, preserved him for higher things. The king handed him there the bond, to see the seal, and asked if he had sealed it. He looked at the seal intently, and answered him humbly, and said, "How foolish am I! My seal is not always with me; I have another to bear it. Therefore if it be your will, in order to see this letter and be advised of it, I ask respite till to-morrow when ye take your seat, and then without longer delay, I shall produce this letter here before your full council. For this I give in pledge my whole inheritance."

The king thought him worthy enough of trust, since he gave his lands in pledge, and he let him go with the letter, to produce it, as was agreed.

BOOK II

THE BATTLE OF METHVEN

THE Bruce went swiftly to his inn, right blithe, ye may well believe, that he had got that respite.[1] He called his marshal to him quickly, and bade him look to it that he made his men good cheer in every way, for he would be in his chamber a very great while, in private, with a clerk and no others. The marshal went to the hall, and did his lord's command. But the Lord Bruce, without more delay, caused two steeds to be brought secretly. He and the clerk, without more company, leapt on unperceived, and day and night, without sojourn, rode till on the fifth day they were come to Lochmaben.

There they found his brother Edward, who marvelled, I warrant, that they came home so privately. He told his brother the whole tale, of what had happened, and how he had escaped by chance.

[1] Wyntoun adds that the Duke of Gloucester sent Bruce a piece of money and a pair of spurs as a strong hint at this juncture.

It so fell that at the same time Sir John the Comyn made sojourn at Dumfries, close by. The Bruce mounted and rode thither, thinking, without more delay to quit him for his betrayal. He rode thither forthwith, and met Sir John the Comyn in the Greyfriars at the high altar, and with laughing countenance shewed him the bond; then with a knife, on that very spot, reft the life of him.

Sir Edmund Comyn too was slain, and others as well of much account. Nevertheless some say that the strife befell otherwise. But whatever made the conflict, well I know Comyn died of it.

There is no doubt that Bruce sinned there greatly, in giving no heed to the sanctuary of the altar. Therefore such hard mischance befell him that I have never heard tell in romance of a man so sore bested who afterwards came to such welfare.

Now go we again to King Edward. He on the morrow sat with his barons in parliament, and sent bold knights after the Lord Bruce, to his inn. When he had been often called, and they asked his men after him, they said that since yesterday he had remained constantly in his chamber, alone with a clerk. Then they knocked at his chamber, and when they heard none make answer, they broke the door. But they found nothing, though they sought all the chamber. Then they told the king the whole matter, and how Bruce had escaped. He was sore at his escape, and swore in wrath, most stoutly, that he should be drawn and hanged. He menaced as he meant to do, but Bruce thought things might go another way.

And when he, as I have said, had slain Sir John in the kirk, he went again to Lochmaben, and caused men to ride with letters in all directions to his friends. They came to him with their following, and he assembled his own men as well, and purposed to make himself king.

Word sprang over all the land that the Bruce had slain the Comyn. And letters reached, among others, the Bishop of St. Andrews, telling how that baron was slain. The letter told him all the deed, and he read it to his men, and afterwards said to them, "I hope the prophecy of Thomas of Ersildoun shall come true in him, for, so help me God! I have great hope he shall be king, and have all this land under his rule."

James of Douglas, that everywhere and always carved before the bishop, heard the reading of the letter, and he also took good heed to all the bishop said. And when the tables were set aside, and they went to their chamber, Douglas said to the bishop, "Sir, ye see how the English by force disinherit me of my land, and you have been made to understand that the Earl of Carrick claims to govern the kingdom, and that, because of the man he has slain, all Englishmen are against him, and would disinherit him gladly. Nevertheless I would go dwell with him. Therefore, sir, if it please you, I would take good and ill with him. Through him I trust to win my lands, despite the Clifford and his kin."

The bishop heard and had pity, and said, "Sweet son, so God help me, I would gladly that thou wert there, but, that I be not blamed, thou must go about the matter in this way. Thou shalt take my palfrey Ferrand, for there is no horse in this country so stout and well in hand. Take him as by thine own will, as if I had given no consent, and if his groom make any scruple, do thou take the horse in spite of him. So shall I be well excused. Almighty God, for his greatness' sake, grant that him thou goest to, and thou thyself, may be enabled to defend yourselves from your enemies!"

He gave him silver to spend, and his blessing, and bade him go his way, for he would say nothing till he was gone.

Douglas then made his way straight to the steed, as the bishop had bidden. The groom there resisted him angrily, but he, waxing wroth, felled him with a blow of his sword. Then, without longer stoppage, he saddled the horse hastily, and quickly leapt on his back, and rode forth without farewell.

Dear God, our Heavenly King, save him, and shield him from his foes!

All alone he took the road towards Lochmaben. And near Arickstone[1] he met the Bruce riding with a great company to Scone, to be enthroned and made king. And when Douglas saw him coming, he rode forward in haste, and greeted him, and made obeisance right courteously, and told him all his condition, what he was, and how Clifford held his inheritance. Also that he was come to do homage to him as his rightful king, and was ready in everything to share his fortune.

And when the Bruce had heard his desire he received him with much pleasure, and gave him men and arms. He felt assured he should be worthy, for his fathers all were doughty men.

Thus they made their acquaintance, that never afterwards by chance of any kind was broken while they lived. Their friendship waxed ever more and more, for Douglas served always loyally, and Bruce, valiant, strong, and wise, right gladly and well rewarded his service.

The Lord Bruce rode to Glasgow, and sent about till he had a great following of friends. Then he rode in haste to Scone, and without

---

[1] At the head of Annandale.

longer delay was made king, and set in the king's
seat, in the manner of that time.[1] But of the
nobles' great array, their service, and their royal
state, ye shall hear nothing now from me, except
that Bruce took homage of the barons who came
thither, and afterwards went over all the land
acquiring friends and friendship to maintain the
enterprise he had begun. He knew, ere all the
land were his, he should find hard enough fighting
with the English king. For there was none living
so fierce, so unscrupulous, and so cruel.

And when King Edward was told how the bold
Bruce had made end of the Comyn, and how he
had afterwards made himself king, he went very
nigh out of his mind, and called to him Sir
Aymer the Valence,[2] a knight wise, strong, and
capable, and bade him take men-at-arms, and go
to Scotland in all haste, and burn and slay and
raise the devil, and promise all Fife as a reward
to the man who should either take or slay his
enemy, Robert the Bruce.

Sir Aymer did as he bade. He had with him a
great company of knights. With him was Philip
the Mowbray and Ingram the Umphraville, a wise
and prudent and chivalrous knight, and they had
in their company the chief part of Scotland. For

---

[1] Bruce was twice crowned, on March 25, 1306, and again on
Palm Sunday, two days later.

[2] Earl of Pembroke, third son of the half-brother of Henry III.

at that time much of the country was still in English hands.

The Scots then went in a body to Perth, which at that time was walled all about, with many high embattled towers to defend it against assault. Therein dwelt Sir Aymer with all his chivalry. King Robert knew he was there, and the mettle of his captains, and assembled all his following. He had many of the greatest valour, but their foes were more than they, I have heard, by fifteen hundred. Nevertheless he had there at need full many doughty men, and barons bold as the wild boar. With him were the Earls of Lennox and Atholl, also Edward Bruce, Thomas Randolph,[1] and Hugh de la Haye, with Sir David the Barclay, and Fraser, Somerville, and Inchmartin. James of Douglas was there besides, though of little might as yet, and many other folk strong in battle, such as good Christopher Seton,[2] and Robert Boyd, a knight of great renown. I cannot tell the names of all. Though few, they were stout and full of valour.

In fair battle array they came before Saint Johnstoun,[3] and bade Sir Aymer come forth to

[1] Nephew of Bruce, and afterwards Regent.

[2] Bruce's brother-in-law, afterwards captured in Loch Doon and executed by Edward.

[3] The old name for Perth, from the still existing Kirk of St. John.

fight. And he, trusting in the might of those
with him, called his men hurriedly to arms. But
Sir Ingram the Umphraville thought it too great
a peril to go forth in open battle, while their
assailants were so arrayed, and he said to Sir
Aymer, "Sir, if ye will take my counsel ye shall
not go forth to attack them while they are
prepared for battle, for their leader is wise and
able, and a noble knight of his hands, and in his
company he has many a good man and stout.
There will be hazard in the attack while they are
so well arrayed. Only the greatest force would
put them now to flight. For when folk are well
arrayed, and fully prepared for battle, provided
they be all good men, they are far more assured
and to be feared than when they are somewhat
out of order. Therefore, sir, ye may say to them
that this night, if they will, they may go to their
quarters, and rest and sleep, and that to-morrow,
without longer delay, ye shall issue forth to battle,
and fight them, unless they fail to appear. So
shall they go to their quarters, and some shall
go foraying, and those that remain in quarters,
seeing they come off the march, shall shortly be
unarmed. Then in our best array may we, with
all our fair chivalry, ride right boldly upon them,
and they, expecting to rest all night, when they
see us in order of battle coming on them so
suddenly, shall be mightily dismayed, and ere they

be in fighting order we shall hasten to the attack.
Many a man, brave enough when prepared, will
tremble with fear when suddenly assailed."

They did as he advised, and sent to them with-
out, bidding them go to quarters for that night,
and come to battle on the morrow. And Bruce's
men, when they saw they could do no more,
made for Methven, and took lodging in the wood.
A third of them went foraging, and the rest
were soon unarmed, and scattered here and there
to rest.

Then Sir Aymer, with all his folk, issued in
great strength to the fight, and rode at a furious
pace straight upon Methven. The king, who was
then unarmed, saw them coming thus in force,
and cried loudly to his men, "To arms quickly,
and make you ready! our foes are at hand!"

They armed in the greatest haste, and leapt
hurriedly on their steeds. The king displayed his
banner when his men were come together, and
said, "Sirs, now may ye see how yonder folk
deceitfully seek to do by guile what they dare
not by strength. Now I perceive that he who
trusts his foe shall find himself rue it. Never-
theless, though our enemies be many, God may
give us the best of fortune. For numbers do not
make victory. As many a tale tells, a few folk
have often vanquished a host. Let us trust we
shall do the same. Ye are each one strong and

valiant, and accomplished in knightly deeds, and know right well what honour is. Act then so as to save your honour, and remember, he who dies for his country shall find quarters in heaven."

When this was said they saw their foes come riding near at hand in battle array.

Thus on either side they were prepared, and ready to attack. They couched their spears, and rode so rudely together that their weapons were all broken, and many men slain and sore wounded, the blood bursting out at their breast-plates. For the best and stoutest, eager to win honour, plunged into the strenuous conflict and dealt rude blows about them. In that crowd were to be seen brave and stout knights, some wounded and some slain, defiled under the horses' feet. The grass grew red with blood, and they that kept their saddles swept out their sturdy swords, and gave and took such fell strokes that the ranks shook about them. The Bruce's folk showed their knighthood full manfully, and he himself above the rest gave such hard and heavy dints that wherever he came the enemy made way. His followers made hard endeavour to stem the mighty onset of their foes, who by that time had so much the best of the fight that they won ground ever more and more. The king's few folk were nearly overcome, and when Bruce saw them begin to fail, mightily vexed he shouted

his battle-cry, and rushed so furiously into the
fight that all the battle shook. He cut to pieces
all whom he overtook, and dealt them blows
while he could hold out, and cried out to his
followers, "On them! on them! they weaken
fast! this conflict cannot last longer!" And with
that word he hewed away with such good will
and hardihood that whoever had seen him in
that strife could not but own him a doughty
knight.

But though he was bold and stout, and others
as well of his company, no bravery could avail
them, for their followers began to give way, and
fled all scattered here and there. But the true
men, fired with rage, stood their ground and
held the battle, gaining themselves endless honour.

And when Sir Aymer saw the small folk all
flee, one after another, and so few abide to fight,
he rallied a body of knights, and rushed with his
cavalry so boldly into the press that he over-
threw his foes each one. Sir Thomas Randolph
was taken, a young bachelor at that time, and
Sir Alexander Fraser, and Sir David the Berkeley,
with Inchmartin, and Hugh de la Haye, and
Somerville, and many others; and the king him-
self was in direst peril through Sir Philip the
Mowbray, who rode most boldly at him, and
seized his rein, and cried "Help! help! I have
the new-made king!"

With that Christopher Seton, when he saw the king thus seized by his foe, came spurring straight, striking to right and left, and dealt Mowbray such a blow that, though he was of great strength, it made him reel dizzily, and had sent him altogether to the ground but that he held by his horse. Then he let go the king's bridle, and Bruce, raising his battle-cry, rallied his men at hand. These were so few, however, that they could no longer bear the brunt of the fight. They pricked, therefore, out of the press, and the king, vexed to see his men flee, said, "Sirs, since fortune runs against us here, it were best to pass from this danger, till God presently sends us grace, and it yet may happen, if they pursue, we shall requite them somewhat in turn."

To this they all agreed, and retreated at the gallop. Their foes also were weary, and made no chase, but held their way straight to the town with their prisoners, being right glad and joyful for their capture. That night they all lay in the town, none of them, for all their renown and hardihood, daring to lodge without the wall. So sorely did they dread the return of the doughty King Robert.

Presently they wrote to the King of England, telling all they had done. And he was glad of the tidings, and for despite bade hang and draw all the prisoners, many as they were. But this Sir Aymer did not do. To some he gave both land and life to leave the Bruce's fealty, and serve the King of England, to hold their lands off him, and make war on Bruce as their enemy. Thomas Randolph was one of these, who in return for his life became their man. Of others then taken some were held to ransom, some slain, and some hanged and drawn.

In this manner was the Bruce repulsed. He made much mourning for his men slain and taken. He was also so much at a loss that he trusted firmly in none save those of his company. These were so few that five hundred was nearly all his following. His brother, the bold Sir Edward, was always by him, and a bold baron, Sir William the Barondoun. The Earl of Atholl also was there. But always after they were discomfited the Earl of Lennox was absent. He was right hard put to it ere he met the king again, but always maintained himself doughtily as a man of might. The king had also in his company James of Douglas, active, wise, and prudent; also Sir Gilbert de la Haye, Sir Neil Campbell,[1] and many others I cannot name. Many a day they went like outlaws in the mountains, suffering misery, living on flesh and water. He durst not

[1] Ancestor of the house of Argyll. He married Lady Mary Bruce, sister of the king.

go to the plains, for all the common folk forsook
him, and were fain, for their lives, to come again
into the English peace. Thus ever go the people.
None can put trust in the commons unless he be
their protector. So they left Bruce then. Since
he could not defend them from their foes they
turned to the other side. But the bondage they
were brought to feel made them wish heartily for
his success.

He lived thus in the hills till the greater part
of his following were ragged and torn. They
had no shoes but those they made from skins.
Therefore they went to Aberdeen, and there to
meet them came Neil the Bruce, and the queen,
and other fair and noble ladies, each for love
of her husband. For true love and loyalty they
would be partners of their pains, choosing rather
to take sorrow and suffering with them than to
be separated. For love is so powerful that it
makes all sufferings light, and often it gives
tender creatures such strength that they will
endure great sufferings and take any fortune
that may befall, provided that by it they may
succour their loved ones.

We read how, at the taking of Thebes, when
King Adrastus' men were slain in assailing the
city,[1] the women of his country came to fetch

[1] The incident belongs to the war of the Thebans against the
Argives, and is narrated in the *Thebais* of Statius, lib. xii.

him home. When King Capaneus, with the help
of Menestius, who came by chance riding thereby,
with three hundred in company, and at the
king's prayer joined the attack, had failed to take
the town, the women pierced the wall with
pikes, so that the assailants all entered, and
destroyed the tower, and slew the people. After-
wards, when the duke had departed, and all the
king's men were slain, the women carried him
to his country, where no man but he was left
alive. Much comfort is there in women, and
great solace in many ways.

So it proved here, for their coming right greatly
rejoiced the king. Nevertheless he himself kept
watch each night, and took his rest during the
day.

There he sojourned for some time, and mightily
refreshed his men, till the English heard that he
lay there with his following, at ease and secure.
They hastily got together their host, and trusted
to surprise him. But he, wise in all he did,
knew of their muster, and where they were.
He knew they were so many that he could
not fight against them. Hastily he caused his
men to be set in array, and prepared to ride
from the town. The ladies rode by his side, and
they made their way to the hills. There they
had great lack of provision, but the stout James
of Douglas ever laboured and busied himself to

procure the ladies food, and would get it in
many ways. Sometimes he brought them venison,
and sometimes he made snares to take pike and
salmon, as well as trout, eels, and minnows.
Sometimes a foray was made, and provision
procured in that way. Each man strove to get
food for the ladies, but there was not one of
them all of more service than James of Douglas.
The king himself was often helped by his shrewd-
ness and activity. Thus they contrived to live till
they came to the head of the Tay.

BOOK III

THE KING A FUGITIVE

IN that region dwelt the Lord of Lorne, the
king's deadly enemy for the sake of his uncle,
John Comyn.[1] He planned to take a cruel ven-
geance. When he knew the king was so near
he mustered his men, and was joined by the
barons of Argyll. They were a force of a full
thousand or more, and made to surprise the
king.

Bruce was well aware of their coming. He
had all too few with him, nevertheless he boldly
awaited them, and a large number at their first
meeting were laid low. The king's men bore
themselves right well, and slew, and felled, and
dealt sore wounds. But the men of the other
side, being every one on foot, fought so fiercely
with axes that they slew many of the horses of
Bruce's men, and gave wide wounds to some of

[1] Alastair MacDougal, Lord of Lorne, had married Comyn's
third daughter, and was therefore his son-in-law, not his
nephew.

the riders. James of Douglas was hurt, and also Sir Gilbert de la Haye.

The king, seeing his men dismayed, shouted his battle-cry, and charged the enemy so boldly that he drove them back, and overthrew many. But when he saw they were so numerous, and saw them deal such dread strokes, he feared to lose his men. Therefore, rallying his followers about him, he said, "Sirs, it were folly for us to combat more, for many of our steeds are slain, and if we fight further we shall lose some of our small band, and be ourselves in peril. Therefore methinks we are best advised to withdraw, defending ourselves, till we come out of danger, for our stronghold[1] is near at hand."

They withdrew then in a body. The retreat however, was not cowardly, for they held together, and the king devoted himself to defending the rear. With such valour did he do this that he rescued all the fleeing host, and so stopped the pursuers that none durst leave the main body. So well did he defend his men, and so stoutly did he prove his prowess, and so often did he turn to face his foes, that whoever had seen him then must have held him indeed worthy to be king of a great realm.

[1] Local tradition has it that after this fight at Dalree, Bruce took refuge in the island castle in Loch Dochart, a few miles to the east.

When the Lord of Lorne saw his men stand
in such awe of the Bruce that they durst not
follow the pursuit, he was mightily vexed, and
for wonder that one solitary man should baulk
them, he said, "Methinks, MacMurdoch,[1] as Gaul,
the son of Morni,[2] was wont to save his followers
from Fingal, so this leader has saved his folk
from us!"

The comparison thus made was but indif-
ferent. More aptly might he have likened Bruce
to Gaudifer of Larissa in the fray in which
the mighty Duke Betys assailed the forayers in
Gadyris.[3]   When King Alexander succoured his
men, Duke Betys took flight and would not abide
the battle, but Gaudifer, bold and stout, gave
himself so valiantly to save the fugitives and
dismay the pursuers, that he bore to earth Alex-
ander himself, with Ptolemy and Caulus, as well
as Dauclene and others besides. But at last he
was slain there himself, and in this the likeness
failed; for Bruce right chivalrously defended all
his company, and was set in the greatest danger,
and yet escaped whole and sound.

---

[1] The unknown person here addressed by Lorne was probably
the chief of the MacMurdochs, or Murchisons, a sept afterwards
famous in the region.

[2] A famous hero of the Ossianic poems.

[3] The reference is to an episode in the romance of Alexander
the Great, one of the favourite sources of entertainment in
Bruce's time.

There were two brothers, the boldest in all
that country, who had sworn that if they could
see the Bruce in a place where they might come
up with him, they should either die or slay him
there. Their name was MacIndrosser, or "sons
of the door-ward."[1] They had a third man in
their plot, right stubborn, wicked, and fierce. When
they saw the well-known figure of the king
riding thus behind his people, and saw him so
often face about, they waited till he was entered
in a narrow place, between a loch and a hillside,
a place so strait that he could not well turn
his horse.[2] Then they went wildly at him. One
seized his bridle, but the king dealt him such a
stroke that arm and shoulder flew from him.
With that another took him by the leg, thrusting
his hand between the foot and stirrup. And
when the king felt the hand there he stood
firmly in his stirrups, and struck spur into his
steed, so that it dashed quickly forward, and the
man lost his footing, while, despite him, his hand

[1] De Soulis, one of the fifteen competitors for the Scottish
crown, based his claim on his descent from Alan the Durward of
Alexander II.'s time, who married an illegitimate daughter of
that king. The Durwards were therefore as bitter enemies of
Bruce as Comyn and Baliol.

[2] The Battle of Dalree took place, according to the chronicler
Fordoun, Aug. 11, 1306. It was fought in the valley of the
Dochart, near St. Fillan's Pool, a mile or so below Tyndrum.
Bruce was probably attacked by the MacIndrossers in the narrow
pass between the moraines and the river.

remained under the stirrup. At that moment the third, bounding up the hillside, leapt on the horse behind the Bruce. The king was then in the greatest difficulty. Yet, with presence of mind as in all his deeds, he set himself to do an unheard of feat. Forthwith he lifted the man at his back, against his will, and in spite of all his efforts, laid him straight in front, then with the sword gave him such a stroke that he cleft the skull to the brain. The man crashed to the earth all red with blood, slain on the instant. Then the king struck hard at the other whom he dragged at his stirrup, and slew him at the first blow. In this way he delivered himself from all these three fierce foes.

When the men of Lorne saw the Bruce so stoutly fend himself none dared assail him further, so greatly did they fear his strength. There was a baron, MacNaughton, who in his heart took great heed of the king's feats of arms, and admired him greatly in secret. He said to the Lord of Lorne, "Assuredly ye now behold retreating the starkest man of might that ever ye saw in your life. For yonder knight, by his doughty act and amazing manhood has slain in short space three men of great strength and pride, and so dismayed all our host that no man dare go after him, and so often does he turn his steed that it would seem he has no dread of us."

Then said the Lord of Lorne, "I'faith, it seems
to pleasure thee that he slays our folk in yonder
fashion."

"Sir," said MacNaughton, "God knows, saving
your presence, it is not so. But whether he be
friend or enemy that wins the praise of knightly
deed, men should speak loyally thereof. And
assuredly, in all my time, I never heard tell, in
song or romance, of one who so quickly achieved
such a great feat of arms."

While they spoke thus of the king, he rode
after his people, and led them to a safe place
where he had no fear of his foes.[1] And the men
of Lorne departed lamenting the hurt they had
suffered.

That night the king set watch and gave order
that his folk should eat, and bade them take
comfort and make merry as they might. "For
dejection," said he, "is the worst thing possible.
Through much dejection men fall to despairing,
and if a man be in despair, then is he van-
quished utterly. If the heart be discouraged the
body is not worth a mite. Therefore," said he,
"above everything, keep you from despair, and
think, though we now suffer hurt, that God may

[1] After the fight at Dalree Bruce is said by tradition to have taken
refuge in the castle on the island in Loch Dochart. Another
tradition says that he retreated farther, to a great cave at the
head of Balquhidder.

yet give us good relief. We read of many that were far harder bested than we are yet, and God afterwards lent them such grace that they came fully to their intent. Rome was once thus hard beset, when Hannibal, after vanquishing the Roman army,[1] sent to Carthage three bushels of rich stone rings taken from the fingers of knights, and forthwith marched upon Rome to destroy the whole city. Great and small within the city would have fled before his coming had not the young Scipio threatened to slay them if they took flight, and so turned them again. Then, to defend the city, he freed the slaves, and made them knights every one, and took from the temples the arms borne by their fathers, which had been offered there in name of victory. And when these stalwart and active carls were armed and arrayed, and saw that they were free, they determined rather to die than let the town be taken, and with common assent, as one man, they marched forth to fight Hannibal, where he stood in great might arrayed against them. But by God's grace there fell so heavy and terrible a rain that even the stoutest could not withstand it, but sped in haste, the one side to their tents, the other to the city. Thrice in this way the rain stopped the battle. When Hannibal saw this miracle he left the town with all his great armed

[1] At the battle of Cannae, 2nd Aug. 216 B.C.

host, and went his way; and he was afterwards
so assailed by the forces of that city that he lost
both land and life.

"By the example of these few, who so valiantly
overcame such a mighty king, ye may see
that no man should despair, nor let his heart
sink for any misfortune that may befall. For
none knows in how little space God may be
gracious. Had the people of Rome fled, their
foes would quickly have taken the city. There-
fore should men, in time of war, set their
endeavour always to withstand the might of
their enemies, either by force or stratagem, and
expect ever to compass their design, and if the
choice lie before them—to die or to live as
cowards—they should rather die valorously."

In this fashion the king encouraged his fol-
lowers. And, to fortify them he brought to
mind old tales of men sore bested, and battered
hard by fortune, who yet won success at last.
"They that would keep their hearts undismayed,"
he said, "should ever steadily expect to bring
their enterprise to a successful end. Thus did the
valiant Cæsar, who laboured always so busily,
and with all his might, to accomplish his intent,
and who deemed that he had done nothing
at all so long as ought remained to do. For
this reason, as may be seen in his story, he
achieved great things. From Cæsar's unbending

will it may be seen—and the thing also stands
to reason—that he who forms his plan firmly,
and pursues it steadily, without fainting or
tempting of Providence, provided the thing be
feasible, and unless he be the more unfortunate,
shall achieve it in part, and if he live long
enough, may accomplish it all. Therefore should
none despair of achieving the greatest purpose.
If it happen that he fail in it the fault lies in
his effort."

Thus he spoke to them, and feigned to make
better cheer than he had ground for; for his
cause went from ill to worse. They were ever in
such difficult journeying, that the ladies began to
fail, and might no longer endure the toil. There
were others also in the same plight. John, Earl
of Atholl, was one of these. When he saw the
king defeated twice, and so many rise against
him, and life in such toil and peril, his heart
began altogether to fail him. And one day he
said to the king, "If I durst speak to you, we
live in so much fear, and have often such want
of meat, and are ever in such journeying, with
cold and hunger and want of sleep, that for
myself I count not life worth a straw. These
sufferings I can no longer endure, and though I
should die for it I must rest, wherever it be.
Leave me therefore, I beg of you."

The king saw that he was overcome as he

said, and outwearied with toil, and answered,
"Sir Earl, we shall take order soon what may
best be done. Wherever ye be God grant you
defence from your enemies!"

With that he forthwith called those most privy
to him, and among them they thought it best
that the queen, the earl, and the ladies should
at once go to Kildrummy with Neil the Bruce.
For it was thought they might dwell securely
there so long as they were well provisioned, since
the castle was so strong that it could hardly be
taken by force while there were men and meat
inside.

Forthwith they did as they agreed. The queen
and all her company mounted and fared forth.
Men there might have seen the ladies weep at
the leave-taking, and their faces wet with tears,
and knights, for their love's sake, sigh and weep
and make lament. They kissed their loves at
parting, and the king bethought him of a plan.
Thenceforth he would go on foot, and take good
and evil fortune as a foot soldier, and would
have no horsemen with him. So he gave all his
horses to the ladies, who needed them.

The queen rode forth on her way, and came
safely to the castle, where her people were well
received, and comforted well with meat and drink.
But no comfort could keep her from thinking
of the king, who was so sore bested that he had

but two hundred with him. The relief greatly
helped the queen's little band. God Almighty
help the king!

The queen dwelt thus in Kildrummy, and the
king and his company, after sending away their
horses, wandered among the high mountains and
endured much suffering, for it was near winter,
and so many enemies were about them, that all
the country warred against them. Such dire hard-
ship assailed them then, with hunger, cold, and
bitter showers, as indeed none living can describe.
The king saw how hard pressed his people were,
and the sufferings they endured, and he saw
winter coming near, and felt he could not hazard
the cold lying out in the hills, and the long sleep-
less nights. He resolved to go to Cantyre, and
sojourn there till winter was past, when without
more delay he should return to the mainland, and
drive his fate to a final issue. And since Cantyre
lies in the sea, he sent before him Sir Neil
Campbell, to get boats and food, setting a certain
time when he should meet him at the coast.

Sir Neil Campbell, with his company, departed
forthwith, leaving his brother with the king, and
he so wrought that in twelve days he procured
boats in plenty, and a great abundance of
victuals, thus making noble provision. His kins-
men dwelt in that region, and they helped him
right willingly.

After he was gone the king took his way to
Loch Lomond, and came there on the third day.[1]
But no boat could be found at the place to bear
them over the water. Then were they greatly
disheartened, for it was far to go about, and
they were in doubt besides that they might
meet their wide-spread enemies. Therefore they
sought busily and diligently along the loch-side,
till at last James of Douglas found a little
sunken boat, and drew it with all speed to land.
But it was so small that it could carry but three
at a time over the water.

They sent word of it to the king, who was
joyful at the discovery. He went first in the
boat, and Douglas with him. The third was one
who rowed them quickly across, and set them
on dry land. The boat was rowed so constantly
to and fro, fetching over always two at a time,
that in a night and a day all were brought
across. For some of them could swim well, and
bear a burden on their back, and so with swim-
ming and rowing, all were brought over, with
their baggage. The king, the while, merrily read
to those beside him the romance of the valiant
Fierabras,[2] who was gallantly overcome by the

[1] A cave in Craigroyston, under Ben Lomond, is pointed out as
the place where Bruce took up quarters.

[2] The famous Romance of Fierabras was printed for the Roxburgh
Club in 1854.

doughty Oliver; and how the Twelve Peers of
France were besieged in Egremont by King Balan
and more thousands than I can say. And they
within were only eleven, and a woman,[1] and were
so beset that they had no food but what they
won from their foes. Yet they so bore them-
selves that they held the tower manfully till
Richard of Normandy, despite his enemies, apprised
the king.[2] He was joyful at the tidings, for he
supposed they had all been slain. Therefore he
turned again in haste, and won the bridge Man-
treble, and passed the river Flagot, and presently
severely defeated Balan and all his fleet, and
freed his men, and won by his valour the nails
and spear and crown that Jesus had borne, and
a great part of the cross.[3]

Thus the Bruce encouraged those beside him
and made them sport and diversion till all his
people were ferried across.

When they had passed the broad water, though
they had many enemies they made merry and
were blithe. Nevertheless full many times they
had the greatest lack of food. For this reason,
in order to get venison they went in two parties.
The king himself was in one, and Sir James of
Douglas in the other. They took their way to

---

[1] Florippa, daughter of Balan.   [2] Charlemagne.

[3] Relics carried off from Rome by Fierabras, and thus recovered
by Charlemagne.

the hills, and hunted a great part of the day,
and searched woods, and set snares; but they
got little to eat.

It happened by chance at that time that the
Earl of Lennox was among the hills, near that
place, and when he heard the horn-blowing and
shouting he wondered what it could be, and he
enquired in such a way that he knew it was
the king. Then, without more delay, with all
his company he went straight to the Bruce.
He could not have been more glad and joyful,
for he believed the king was dead, and was so
much at a loss that he durst rest nowhere.
Since the king was defeated at Methven he had
heard no certain news of him. Therefore with
the greatest delight he very humbly greeted
him, and Bruce welcomed him right gladly, and
kissed him very tenderly, and all the lords were
right joyful of that meeting, and kissed him in
great delight. It was most touching to see how
they wept for pity and joy when they met their
friends that they thought dead. They welcomed
him most heartily, and he for pity wept again,
being never so glad of a meeting.

Though I say they wept, it was no real
weeping. For I trow, verily, that weeping comes
to men as a displeasure, and that none weep
without vexation, except women, who can wet
their cheeks with tears when they list, though

often enough nothing hurts them. But I know
that, whatever such weeping may be called, great
joy or pity may cause men to be so moved that
water will rise from the heart and wet the eyes
like tears, though it be not so in fact. For when
men indeed weep the heart is sorrowful or vexed,
but weeping for pity, I trow, is but an opening
of the heart shewing the tender ruth it contains.

The barons thus by God's grace were come
together. The earl had food in plenty, which he
gladly gave them, and they ate it very gladly,
asking for it no sauce but appetite, for their
stomachs were well scoured. They ate and drank
what they got, and gave praise and thanks to
God with glad hearts that they had met their
friends. The king then earnestly enquired how
the earl and his folk had fared since he saw
them. And they related the piteous adventures
and distresses and poverty that had befallen
them. The king had great sympathy with them,
and told them in return the sorrowful distress,
toil, and suffering he had himself endured. There
was none, high or low, among them but felt
pity and pleasure at the remembering of these
past perils. For when men are at their ease it is
wondrous pleasant to speak of bygone suffering,
and the recounting of their old distress gives
them encouragement and comfort. In this there
is no blame, dishonour, shame, or wickedness.

After the meal, and when he had done asking
questions, the king rose and got ready, with his
company, and made haste towards the sea, where
Sir Neil Campbell met them with food, sails,
oars, and all things to speed their passage. Then
they embarked, without more ado, some taking
the helm and some the oar, and rowed by the
Isle of Bute. There might be seen many a noble
youth casting his eyes along the coast as he rose
on the rowing oars; and fists, strong and square,
used to the spanning of spears, might be seen
spanning oars so earnestly that the skin often
was left on the wood. For all were employed,
knight and knave; there was none that could
be spared from steering and rowing, to further
them on their passage.

But at the time when they were taking ship
the Earl of Lennox, I know not by what chance,
was left behind with his galley till the king was
far on his way. And when the people of his
country knew that he lingered behind, they
followed him in boats. He saw that he had not
force enough to fight these traitors, and that he
had no succours nearer than the king's fleet, so
he hastened after it. But the traitors followed
him so fast that they were near overtaking him.
In spite of all he could do they came ever
nearer and nearer. And when he saw them so
near that he could even hear their threats, and

them still coming nearer, he said to his men: "Unless we find some stratagem we shall very shortly be overtaken. Therefore I counsel that, without waiting longer, we cast into the sea everything save our armour, and when the ship is so lightened we shall make such speed that we shall easily escape them. For they will delay to pick up our belongings, and we shall row without resting till we be escaped."

They did as he planned, and lightened their ship, and rowed with all their might, and she, being lightly built, sped sliding through the sea. And when their enemies saw the things floating more and more about them, they took them, and presently turned again, and so lost all their trouble.

When the earl was thus escaped, with his followers, he hastened after the king, who had then arrived in Cantyre. The earl told him all his adventure, how he had been chased at sea by those who should be his own people, and should certainly have been taken had he not heaved out all he had to lighten the ship, and so escaped.

"Sir Earl," said the king, "since thou hast escaped we shall make no complaint of the loss, but I will say one thing, that it is folly to pass often from my host. For constantly, when thou art away, thou art stiffly assailed. Therefore

D

methinks it were best for thee always to keep near me."

"Sir," said the earl, "it shall be so. I shall in no wise pass far from you till by God's grace we are strong enough to hold our purpose against our foes."

Angus of Islay was at that time lord of Cantyre. He right well received the king, and undertook to be his man, and him and his in many ways he devoted to his service. For greater security he gave him his castle of Dunaverty[1] to dwell in at his pleasure. The king thanked him greatly, and accepted his service. Notwithstanding, in many ways he ever feared treason, and therefore, I have heard tell, trusted securely in none till he knew him utterly. But whatever fear he had, he showed always a fair countenance, and in Dunaverty he dwelt three days and more.

Then he made his men prepare to go over sea to Rathlin. This is an island midway between Cantyre and Ireland, where the tides run as strong and perilous to sea-farers as is the Race of Brittany or the Strait between Morocco and Spain. They set their ships to the sea, and made

[1] The ruined stronghold of Dunaverty still stands on its tremendous precipice at the extremity of Cantyre. It was here at a later day that Alister M'Donald, " Colkitto," the lieutenant of Montrose, with three hundred Highlanders, after a gallant defence surrendered to the Covenanting general on assurance of their lives, and were afterwards put to death.

ready anchors, ropes, sails, and oars, and all
things needed for a voyage. When they were
prepared, they set out with a fair wind. They
hoisted sail and fared forth, and quickly passed
the Mull, and soon entered the tide-race. There
the stream was so strong that wild breaking
waves were rolling as high as hills.

The ships glided over the waves, for they had
the wind blowing from the right point. Never-
theless had one been there he must have seen a
great commotion of ships. For at times some
would be right on the summit of the waves, and
some would slide from the heights to the deeps,
as if they would plunge to hell, then rise sud-
denly on a wave while other ships at hand sank
swiftly to the depths. Much skill was needed to
save their tackle in such a press of ships, and
among such waves; for, ever and anon, the
waves bereft them of the sight of land when
they were close to it, and when ships were
sailing near, the sea would rise so that the
waves, weltering high, hid them from sight.

Nevertheless they arrived at Rathlin, each one
safely, and each blithe and glad to have escaped
the hideous waves. There they landed, armed in
their best fashion. When the people of the
region saw armed men arrive in their island in
such number they fled hastily with their cattle
towards a very strong castle in the country near

that place. Women were to be heard crying
aloud and seen fleeing with cattle here and there.
But the king's folk, who were swift of foot, over-
took and stopped them, and brought them back
to the Bruce without any of them being slain.
Then the king so dealt with them that they all,
to please him, became his men, and faithfully
undertook that they and theirs, under all circum-
stances and in all things, should be at his will.
Also, while he chose to remain there, they would
send victuals for three hundred men, and would
hold him as their lord, but their possessions were
to be their own, free, against all his men.

The covenant was thus made, and on the mor-
row all Rathlin, man and page, knelt and did
homage to the king, and therewith swore him
fealty and loyal service. And right well they
kept the covenant, for while he dwelt in the
island they found provision for his company, and
served him very humbly.

BOOK IV

THE DEATH OF EDWARD I

IN Rathlin we now leave the king, at rest from strife, and for a time speak of his foes. They, by their strength and power, made such persecution, severe, strict, and cruel, of those that loved him, kin or friends, as is piteous to hear. For they spared none of any degree, churchman or layman, whom they believed his friend. Bishop Robert of Glasgow, and Marcus of Man[1] both they loaded with strong fetters and shut in prison. And valiant Christopher of Seton was betrayed in Loch Doon, by MacNab, a false traitor and disciple of Judas, who was ever, night and day, in his house, and well entertained. It was far worse than treachery to betray a man so noble and of such renown, but the traitor had no ruth of that. For his deed may he be doomed in hell! When Seton was

---

[1] Man then belonged to Scotland and was included in the Bishopric of the Isles. Its bishopric is still known as that of Sodor (the Southern Isles) and Man.

betrayed the English rode straight with him at
once to England, to King Edward, and he, with-
out pity or mercy, had him drawn, headed, and
hanged.[1] It was a great sorrow indeed that so
valiant a person as he should in such fashion be
hanged. Thus ended his valour.

Sir Ranald of Crauford also, and Sir Bryce the
Blair, were hanged in a barn at Ayr.

The Queen and also Dame Marjory, her daugh-
ter,[2] afterwards happily wedded with Walter,
Steward of Scotland, would in no wise lie longer
in Kildrummy Castle to abide a siege, but rode
rapidly, with knights and squires, through Ross to
the Girth of Tain.[3] But they made the journey in
vain, for the people of Ross, not desiring to bear
the blame and danger of harbouring them, took
them out of the Girth, and sent them every one
to England, to King Edward. He caused all the
men to be drawn and hanged, and put the ladies
in prison, some in castles and some in dungeons.
It was pitiful to hear of folk so afflicted.

There were at that time in Kildrummy warlike
and bold men, Sir Neil the Bruce and the Earl
of Atholl. They victualled the castle well with

[1] He was really executed at a spot long known as Kirsty's
Mount, near Dumfries. Bruce erected a chapel at the place.

[2] The Queen was Bruce's second wife Elizabeth, daughter of
the Earl of Ulster. Marjory was the daughter of his former
wife, Isabella.

[3] The sanctuary of St. Duthac.

meat, and laid in fuel, and so strengthened the
place that it seemed to them no force could take
it. And when it was told the King of England
how they prepared to hold that castle he was
much enraged. He forthwith called to him his
eldest son and heir-apparent, a young bachelor
strong and fair, called Sir Edward of Carnarvon,
the starkest man of his time, then Prince of
Wales. He also called two earls, Gloucester and
Hereford, and bade them march to Scotland, and
set strong siege to the castle of Kildrummy;
and he ordered them to destroy altogether, with-
out ransom, all the holders of it, or bring them
prisoners to him.

When they had taken all his commands they
immediately gathered a host, and hastened to
the castle, and besieged it rigorously. They made
many bold assaults upon it, yet failed to take it,
for those within were right valiant, and defended
themselves doughtily, driving off their enemies
many times, with wounds and slaughter. Often,
too, they sallied forth, and fought at the out-
works, and wounded and slew their foes. Indeed,
they so bore themselves that the besiegers de-
spaired, and thought of returning to England. For
they saw the castle stand so strong, and knew
it was provisioned well, and found the garrison
so defend themselves, that they had no hope of
taking the place. Neither had they done this all

that season if false treason had not been there. But a traitor was within, a false rascal and lying fellow, Osborne by name, who did the treachery. I know not for what reason, nor with whom he made the plot, but they that were within the castle have said that he took a hot coulter glowing and burning from a fire, and went into the great hall that was filled full with corn, and threw it high upon a heap.

The deed was not long hidden. Neither fire nor pride, they say, can go long without discovery. The pomp of pride shows ever forth, or the great boast that it blows abroad, and no man can so cover fire but that flame or smoke shall discover it. So it fell here, for clear flame soon showed through the thick wood floor, first like a star, then like a moon, and soon afterwards a broader gleam. Then the fire burst out in blazes, and the smoke rose right wondrous fast. The flame spread over all the castle so that no power of man could master it. Then those within drew to the wall, which at that time was battlemented within as it was without. Without doubt that battlement saved their lives, for it broke flames that would have overtaken them.

When their foes saw the mischance they in a little while got to arms, and made diligent attack on the castle at the places where the fire blasts

would let them. But the garrison, as they had
need to do, made such great and stout defence,
shunning no perils, that they full often drove
back their enemies. They toiled to save their
lives, but fate, that ever drives the world's
business to an end, so harassed them, assailing
them on two sides, within with fire that broiled
them, without with folk that attacked them, that
in spite of them their enemies burned the gate.
Yet because of the heat of the fire the assailants
durst not enter hastily. Therefore they rallied
their men, and, since it was night, went to rest
till daylight on the morrow.

The garrison were indeed in evil case. Never-
theless they still valiantly defended themselves,
and wrought so manfully that before day, with
great labour, they had again walled up the gate.
At daylight on the morrow, when the sun was
risen and shining bright, the enemy came arrayed
in full order of battle, prepared to make assault.
But the garrison, being so placed that they
had neither victual nor fuel wherewith to hold
the castle, made parley first, and then yielded
themselves to the king's will, at that time most
bitter against the Scots. This was soon after-
wards well known, for they were all hanged and
drawn.

When this covenant had been made and surely
confirmed, the besiegers took the garrison, and

shortly wrought so that a quarter of Snowdoun[1]
was thrown to the ground. Then they made
their way towards England.

Now when King Edward heard how Neil the
Bruce held Kildrummy so stoutly against his son,
he gathered a great armed force, and marched
hastily towards Scotland. And as he was riding
with a great rout towards Northumberland, he
was seized with a sickness which beset him so
sore that he could neither walk nor ride. He
was forced, despite himself, to tarry at a hamlet
near by, a little mean place.

With great trouble they brought him there.
He was so bested that he could not draw his
breath except with great difficulty, nor speak
unless it were very low. Nevertheless he bade
them tell him what place it was where he lay.

"Sir," they said, "the men of the country call
this place Burgh-in-the-Sand."

"Call they it Burgh? alas!" said he, "my hope
is now at an end. For I thought never to suffer
the pains of death till I, by much might, had
taken the burgh of Jerusalem. There I thought
to end my life. In Burgh I knew well I should
die, but I was neither wise nor cunning enough
to take heed of other 'burghs.' Now may I nowise
farther go."

---

[1] Snowdoun was an old name for Stirling, but here it means
Kildrummy.

Thus complained he of his folly, as he had reason to do, surely enough, when he had thought to know certainly that which can be known assuredly by none. Men said he kept a spirit that made answer to his questions; but he was foolish, if not worse, to give trust to that creature. For fiends are of such nature that they bear envy to mankind. They know well and certainly that men shall win the seats from which they were thrown down for their pride. Ofttimes therefore will it happen that when fiends are forced, by dint of conjury, to appear and make answer they are so false and cruel that they give answer with double meaning, to deceive those that trust them.

I will give example in the case of a war that fell out between France and the Flemings. The Earl Ferrand's[1] mother was a necromancer, and she raised Satan, and asked him what should be the issue of the fighting between the French king and her son. And he, as he was ever wont, made deceitful answer in these verses:

"Rex ruet in bello tumulique carebit honore;
Ferrandus, comitissa, tuus, mea cara Minerva,
Parisios veniet, magna comitante caterva."

This, in English, is the speech he made: "The

[1] Ferrand, Prince of Portugal, who became Earl of Flanders in right of his wife Jane, daughter of Baldwin IX. Along with Otho IV. of Germany he was defeated by Philip Augustus of France, at Bouvines, between Lille and Tournay, July 27, 1214.

king shall fall in the battle, and shall lack the honour of burial; and thy Ferrand, my dear Minerva, shall, without doubt, march to Paris, followed by a great company of noble and valiant men."

This is the sense of the saying he showed her in Latin. He called her his dear Minerva, for Minerva was ever wont to serve him fully in every way; and since Earl Ferrand's mother made him the same service, he called her his Minerva. In his subtlety also he called her dear, to deceive her, that she should the more quickly take out of his speech the meaning which pleased her most.

His double speech so deceived her that through her many came by their death. For she was blithe of his answer, and quickly told it to her son, and bade him speed to the battle, for he should without doubt gain the victory. And he, hearing her counsel, sped fast to the fighting, where he was discomfited, disgraced, taken captive, and sent to Paris. At the same time, in the fighting the king was both unhorsed and lamed by Ferrand's knights; but his men quickly horsed him again.

And when Ferrand's mother heard how her son fared in the battle, and that he was discomfited, she called up the evil spirit, and asked why he had lied in the answer he made her. But he said that he had wholly spoken truth: "I told thee the king should fall in the battle, and so he did; and should lack burial, as men may see. And I said thy son should go to Paris, and he did so, assuredly, followed by such a company as he never had in his life before. Now seest thou I spake no falsehood?"

The lady was confounded, and durst say no more to him. Thus, through double meaning, and the deceiving of one side, that strife came to the end it did.

Just so it fell in King Edward's case. He expected to be buried in the burgh at Jerusalem, yet he died at Burgh-in-the-Sand in his own country.

And when he was near death the folk that had been at Kildrummy came, with the prisoners they had taken, and were admitted to the king. And to comfort him they told how the castle was yielded to them, and how the defenders were brought to his will, to do with them whatever he thought good; and they asked what they should do with them.

Then looked he awfully at them, and said grinning, "Hang and draw!"

It was a great marvel, among those who saw, that he, who was near death, should answer in such fashion, without remembrance of mercy. How could he trustfully cry on Him who truly judges all things, to have mercy on himself, who thus cruelly, at such a pass, had no mercy? His men did his command, and he died soon afterward, and was buried, and his son became king.[1]

To King Robert again we go, who lay in Rathlin with his company till the winter was near gone, and took his provision from that island.

James of Douglas was vexed that they should lie idle so long, and he said to Sir Robert Boyd, "The poor folk of this country are at great charge for us, who lie idle here. And I hear say that in Arran, in a strong castle of stone, are Englishmen who by force hold the lordship of the island. Go we thither, and it may well befall that we shall trouble them in some way."

Sir Robert said, "To that I agree. There were little reason in lying longer here. Therefore will we pass to Arran, for I know that country right well, and the castle also. We shall come there so privily, that they shall have no sight or news of our coming. And we shall lie ambushed near, where we may see their coming out. So it shall nowise fail but we shall do them damage of some sort."

With that they made ready anon, and took

[1] Barbour makes Edward die in the winter of 1306. As a matter of fact his death did not take place till July 7, 1307, after the battle of Loudoun Hill, described in Book VIII.

their leave of the king, and went forth on their way.

They came soon to Cantyre, then rowed always by the land till near night, when they made their way to Arran. There they arrived safely, and drew their galley under a hillside, and there covered it up. Their tackle, oars, and rudder they hid in the same fashion, and held their way in the dead of night, so that, ere daylight dawned, they were in skilful ambush near the castle. There, though they were wet and weary, and hungry with long fasting, they planned to hold themselves all privy till they could see their proper chance.

Sir John the Hastings was at that time in the castle of Brodick, with knights of high pride, and squires, and good yeomanry, a very great company. And often at his pleasure he went hunting with his followers, and held the land in such subjection that none durst refuse to do his will. He was still in the castle when James of Douglas laid his ambush, as I have said.

By chance it so happened at that time that close to the place of the ambush the under-warden had arrived the evening before with three boats loaded with victual and provision, clothing and arms. Douglas soon saw thirty and more Englishmen go from the boats loaded with sundry stuff. Some carried wine and some arms.

A number were loaded with stores of different sort, and various others marched idly by them, like masters.

The men in ambush saw them, and without fear or awe, broke from hiding, and slew all they could overtake. Then rose an outcry loud and terrible, for the men of the boats, in fear of death, roared aloud like beasts. Douglas's followers slew without pause or mercy, so that very nigh forty English lay dead.

When those in the castle heard the outcry and uproar they sallied forth to the fight. But Douglas, seeing them, rallied his men, and went hastily to meet them. And when the garrison saw him come fearlessly at them, they fled without more fighting, their assailants following them to the gate, and slaying them as they passed in. But those in flight barred the gate so quickly that the pursuers could not get at them further. Therefore they left them and turned again to the sea, where the men were slain before. And when the English in the boats saw them coming, and knew in what fashion they had discomfited their fellows, they put hastily to sea, and rowed diligently with all their might. But the wind was against them, and it raised such breakers that they could in no wise get out to sea. Neither durst they come to land, but held themselves plunging there so long that two of the three boats were swamped. When Douglas saw this, he took the arms and clothing, victual, wine, and other stores which he found at the place, and went his way, right joyful and pleased with the plunder.

Thus James of Douglas and his company, by God's grace, were fully furnished with stores of arms, clothing, and provisions. Then they held their way to a narrow place,[1] and stoutly maintained themselves, till on the tenth day the king with all his following arrived in that region.

Bruce reached Arran with thirty-three small galleys, and landed and took up his quarters in a steading.[2] There he enquired particularly if any had tidings of strangers in the island.

"Yes, sir," said a woman, "I can indeed tell you of strangers arrived in this country. A short while since, by their valour, they discomfited our warden and slew many of his men. In a strong place at hand the whole company has its resort."

"Dame," said the king, "do thou make known to me the place of their retreat, and I shall reward thee indeed; for they are all of my

[1] At the head of Glen Cloy the earthworks of Douglas's camp are still pointed out.

[2] According to tradition he lodged first in the King's Caves under the headland of Drumadoon, on the west side of the island. Rude carvings on the cavern walls are still shown as the work of his men.

E

house, and most glad would I be to set eyes on them, as, certainly I know, would they be to set eyes on me."

"Sir," said she, "I will blithely go with you and your company till I show you their quarters."

"That is enough, my fair sister," said the king. "Now let us go forward."

Without more delay then they marched after her, till at last she showed the king the place in a woody glen. "Sir," she said, "here I saw the men ye ask after make their lodging; here I trow, is their retreat."

The king then blew his horn, and made the men beside him keep still and hidden. Then again he blew his horn.

James of Douglas heard him blow, and at once knew the blast, and said, "Assuredly yonder is the king; many a day have I known his blowing."

Therewith the Bruce blew a third time. Then Sir Robert Boyd knew it, and said, "Yonder, for certain, is the king. Go we forth to him with all speed."

They hastened then to the king, and saluted him most courteously. And Bruce welcomed them gladly, and was joyful of their meeting, and kissed them, and enquired how they had fared in their hunting. And they told him everything truly, and praised God that they had met.

Then, gay and glad at heart, they went with the
king to his quarters.

Next day the Bruce said to his privy company,
"Ye know right well how we are banished out
of our country by English force, and that the
land which is ours by right the English seize by
violence; also that they would, if they could,
destroy us all without mercy. But God forbid
that it should befall us as they menace, for then
were there no recovery. Human nature bids us
bestir ourselves to procure vengeance, and there
are three things that urge us to be valiant,
active, and wise. One is the safety of our lives,
which should in no wise be spared if our foes had
us at their will. The second is that these foes
hold our possessions by might against right. The
third is the pleasure that awaits us if it happen,
as well may, that we gain the victory and have
strength to overcome their cruelty. Therefore
we should uplift our hearts, and let no mischance
downcast us, and press always towards a goal
so full of honour and renown. So, lords, if ye
agree that it is expedient, I shall send a man to
Carrick,[1] to spy and enquire how the kingdom
is inclined, and who is friend or foe. And if he
sees we may go ashore, he shall make a fire on

---

[1] The mother of Bruce was Countess of Carrick in her own
right, but the lordship, with the castle of Turnberry had been
given by Edward to Henry Percy.

a certain day on Turnberry Point, for a signal that we may land safely. And if he sees we may not do this he shall on no account make the fire. Thus we shall have sure knowledge whether to pass over or remain."

To this proposal all were agreed. Then forthwith the king called to him one in his confidence, a native of his own country of Carrick, and charged him in every way as ye have heard me set forth, appointing him a certain day to make the fire if he saw it possible for them to carry on war in that region. And the man, right eager to fulfil his lord's desire, for he was valiant and true, and could keep secrets well, declared he was ready in everything to fulfil the king's command, and said he should act so wisely that no reproof should touch him afterwards. Then he took leave of the king, and went forth upon his way.

This messenger, Cuthbert by name, soon arrived in Carrick, and passed through all the countryside, but he found few therein who would speak well of his master. Many of them durst not for fear, and others were enemies of the noble king to the very death. These afterwards rued their hostility. The whole land, both high and low, was then in possession of Englishmen who hated above everything the doughty king, Robert the Bruce. All Carrick was then given to Sir

Henry Percy, who lay in Turnberry Castle with nigh three hundred men, and so daunted the whole land that all obeyed him.

Cuthbert beheld their cruelty, and perceived the people, rich and poor, so wholly become English, that he durst discover himself to none. He determined to leave the fire unmade, and to hasten to his master, and tell him the whole dire and piteous state of affairs.

In Arran the king, when the day was come that he had set his messenger, looked diligently for the fire. And as soon as the moon was past he bethought him surely that he saw a fire burning brightly by Turnberry. He showed it to his company, and each man felt sure that he saw it. Then the people cried with blithe heart, "Good king, speed you quickly that we arrive early in the night without being discovered!"

"I agree," said he. "Now make you ready. God further us in our journey!"

Then very shortly the men might be seen launching all their galleys to the sea, and bearing to the water's edge oar and rudder and other needed things.

And as the king was passing up and down on the land, waiting till his men were ready, his hostess came to him. And when she had greeted him, she spoke privately to him, and said, "Take good heed to my words, for, ere ye go, I shall show you a great part of your fortune, and above everything I shall especially make known to you the issue of your enterprise; for in this world there is indeed none who knows the future so well as I.

"Ye pass now forth on your voyage to avenge the harm and outrage that Englishmen have done you; and ye know not what fortune ye must encounter in your campaign. But be assured, without falsehood, that after ye have now landed, no force or strength of hand shall cause you to pass out of this country till all is yielded to you. Within a short time ye shall be king, and have the land at your pleasure, and overcome all your enemies. Ye shall endure many sufferings before your enterprise is at an end, but ye shall overcome them each one. And, that ye may surely believe this, I shall send with you my two sons to share your toils; for I know well they shall not fail to be right well rewarded when you are exalted to your high place."

The king, who had listened to all her tale, thanked her greatly, for she encouraged him in some sort. Nevertheless he did not altogether put faith in her words, for he marvelled greatly how she should know so much for certain. And, indeed, it is wonderful how any man may, by means of the stars, know determinately all or part of things to come, unless he be inspired by

Him who in His foreknowledge evermore sees all things as if in His presence. David was thus inspired, and Jeremiah, Samuel, Joel, and Isaiah, who, through His holy grace told many things that afterwards befell. But these prophets are so thinly sown that none is now known on earth. Yet many folk are so curious and so desirous after knowledge that, in order to learn the future, by their great learning, or by their devilry, they make search in two ways.

One is astrology, whereby learned clerks know conjunction of planets, and whether their courses lie through mansions blest or sorrowful, and how the disposition of the whole heavens should act on things here below, in different regions or climes, according as the beams strike evenly or awry. But methinks it were a mighty feat for any astrologer to say "this shall befall here and on this day." For though a man during his whole life studied astrology, so that he broke his head on the stars, wise men say he should not in all his lifetime make three certain predictions, but should ever be in doubt till he saw how the matter fell out. There is, therefore, no certain foreknowledge. Even if these students of astrology knew all men's nativities, and also the constellations that gave them natures preordained to good or ill, and if they, by craft of learning, or sleight of astrology, could tell the peril that

threatens them, I trow they should fail to tell
the issue of events. For howsoever a man be
inclined to virtue or wickedness, he may full
well, either by training or reason, restrain his
desire, and turn himself all to the opposite. It
has often been seen that men, naturally given
to evil, have by their great wisdom driven
away their evil, and become of great renown,
despite the constellations. Thus we read that if
Aristotle had followed his preordained character
he should have been covetous and false, but his
wisdom made him virtuous. And since men may
in this way work against the course of stars
which has chief control of their fate, methinks
their fate no certain matter.

Another method of divining the future is by
necromancy. This in sundry ways teaches men
by strong conjurations and exorcisings to cause
spirits to appear to them and give answer in
various fashion. Thus aforetime the Pythoness
did, who, when Saul was cast down by the might
of the Philistines, raised very soon by her great
sleight, the spirit of Samuel, or the Evil Spirit
in his stead, who gave her right ready answer,
though she knew nothing herself.

Man is ever in fear of things he has heard
told, and especially of the future, till he has
certain knowledge of the end. And since he is
in such uncertainty, without sure knowledge,

methinks that man lies greatly who says he knows things to come. But whether she who told the king how his enterprise should end guessed or knew it for certain, it fell out afterwards wholly as she said; for presently he was king, and of full great renown.

BOOK V

THE RETURN OF THE KING

THIS was in spring, when winter, with its
hideous blasts, was over, and small birds,
like the throstle and nightingale, began merrily
to sing, with their many different notes and
pleasant melody; when the trees were beginning
to bourgeon and blossom, and spread again the
canopy that wicked winter had reft, and all the
woods were beginning to grow green. Then it
was that the noble king, with his fleet and small
following—three hundred they might be—put to
sea from Arran a little before evening.

They rowed diligently with all their strength,
till night fell upon them, and it grew very dark,
so that they knew not where they were. For
they had no needle or loadstone, but rowed
always in one direction, holding a straight course
towards the fire, which they saw burning light
and clear. It was chance only that led them,
but they so sped that they shortly arrived at
the fire, and landed without delay.

But Cuthbert, who had seen the fire, was full of wrath and grief, for he durst not put it out, and he was in fear that his lord might cross the sea. Therefore he awaited their coming, and met them as they arrived.

He was forthwith brought to the king, who asked him how he had fared. And with sore heart he told how he had found none well disposed, but all on the enemy's side. Also that the Lord Percy, with nigh three hundred in his company, filled with pride and hatred, was in the castle at hand. More than two-thirds of his host, however, were quartered in the village outside. "And they hate you more, Sir King, than they hate aught else."

Then said the king, in the greatest wrath, "Traitor! Why madest thou the fire?"

"Ah, sir," he answered, "as God sees me, that fire was never made by me, nor knew I of it till night. But from the time I knew of it, I felt sure that you and your whole company would forthwith put to sea. Therefore I came to meet you here, and to tell the perils I know of."

At these words the king was vexed, and in haste asked his council what they thought it best to do.

To this the first answer was made by the bold Sir Edward, his brother. "I tell you assuredly," said he, "that no peril that can appear shall drive me again to sea. My fortune I will take here, whether it be good or bad."

"Brother," said Bruce, "since thou wilt have it so, let us take together what God will send, suffering or comfort, weal or woe. And since it seems that Percy seeks to seize my heritage, and his host, filled with hatred for us, lies so near, let us avenge some of the hate. This we may very soon do, for they lie unguardedly without fear of us or of our coming here. And though we slew them all while they slept none should blame us for the deed. For a soldier should take no account whether he overcomes his foe by strength or subtlety, so long as he keeps good faith."

When this was said they went their way, and soon came to the village. So secret were they and noiseless, that none perceived their coming. They spread quickly through the place, and battered down doors, and slew all they could overtake. Their enemies, seeing they could make no defence, made most piteous shout and outcry; but they slew them without mercy, being of a mind to avenge the sorrow and evil that they and theirs had wrought. They pursued them with such dire intent that they slew everyone except only Macdowal, who escaped by cunning and the darkness of the night.[1]

[1] Macdowal of Galloway had seized two of Bruce's brothers, Thomas and Alexander, and delivered them up to Edward.

In the castle the Lord Percy heard the noise and shouting. So did the men that were within with him, and in great fear they ran to arms. But none of them were so bold as sally forth to the outcry. In this terror they passed the night, till at daylight on the morrow the greater part of the uproar, slaughter, and outcry ceased. The king then caused the whole of the plunder to be shared among his men, and remained three days quietly in that place.

Such was the foretaste he gave the enemy at the very beginning, when he was newly arrived.

After his coming Bruce dwelt in Carrick for a time, to see who should be friend or foe. But he found little kindliness, for, though some of the people were inclined to him, the English so ruled them with danger and fear that they durst show him no friendship.

But a lady of that country, who was his near kinswoman,[1] was wondrous glad at his arrival, and made great haste to join him, bringing fifteen men, whom she gave to the king to help him in his warfare. He received them with much pleasure, and very greatly thanked her, and forthwith asked tidings of the queen and all the friends he had left in the country when he crossed the sea.

---

[1] According to Fordoun the lady was "a certain noblewoman, Christian of the Isles, and it was by her help and power and goodwill that Bruce was enabled to return to Carrick."

And sighing full sore she told him how his brother was taken in the castle of Kildrummy, and afterwards villainously destroyed. Also of the Earl of Atholl,[1] and how the queen and others belonging to his party were taken and led into England and thrown cruelly into prison, and how Christopher of Seton was slain. Weeping she told these things to the king, and he was sorrowful at the tidings. And when he had thought a little while, he said these words:

"Alas! for love of me and for much good loyalty these noble and valiant men are villainously destroyed! But if I live in my full strength their death shall be right well avenged. Albeit the King of England thought the kingdom of Scotland too small for him and me, I will have it all mine. But for good Christopher of Seton, who was of such noble renown, it was piteous that he should die except where he could have proved his valour."

Thus the king sighed and mourned. And the lady took her leave and went home, and many a time she helped Bruce both with silver and with such food as she could get in the country. He also harried the land often, and made all his own that he found, and afterwards drew to the hills, the better to withstand the strength of his enemies.

---

[1] Atholl was executed in London.

During all that time Percy, with a most harmless company, lay in Turnberry Castle, in such dread of King Robert that he durst not sally forth to pass to the castle of Ayr, which was full of Englishmen. But he lay lurking as in a den till the men of Northumberland should come with arms and strength, as he had sent word, to convoy him to his own country. His friends there had hastily come together, over a thousand men, and they took counsel among themselves whether they should go or stay. They were wondrous fain to shun a journey so far into Scotland. A knight, Sir Walter the Lisle, said it was too great a peril to go so near the wandering folk, and his word so dismayed them all that they would have altogether given up the journey, had not a knight of great courage, Sir Roger of St. John, encouraged them with all his strength of mind, and spoken such words to them that they held their way all together to Turnberry. Then Percy took horse, and spurred with them into England, where he reached his castle without disturbance or hurt. There I trow he was like to lie a while ere he sought to go and ravage Carrick further. For he knew he had no right on his side, and he also dreaded the might of the king, who was then wandering in Carrick, where the chief strength of the land lay.

Then one day Douglas came to the Bruce, and

said, "Sir, with your leave I would go see how they fare in my country, and how my men are treated. For it troubles me wondrous sore that Clifford so peaceably enjoys and holds the lordship that should by every right be mine. But while I live and have power to lead a yeoman or a hind, he shall not enjoy it without a struggle."

"Certes," said the king, "I cannot see how it can yet be safe for thee to journey into that country, where the English are so strong, and thou knowest not who is thy friend."

"Sir," said he, "needs must that I go, and take the fortune God will give, whether it be to live or die."

"Since thou hast so great a desire to go," the king replied, "thou shalt go forward with my blessing, and if any trouble or hurt happen thee, I pray thee speed at once to me, that we take together whatever may befall."

"I agree," said Douglas, and therewith he bowed low and took his leave, and passed towards his own country.

He set out for his heritage with two yeomen and no more. It was a small force to take to win a land or castle. Nevertheless he was eager to make a beginning with his enterprise. For much lies in a beginning. A good and bold beginning, if wisely followed up, oft-times causes an unlikely matter to come to a right happy issue.

It did so here. But he was wise, and saw he could in nowise harry his foes with equal force. Therefore he planned to work by stratagem.

It was evening when he entered his own country of Douglasdale. There was a man dwelt near by, Thomas Dickson by name, who was strong in friends and rich in goods and cattle. He had been loyal to the father of Douglas, and to Douglas himself in his youth, and had done many thankworthy deeds. To this man he sent, and begged him to come by himself to speak privately with him. He came without difficulty, and when Douglas told him who he was he wept for joy and pity, and had him straight to his house, and kept him and his company in a chamber secretly, so that none knew of them. There they had plenty of meat and drink and all else that might pleasure them.

Dickson wrought then so shrewdly that he caused all the true men of the country who had followed the father of Douglas to come one by one and do him homage, and he did so first himself.

Douglas was right glad of heart that the good men of his country were willing to be so bound to him. He enquired of the state of the country, and who held the castle, and they told him everything. Then they arranged among them privately that he should keep still in hiding till

F

the third day after, which was Palm Sunday; for
then the folk of the countryside would be
assembled at the kirk, and the men of the castle
would also be there to bear their palms, fearing
no hurt because they thought everything was at
their will. Then should he come with his two
men, but in order that men should not know
him, he should have a mantle old and bare, and
a flail as if he were a thresher. Nevertheless
secretly under the mantle he should be armed,
and when the men of his country, who should
all be ready before him, heard him shout his
battle-cry, they should assail the English in the
midst of the kirk with all their might, so that
none should escape. By this means they trusted
to take the castle, which was near hand.

When this was planned and agreed each one
went to his house, and kept the news secret till
the day of their coming together.

On the Sunday the people held their way to
St. Bride's Kirk, and the men of the castle, every
one except a cook and a porter, passed out to
carry their palms. James of Douglas had word
of their coming, and hastened to the kirk. But
too hastily, before he reached it, one of his men
cried "Douglas! Douglas!" And Thomas Dickson,
being nearest the men of the castle, who were
all in the chancel, when he heard the shout of
"Douglas!" drew his sword and rushed among

them. Only one other was with him, and they were soon slain.

With that Douglas, coming up, raised the cry loudly upon them. They held their chancel right stoutly, and defended themselves well, till several of their men were slain. But Douglas bore himself so well that all the men with him were encouraged by his prowess, and he spared himself in no way, but so approved his might in battle, and by his bravery and strength so keenly helped his men, that they won entrance to the chancel. Then they drove at their enemies so boldly that shortly two-thirds of them lay dead or dying. The rest were soon seized, so that of thirty was left none that was not slain or a prisoner.

James of Douglas, when this was done, took the prisoners, and, before any noise or outcry could arise, went hastily to the castle with his men. And in order to surprise those left in the castle, he sent before him five or six, who found the whole entrance open, and took the porter at the gate, and afterwards the cook. With that, Douglas reached the gate, and entered without hindrance, and found the meat all ready prepared, with tables set and cloths laid. The gates then he caused to be shut, and sat and ate at full leisure. Then they packed up all the goods they thought they could take away, especially weapons and armour, silver treasure and clothing. And

the victual that could not be packed up he
destroyed in this manner. All the provender,
except salt, such as wheat, malt, flour, and meal,
he caused to be brought into the wine-cellar and
thrown all together on the floor, and he caused
each of the prisoners he had taken to be beheaded
there. Afterwards he struck out the heads of the
tuns, and made a foul mixture, for meal, malt,
blood, and wine ran all together in a mess
unseemly to see. Therefore, because such things
were mingled there, the folk of that country
called it "the Douglas Larder." Then he took
the salt and dead horses, and fouled the well,
and afterwards burned everything that was not
stone, and passed forth with his followers to his
place of retreat. For he bethought him that if
he held the castle it should soon be besieged, and
this he deemed too great a peril, since he had no
hope of rescue, and it is too dangerous a venture
to be besieged in a castle wanting these three
things—victual, or men-at-arms, or good hope of
rescue. And because he feared these things
should fail him he chose to fare forth where
he could be at liberty, and so drive forward his
destiny.[1]

Thus was the castle taken, and each one in it
slain. Douglas then caused his following to

[1] Referring to this policy, he said he would "rather hear the
lark sing than the mouse squeak."

quarter separately in many places, and in order
that it should be less known where they were,
they dispersed here and there. The wounded he
caused to lie in secret hiding, and had surgeons
brought to them till they were whole. Himself
with a small company, sometimes one, or two,
or three, or quite alone, went in hiding about
the country. So feared he the might of the
English that he durst not come in sight; for at
that time they were ruling everything as over-
lords throughout the land.

But the tidings of the deed Douglas had done
soon spread, and came to Clifford's ear. He was
vexed at his loss and lamented his men who had
been slain, and forthwith made up his mind to
build the castle again. Therefore, being a man
of great power, he got together a large company,
and went straightway to Douglas, and quickly
built up the castle, and made it stout and strong,
and put men and victual therein. Then he left
one of the Thirlwalls behind as captain, and went
again to England.

The king was still in Carrick with a very small
gathering, not more than two hundred men.
But Sir Edward his brother was in Galloway,
not far away, with another company. They
held the strong places of the country, for they
durst not yet take on hand to ride over the land
openly.

Sir Aymer de Valence, Warden of Scotland under the English king, was lying in Edinburgh when he heard of the coming of King Robert and his force into Carrick, and how he had slain the Percy's men. Then he assembled his council, and with its approval, sent to Ayr, to assail Bruce, a stout knight, Sir Ingram Bell, and a great company with him.

And when Ingram was come there it seemed to him not expedient to move to attack Bruce in the high country. Therefore he thought to work by stratagem, and lay still in the castle, till he got word of a man of Carrick, who was cunning and active and of great strength, such as the men of that country are. This man was in King Robert's confidence, being his near kinsman, and when he would, could without difficulty enter the king's presence. Nevertheless he and his two sons dwelt yet in the country, as they would not have it known that they were intimate with the king. They gave him warning many a time, when they saw anything to his hurt. For this he trusted them. The man's name I cannot tell, but I have heard sundry men say, forsooth, one of his eyes was out, but he was so sturdy and stout as to be the most doughty man then in Carrick.

And when Sir Ingram was assured that this was no lie, he sent after him, and the man came

at his command. Sir Ingram, who was cunning
and sagacious, dealt with him in such wise that
he made a sure undertaking by treason to slay
the king. For this service he was to have, if he
carried out their plan, forty pounds worth of
land settled on himself and his heirs.

The treason thus undertaken, he went home
and waited an opportunity to fulfil his wicked-
ness. Then was the king in great peril, knowing
nothing of the treason, for the man he trusted
most of all had falsely undertaken his death,
and none can do a treason more readily than he
whose loyalty is trusted. The king trusted him.
For this reason he would have accomplished his
felony had not the Bruce, by God's grace, got
knowledge of his attempt, and why, and for how
much land he had undertaken the slaughter.

I know not who gave the warning, but at all
times it was the king's fortune that when men set
out to betray him he got knowledge of it. Many
a time, I have heard tell, women with whom he
dallied would tell him all they could hear, and
so it may have happened in this case. But, how-
ever it befell, indeed, I trow he was the more
wary.

This traitor ever had it in his thought, night
and day, how he could best bring to an end
his treasonable undertaking. Till at last he
bethought him, and recalled to mind that it was

the king's custom to rise early every day and
pass far from his host, where he would be
private, and seek a covert by himself, or have
at most one with him. There thought the traitor,
with his two sons, to surprise and slay the king,
and then flee away to the forest. Yet they failed
of their purpose.

Nevertheless they went all three into a secret
covert where the king was wont to go. There
they hid till his coming. And in the morning,
when it was his pleasure, the king rose, and
went straight to the covert where the three
traitors were lying. He had no thought then
of treason, but he was wont, wherever he went,
to bear his sword about his neck, and this
availed him greatly here. For had not almighty
God set help in his own hand he had without
doubt been slain. A chamber page went with
him, and thus, without more followers, he passed
to the covert.

Now, unless God helped the noble king he was
near his end. For the covert he went to was on
the farther side of a hill, where none of his men
could see. Thither went he and his page. And
when he was come into the wood he saw these
three come sturdily against him, all in a row.

Then he said quickly to his boy, " Yonder men
will slay us if they can! What weapon hast
thou ? "

"Ah, sir! indeed I have but a bow and a bolt."

"Give me them both quickly!"

"Ah, sir! what will ye then that I do?"

"Stand afar and behold us. If thou seest me get the upper hand thou shalt have weapons plenty; and if I die withdraw thee quickly."

With these words, without delay he seized the bow out of his hand, for the traitors were coming near. The father had a sword only, the second man carried both sword and hand-axe, the third had a sword and a spear. The king saw by their bearing that all was true that had been told him.

"Traitor," he said, "thou hast sold me. Come no further, but hold thee there. It is my will that thou come no further."

"Ah, sir! bethink you," said he, "how near I should be to you. Who should come so near to you as I?"

The king said, "I will assuredly that at this time thou comest not near. Thou may'st say what thou wilt at a distance."

But the man, with false, flattering words, was, with his sons, ever advancing. When the king saw he would not stop, but ever came on, feigning falsely, he strung the bolt and let it fly, and hit the father in the eye, piercing to the brain, and he fell backward on the spot. The brother who bore the hand-axe, when he saw his father lying there, made a spring at the king, and struck at him with the axe; but the Bruce had his sword up and dealt him a blow with such downright force, that he clave the head to the brain, and laid him dead on the ground. The second brother, who carried the spear, saw his brother fall, and full of grief made a rush at the king. But the Bruce, who feared him somewhat, waited the spear as it came, and with a swift blow struck off its head, and ere the other had leisure to draw his sword, gave him a stroke that clove his skull, and he fell of a heap all red with blood.

When the king saw they were all three lying dead he wiped his brand. With that his boy came running fast, and said "Our Lord be praised, who granted you strength and might to lay low in so little space the felony and pride of these three!"

The king said, "As Our Lord sees me! they had been valiant men all three had they not been full of treachery. But that wrought their confusion."

BOOK VI

ADVENTURES OF THE FORD AND THE SLEUTH-HOUND

THE king went to his quarters, and tidings of his deed soon came to Sir Ingram Bell, who perceived that his subtlety and guile had wholly failed in that case, and was therefore sore vexed. He went back then to Lothian, and told Sir Aymer the whole matter. Sir Aymer was vastly astonished that any man could do so sudden and great a feat of arms as the king, who single-handed had taken vengeance on the three traitors.

"Certes," he said, "I can see how of a surety fate helps always the brave. Ye may know it by this deed. Had he not been so desperately brave he had not so undauntedly and so quickly seen his advantage. I fear his great prowess and endeavour will bring to pass what men meanwhile full little dream of."

Thus he spoke of the king.

Meanwhile Bruce ever, without rest, journeyed here and there in Carrick. His men were so scattered, to procure their needs and to spy the country, that not sixty were left with him. And when the people of Galloway knew for certain that he had only a small following, they made a secret gathering of over two hundred men. They took a sleuth-hound with them, for they planned to surprise him, and if he chanced to flee, to follow him with the hound that so he should not escape.

They thought to surprise him in the evening suddenly, and they held their way straight for the place where he was. But he, having his watches always set on every side, had word of their coming long ere they drew near, and knew who and how many they were. He settled, as it was near nightfall, to withdraw with his company from the place. Since it was night he thought the enemy should not be able to see the way by which he and his men went off.

He did as he planned, and made his way down to a morass on a running water, and in a bog, over two bow-shots from the spot where they had passed the water, he found a very strait place. "Here," said he, "ye may tarry, and lie down and rest you all a while. I will go and keep watch for you secretly if I hear aught of their coming, and if I should hear anything I shall have you warned, so that we shall not be taken at advantage."

The king took his way, and took two servants with him, and left Sir Gilbert de la Haye with his followers. He came to the water, and listened very intently if he might hear anything of the coming enemy; but he could hear nothing yet. Then he went along the water a great way in each direction, and saw that the banks stood high and the water ran deep through mud, and he found no ford which men could pass except where he himself had crossed. There, too, the ascent was so narrow that two men could not press up together, nor by any means manage to land abreast.

His two men he then bade hasten back to lie and rest with their fellows, while he should keep watch there.

"Sir," said they, "who shall be with you?"

"God alone," he answered. "Pass on, for I wish it so."

They did as he bade, and he remained alone.

When he had waited there awhile he heard far off as it were the questing of a hound coming ever nearer and nearer. He stood still to listen more, and the longer he waited he heard it coming nearer. But he thought he would stand till he heard further token, for he would not waken his followers because of a hound's questing. So he made up his mind to wait and see what folk they were, and whether they came straight for him, or passed by another way.

The moon was shining clearly, and he stood long listening, till he saw at hand the whole rout coming at the greatest speed.

Then he hastily bethought him that, if he went to fetch his company, the enemy should everyone have passed the ford ere he could return, and that then his only choice must be either to flee or die. But his heart, ever stout and proud, counselled him to make a stand alone, and stop them at the ford side, and defend the up-coming. He was clad in armour, and need not dread their arrows, and if he put forth his strength he might discomfit them all since they could only come one by one.

He did as his heart bade him. Stark and extraordinary was his courage, when so stoutly, all alone, with little advantage of ground, he took on hand to fight two hundred and more.

Therewith he went to the ford, and they on the other side, seeing him stand singly there, rode in a throng into the water; for they had little doubt of the upshot, and made at him with the greatest speed.

He smote the foremost so hard with his sharp-cutting spear that he bore him to the earth. Then the rest came on in a furious rush. But the horse of him that was overthrown hindered them in taking the bank, and when the king saw this he stabbed the horse, and it lashed out and fell at the up-coming. At that with a shout the others came on. But he, stalwart and doughty, met them boldly at the bank, and dealt them such blows that he slew five in the ford. The rest then drew back a space, dreading his strokes wondrous sore, for he spared them no whit.

Then said one of them "Certes, we are to blame. What shall we say when we come home, when one man withstands us all? Who ever knew so foul a thing happen to any as to us if we leave matters thus?"

With that they all together gave a shout and cried "On him! he cannot last!" Then they pressed him so eagerly that, had he not been the better man he had without doubt been slain. But he made such stout defence that where his stroke fell straight nothing could stand against it. In a short space he laid so many low that the passage was stopped up with slain horses and men, and his enemies, for that hindrance, could not reach the bank.

Ah, dear God! whoever had been by, and seen how he so boldly bore himself against them all, I wot well they should have hailed him the best living in his time. And, if I may tell the truth, I have heard of none in times past who single-handed stopped so many.

History tells the story of Tydeus, sent by Polynices to his brother Etiocles, to ask possession of his heritage of Thebes for a year. They had come to strife because they were twins, for each sought to be king. But the barons of their country had caused them to agree that the one should be king a year, and then the other, and that the followers of the second brother should not be found in the country while the first was reigning. Then the second should reign a year, and the first should leave the land while he reigned. Thus always by turns each should reign a year. To ask possession by this agreement Tydeus was sent to Thebes, and he spake so for Polynices that Etiocles of Thebes bade his constable take fifty well-armed men, and go forth to meet Tydeus in the way, and slay him at once. The constable set forth, and took nine and forty with him, so that with himself they made fifty. In the evening secretly they set an ambush in the way by which Tydeus must pass, between a high crag and the sea. And he, knowing nothing of their ill intent, took his way towards Greece. And as he rode in the night time he saw by the moon's light a shining of many shields, and marvelled what it might be. With that they all together gave

a shout, and he hearing so sudden a noise
was somewhat afraid. But in a moment he
right boldly plucked up his spirits, for his
noble and valiant heart gave him assurance in
that need. He struck his steed with the spurs,
and rushed among them. The first he met he
overthrew, then he swept out his sword, and
dealt many blows about him, and very soon slew
six. Then they killed his horse under him, and
he fell. But he rose quickly, and striking about
him, made room, and slew a number, though he
was wounded wondrous sore. With that he
found a little road striking up toward the crag.
Thither he sped, defending himself doughtily,
till he climbed somewhat into the crag, and
found a well-enclosed place where only one
could attack him. There he stood, and gave
them battle. And they everyone made assault,
and often it befell that, when he slew one, as
the man was hurled to the ground he would
bear down four or five. There he stood and
defended himself thus till he had slain of them
more than half. Then he saw beside him a
great stone that by long rains was loosened and
ready to fall. And when he saw them all
coming, he tumbled the stone down on them,
and therewith slew eight men, and so dismayed
the rest that they nigh owned themselves
beaten.

G

Then he no longer kept his fastness, but ran
on them with naked sword, and hewed and
slew with all his main, till he had slain nine
and forty. Then he took the constable, and
made him swear that he would go to King
Etiocles and tell the chance that had befallen
them.

Tydeus bore himself doughtily, who thus over-
came fifty. Ye who read this, judge whether
there should not be more praise for the Bruce,
who deliberately undertook such a deed of valour
as by himself fearlessly to oppose these two
hundred men, or for Tydeus, who suddenly, after
they had raised the shout against him, took
courage, and alone slew fifty men. They did
their deeds both in the night, and fought both
in the moonlight; but more were discomfited by
the king, and more were slain by Tydeus. Judge
now whether Tydeus or the king should have
the greater praise.

In the manner I have described, the king,
stout, stark, and bold, fought at the ford's side,
giving and taking wide wounds, till he made
such martyrdom that he stopped all the ford,
and none could ride at him. Then the enemy
thought it folly to remain, and wholly took
flight, and made homeward whither they had
come. For with the outcry the king's men
awaked, and in much alarm came to seek their

lord. The Galloway men heard their coming, and fled, and durst no longer remain.

The king's men, fearing for their lord, right speedily came to the ford, and found the Bruce sitting alone, with his basnet off, to take the air, for he was hot. Then they asked him how he fared, and he told them all that had happened, how he was attacked, and how God so helped him that he escaped from his enemies whole. Next they looked how many were dead, and they found lying in that place fourteen slain by his hand. At that they gave diligent praise to God Almighty that they had found their lord whole and well, and said it behoved them in no way to dread their foes, since their chieftain was of such heart and strength that he had undertaken to fight for them himself alone against so many.

Such words spake they of the king, and for his high achievement wondered and delighted to look at him, these men who were wont to be always with him. Ah, how valour is to be prized! If it be constant it makes men renowned. Nevertheless the fame of valour is only to be won by great effort. Oft to defend and oft assail, and to be wise in their deeds makes men win the name of valour. No man can have honour who has not wit to guide his steed, and sense what to undertake or to leave alone. Valour has two

extremes, foolhardiness and cowardice, and they are
both to be avoided. Foolhardiness will venture all,
things to leave alone as well as things to take
up, while cowardice ventures nothing and utterly
forsakes all. It were a marvel if this last fell
out well, any more than want of discretion. For
this reason is valour of such renown, that it is
the mean betwixt these two, and ventures what
should be ventured, and leaves what should be
left alone; and it has such great store of sense
as to see clearly all perils and all advantages.
It would hold altogether to hardihood provided
this were not foolish. For foolish hardihood is
vice, but hardihood mixed with sense is ever
true valour. Without sense there can be no
valour.

This noble king ever mingled manhood with
sense, as men may see by this fray. His sense
showed him the narrow passage of the ford and
the issue from it, and he judged that a valiant
man could never be overcome there. Therefore,
since only one could attack at a time, his stout
heart quickly perceived that the defence could
be undertaken. Thus hardihood, governed by
sense, as he always knit them together, made
him famous for valour, and often overcame his
enemies.

The king remained at rest in Carrick, and
his men who were wandering over the country

gathered eagerly to him when they heard tidings
of this deed. For if he were so assailed again
they wished to take their fate with him.

But James of Douglas was still wandering in
Douglasdale, or near by, in secret hiding. He
wished to see how he that had the castle in
keeping ordered affairs, and he caused many a
hazard to be made to see whether he would
readily sally forth. When he had made sure
that the castellan would sally forth readily with
his company, Douglas secretly gathered those
who were on his side. They were so many that
they durst fight with Thirlwall and all the
strength of the garrison.

He set out in the night for Sandilands, and
there made a secret ambush, and chose a few to
carry out a stratagem. Early in the morning
these men took cattle that were near the castle,
and withdrew them towards the ambush. Then
Thirlwall forthwith caused his men to arm, and
sallied forth with all the garrison, and pursued
after the cattle. He was fully armed at all points
except that his head was bare. He made after
the cattle with his men with all speed fearlessly,
till he got sight of them. Then they spurred
with all their might, following them in disarray
as they fled, till far past the ambush. And Thirl-
wall still chased eagerly on.

Then the men in ambush started out upon him,

one and all, and raised a sudden shout. And the men of the castle, suddenly seeing folk come spurring between them and their place of safety, fell into the greatest affright, and finding they were out of array, some fled and some remained. And Douglas, who had a great company with him, assailed them eagerly, and quickly scattered them, and in a short time so dealt with them that hardly one escaped. Thirlwall, their captain, was slain in the encounter, with most of his men. The rest fled in terror. The followers of Douglas gave keen chase, and the fugitives made with all speed for the castle. The foremost entered headlong, but the pursuers sped so fast that they overtook some at the rear, and slew them without mercy. And when the men in the castle saw them slay their fellows at hand, they barred the gates quickly, and ran in haste to the walls. Douglas's company then rapidly seized all they found about the castle, and passed to their retreat. Thus Thirlwall sallied forth that day.

After this was done James of Douglas and his men made ready all together and went their way towards the king in great haste. For they heard tidings that Sir Aymer de Valence with a great host both of Englishmen and Scots were ready gathered with dire intent to seek the king, who was then with his followers in the most difficult part of Cumnock.

Thither went James of Douglas, and was right
welcome to the king. And when he told the
tidings, how Sir Aymer was coming to hunt him
out of the land with hound and horn as if he
were wolf or thief, or thief's comrade, the king
said, "It may hap that though he come, and all
his power, we shall abide in this country. If he
comes we shall see."

In this fashion spake the king. And Sir Aymer
de Valence gathered a great company of noble
and valiant men, of England and Lothian, and
also took with him John of Lorne and all his
strength, eight hundred and more, valiant and
active men. He had also with him a sleuth-
hound so good that it would turn aside for
nothing. Some men say yet that the king had
reared this hound as a dog for the chase, and
made so much of him as always to feed him
with his own hand, so that the dog followed
him wherever he went, and so loved him that he
would in nowise part from him. How John of
Lorne had the hound I never heard mention made,
but men say it is certain that he had him in his
possession, and through him thought to capture
the king. For he knew he so loved him that
from the moment he should once scent the king
he would turn aside for nothing.

This John of Lorne hated the king for the
sake of Sir John Comyn his uncle. Could he

either slay or take him he would not value his life a straw, provided he could have vengeance upon him.

The Warden then, Sir Aymer, with John of Lorne in his company, and others of good renown—Thomas Randolph was one of these—came into Cumnock to seek the king.

Bruce was well aware of their coming, and was up then in the fastnesses, and full three hundred men with him. His brother was with him at the time, and also James of Douglas. He saw Sir Aymer's rout holding always to the plain and the low ground, and riding always in full battle array. The king, who had no idea they were more than he saw there, had eye to them and nowhere else, and wrought unwittingly. For John of Lorne full subtly planned to surprise him from behind, and marched with all his host round a hill, and kept always within covert, till he came so near to the king as to be almost upon him before he was perceived. The other host and Sir Aymer pressed on the opposite side.

The king was thus in great jeopardy, beset on either side with foes who threatened to slay him, the smaller of these two hosts being stronger far and more in number than his. And when he saw them press towards him he considered hastily what should be done, and said, " Lords,

we have not force at this time, to stand and
fight. Therefore let us separate in three: so all
shall not be assailed; and in three parties hold
our way." And he told his council privately
among themselves in what place their retreat
should be. With that all set off, and took their
way in three bodies.

Then John of Lorne came to the place from
which the king had departed, and he set the
hound on his track. Without stop the beast
held a straight course after the king as if it
knew him, and paid no heed to the two other
companies.

And when the king saw him coming in a
straight line after his company he thought he
was recognized. Therefore he bade his followers
separate yet again into three parties; and they
did so without delay, and held their way in
three directions. Again the hound showed its
great skill, and held ever, without change, after
the rout where the king was.

And when the Bruce saw them so follow all in
a body after him, and not after his men, he
had a great belief that they knew him. Accord-
ingly in haste he bade his men at once scatter,
and each man hold his way by himself. And
they did this. Each man went his separate way,
and the king took with him his foster-brother
and no more, and together these two went on.

The hound always followed the king, and turned aside at no parting, but ever without wavering followed the Bruce's track, where he had passed. And when John of Lorne saw the hound draw so hard after him, and follow these two so straightly; he knew the king was one of them. He bade five of his company, men right bold and active, and the speediest on foot of all in his rout, to run after and overtake him. "And," he said, "let him in nowise escape you!" And the moment they had heard the order they held after the king, and followed him so swiftly that they very soon overtook him.

The king, when he saw them coming near, was greatly troubled, for he considered that, if they were doughty, they might occupy and delay him, and so hold him till the others came up. If he had only had these five to fear, I trow assuredly he would not have very greatly dreaded them.

To his fellow, as he went, he said, "Yonder five are coming fast, they are now very near at hand. Is there any help in thee, for we shall soon be attacked?"

"Yea, sir," he said, "all that I can."

"Thou sayest well," said the king. "I'faith, I see them coming near us. I will go no further, but abide right here, till I am in wind, and see what force they can put forth."

The king then stood right sturdily, and soon

the five came in the greatest haste, with mighty clamour and menace. Three of them went at the king, and the other two, sword in hand, made stoutly at his man. The king met the three that made at him, and dealt such a blow at the first that he shore through ear and cheek and neck to the shoulder. The man sank down dizzily, and the two, seeing their fellow's sudden fall, were affrighted, and started back a little. With that the king glanced aside and saw the other two making full sturdy battle against his man. He left his own two, and leapt lightly at them that fought with his man, and smote off the head of one of them. Then he went to meet his own assailants, who were coming at him right boldly. He met the first so eagerly that with the sharp edge of his sword he hewed the arm from the body.

The strokes that were given I cannot tell, but so fairly it fell out that the king, though he had a struggle and difficulty, slew four of his foemen. Soon afterwards his foster-brother ended the days of the fifth.

And when the Bruce saw that all five were thus bereft of life, he said to his fellow, "Thou hast helped right well, i'faith!"

"It pleases you to say so," said he, "but ye took the greater share to yourself, who slew four while I slew one."

The king said, "As the game has gone, I might do it better than thou, for I had more leisure for it. The two fellows who fought with thee, when they saw me assailed, had no sort of doubt of me, for they thought me straitly beset. And because of that they feared me not, and I could trouble them very much the more."

With that the king looked past him and saw the company of Lorne with their sleuth-hound fast coming near. Then with his fellow he hastened towards a wood that was at hand. God in his great mercy save them!

BOOK VII

ESCAPES AND SURPRISES

THE king, weary, drenched with sweat, and all at a loss, went toward the wood, and soon entering it, held down towards a vale where a water ran. Thither he hastened, and began to rest, and said he could fare no farther.

His man said, "Sir, that cannot be. Abide here, and ye shall soon see five hundred eager to slay you; there are many against two. Since we cannot compass our escape by strength, let us help ourselves all we can by craft."

"Since thou wilt so," said the king, "go forward and I shall go with thee. I have oftimes heard say that if one should wade a bowshot along a stream, he should cause both the sleuth-hound and his leaders to lose the scent. Prove we now if it be so. For were yonder devil's hound away, I should reck nothing of the rest."

They did as he planned. Entering the stream, they held their way along it, and afterwards took to the bank, and went on as before.

And John of Lorne with great array came to the place where his five men were slain. He lamented when he saw them, and said, after a little while, that he should speedily avenge their blood. Otherwise, however, went the game.

He made no delay there, but hastened after the king, and came to the stream side. Here the sleuth-hound stopped, and wavered to and fro, but could go no certain way. And at last John of Lorne perceived the hound had lost the scent, and said, "We have lost this labour. It is useless to go farther, for the wood is both broad and wide, and he is far off by this time. Let us therefore turn back and waste no more labour in vain." With that he rallied his company and took his way to the host.

Thus the noble king escaped. But some say his deliverance fell out in other fashion. They say the king had a good archer, who, when he saw his lord left all alone, ran always by him on foot till he was gone into the wood. Then he said to himself that he should tarry there and see whether he could slay the hound. For he knew full well that if the hound lived John of Lorne and his men would follow the king's trace till they took him. He put his life on the venture to succour his lord, and stood lurking in a covert till the hound came near. Then he slew him swiftly with an arrow, and withdrew through the wood. But, whether the escape of Bruce befell as I first said, or in this fashion, I know that for certain the king got away at the stream.

The Bruce went his way, and John of Lorne went again to Sir Aymer, who had returned with his men from the pursuit. In that chase they had made but little speed, for though they followed right eagerly, they gained but little; nearly all their foes escaped. It is said that in the pursuit Sir Thomas Randolph captured the king's banner, and by that deed earned the greatest praise and esteem from Edward in England.

When the pursuers were rallied, and John of Lorne met them, he told Sir Aymer all that had happened, how the king had escaped, and how he had slain the five men, and then taken to the forest.

When Sir Aymer heard this he crossed himself for wonder, and said, " He is greatly to be esteemed, for I know none living who can so help himself in mischance. I trow he should be hard to slay if he were furnished equally."

Meanwhile the good king and his man held forward on their way till they had passed through the forest. Then they entered a wide upland moor. Ere they had crossed half of it, they saw on one side three men coming, like idle and wandering fellows. They had swords and axes, and one of them bore a great wether bound upon his neck.

They met the king, and greeted him, and he returned their greeting, and asked whither they went. They said they sought Robert the Bruce, if they could meet with him, and wished to find quarters with him.

"If that be your wish," said the king, "go forward with me, and I shall soon bring you to him."

They perceived by his speech and his bearing that he was the king, and they changed countenance and demeanour, and kept not in their first bearing; for they were foes to the king, and thought to come in treacherously, and abide with him till they saw their time, and take his life. They agreed, therefore, to what he said, but he right shrewdly perceived by their bearing that they nowise loved him.

"Comrades," he said, "till we be further acquainted ye must all three go forward by yourselves, and in the same way we two shall follow close behind you."

"Sir," said they, "there is no need to think any ill toward us."

"Neither do I," he answered, "but I desire that ye go before us till we be better known to each other."

"We agree," they said, "since ye will have it so." And they went forward on their way.

Thus they marched till it was near night, when they came to a large farmhouse. There the men slew the wether they carried, and made a fire to roast the meat. And they asked the king if he would eat, and rest him till the meat were prepared. To this he agreed readily, being hungry, I promise. But he said he would sit apart with his companion at one fire, and the three should make another fire in the end of the house.

This they did. They drew to the house end, and sent him half the wether, and roasted their meat quickly and fell to eating right keenly.

The king had fasted long and travelled far, therefore he ate eagerly. And when he had eaten he had a great desire to sleep, which he could not resist. For when the veins are filled the body ever becomes heavy, and heaviness draws to sleep. Being thus overwearied, and seeing that he must needs sleep, he said to his foster-brother, "Can I trust thee to keep watch while I take a little sleep?"

"Yea, sir," he answered, "while I can hold out."

Then the king nodded a little space. He did not sleep altogether, but glanced up often suddenly, for he feared the three men at the other fire, whom he knew to be his foes. Therefore he slept like the bird on the bough.

H

He had slept but little thus when such a heaviness fell on his man that he could not keep his eyes open, but fell asleep and snored loudly.

The king was now in great peril, for should he sleep thus a little while he must surely be slain. The three traitors took good heed that he and his man were asleep, and forthwith they rose up, and drew their swords, and made swiftly at him as he slept, and thought to slay him ere he could wake.

They went a great part of the way towards him, but at that moment, by God's grace, the king blinked up, and saw his man sleeping beside him, and the three traitors coming. He sprang nimbly to his feet, and drew his sword, and met them. And as he went he set his foot heavily on his man. The man wakened, and rose dizzily, but the sleep so mastered him that, ere he got up, one of them coming to slay the king gave him such a stroke that he could help him no more.

Then was the king more straitly beset than he had ever yet been, and but for the armour he wore he had assuredly been slain. Nevertheless he fended himself so in that struggle, that by God's grace and his own manhood he slew the three traitors.

His foster-brother was slain, and he was wondrously at a loss when he saw he was left alone.

He lamented his foster-brother, and cursed all
the other three, and set out alone towards his
meeting-place.

He went forth wrathful and vexed, tenderly
mourning his man, and held his way all alone
towards the house where he had agreed to meet
his men. It was then very late at night. Pre-
sently he came to the house, and found the
goodwife sitting on the settle. She asked him
straightway what he was, and whence he came,
and whither he went.

"I am a wandering man, dame," said he, "that
journeys here through the country."

"All wanderers," she answered, "are welcome
here for the sake of one."

The king replied, "Good dame, who is he that
causes you to have such special liking for wan-
dering men?"

"Indeed, sir," quoth the goodwife, "I shall tell
you. He is our good king, Robert the Bruce,
who is rightful lord of this country. His enemies
now keep him in distress, but I look ere long to
see him lord and king over all the land, so that
no enemies shall withstand him."

"Dame, dost thou love him so well?" said he.

"Yea, sir," she said, "as God sees me."

"Dame," said he, "behold him beside thee, for I
am he."

"Speak ye truly?" she cried.

" Yea, certes, dame ! "

" And where are your men gone, that ye are thus alone ? "

" At this moment, dame, I have none."

" It must in nowise be so," she cried, " I have two bold and active sons. They shall forthwith become your men."

They did as she devised, and there and then became the king's sworn men. Then the woman made him sit and eat. But he had been only a short while at the meal when they heard a great stamping about the house. Then at once they started up to defend the place, but soon afterwards the king knew James of Douglas. Then was he blithe, and bade them quickly open the doors, and his men came in, all that there were. Sir Edward the Bruce was there, as well as James of Douglas, who had escaped from the pursuit, and had met the king's brother, and hastened with him to the appointed trysting place, with a company of a hundred and fifty men.

When they saw the king they were joyful at the meeting, and asked how he had escaped. He told them all that had happened; how the five men had desperately beset him, and how he had passed through the stream, and met the three thieves, and should have been slain sleeping, but that he wakened, through God's grace; and how

his foster-brother was killed. Then all together
they praised God that their lord had escaped.

They talked a while back and forth, till at last
the king said, "Fortune has troubled us this day,
scattering us so suddenly. Our foes will lie
securely to-night, for they think we are so
scattered and in flight here and there that we
shall not be gathered together these three days.
Wherefore if one knew their camping-place, and
came suddenly upon them, he might easily with
a handful of men do them hurt, and escape
without damage."

"By my faith," said James of Douglas, "as I
came hitherward I passed by chance so near their
quarters that I can bring you where they lie.
And if ye make speed ye may yet, before morn-
ing, do them a greater hurt than they have done
us all day, for they lie scattered as they list."

Then all agreed it was best to hasten and come
at them, and they did so forthwith, and came
on them at daybreak, as the light began to
appear.

It so happened that a company had taken
quarters in a village a mile or more from the
host. Two thousand, they were said to be. There
the noble king directed his attack, and presently,
all his force having come up, the sleepers were
assailed and a hideous uproar arose. Others that
heard the cry ran forth in such fear that some

were naked fleeing hither and thither, and some dragged their arms after them. The Bruce's men slew them without mercy, and took such cruel vengeance that in that spot more than two-thirds of them were slain. The rest fled to their host.

When that host heard the noise and cry, and saw its men come fleeing naked here and there so wretchedly, some whole and some sore wounded, it rose in great affright, and each man went to his standard, so that the army was all astir. The king and those with him, when they saw the enemy thus afoot, set out for their place of refuge, and soon reached it.

And when Sir Aymer heard how the king had slain his men and retired, he said, "Now may we clearly see that a noble heart, wherever it be, is hard to overcome by force. For where the heart is valiant it is ever stubborn against difficulty, and I trow no fear can discourage it utterly, so long as the body is free. As much may be seen from this encounter. We deemed Robert the Bruce so discomfited that, as well as could be judged, he should have neither courage nor desire to undertake such hazard. For he was so far mastered as to be left alone, and parted from all his folk, and he was so over-wearied by the pursuit of his assailants that he should have desired rest rather than fighting or marching. But his heart is full of valour, and cannot be conquered."

Thus spake Sir Aymer. And when his companions saw how their labour had been in vain, and how the king had slaughtered their men, and was at full liberty, and that they could not trouble him, it seemed to them folly to remain longer there. They said this to Sir Aymer, and he forthwith determined to go to Carlisle and sojourn there for a time, and keep spies about the Bruce, to know always what he did. His plan was, when he saw his chance, to dash with a great force suddenly at the king. So he took the road for England, with all his company, and each man went to his own house. He himself went to Carlisle with intent to stay there till he saw his opportunity.

Meanwhile Bruce remained in Carrick with all his gathering, and would sometimes go hunting there with his men. So it happened that one day he went to hunt, to see what game was in that country, and it chanced that he sat by a wood side with his two hounds alone, but having his sword, which he always carried. He had sat but a short time there, when he saw coming speedily towards him from the wood three men with bows in their hands, and he straightway perceived by their appearance and manner that they nowise loved him.

He rose and drew his leash to him, and let his hounds go free.

God for his greatness' sake now help the king; for, unless he now be wise and strong he shall be set in great distress. For these three men were assuredly his deadly foes, and had watched busily to see when they could take vengeance on him for John Comyn's sake. That chance they now thought they had, and seeing him alone in the spot, they thought to slay him forthwith. If they could manage, after they had slain the king, to reach the wood again, they should have nothing to fear, they thought, from his men.

They went quickly towards him, and bent their bows as they came near, and he, greatly fearing their arrows, for he was without armour, made haste to speak to them. "Of a sooth," he said, "ye should be ashamed, since I am one and ye are three, to shoot at me from a distance! But if ye be brave men, come near and try me with your swords. Vanquish me in that way, if ye can, and ye shall all win much greater fame."

"By my faith," then said one of the three, "no man shall say we dread thee so greatly that we must slay thee with arrows."

With that they cast away their bows, and came on at once.

The king met them boldly, and smote the fore-

most so hard that he fell dead on the green.
And when the king's hound saw these men thus
assail his master, he sprang at one and took him
so fiercely by the throat that he threw him head
over heels. Then the king, who had his sword
up, and saw himself succoured so well, ere the
fallen man could rise again, attacked him in
such fashion that he broke his back. The third
man, when he saw his fellows thus slain beyond
recovery, took his way to the wood again. But
the king followed quickly, as well as the hound
beside him, and the dog, seeing the man go from
him, dashed swiftly at him, and took him by the
throat, and drew him down. And the king, being
near enough, gave him such a stroke as he rose
that he dropped to the ground stone-dead.

The king's company, which was near, when
they saw their master so suddenly attacked in
this fashion, sped in haste to him, and asked
how the chance befell, and he told them fully
how all the three had assailed him.

"Indeed," said they, "we can well see it is
a difficult venture to take on hand such an
encounter with you, since without hurt you have
so quickly slain these three."

"In truth," said he, "I slew no more than one.
God and my hound slew the other two. Their
treason, indeed, overwhelmed them, for right
stout men were they all three."

When the king thus, by God's grace, had
escaped, he blew his horn, and his good men
rallied quickly to him, and he made ready to
fare homewards, for he would hunt no more
that day.

He lay for some time in Glentrool, and went
very often to enjoy the hunt and get venison
for his men, for the deer were then in season.
All that time Sir Aymer, with a noble company,
lay in Carlisle, watching his chance. And when
he heard for certain that the king was in Glen-
trool, and went to hunt and pleasure himself, he
thought to come upon him suddenly with his
armed force. By leaving Carlisle and making a
forced march, riding all night, and keeping in
cover during the day, he thought he should sur-
prise the king. Accordingly he got together a
great host, folk of the greatest renown, both
Scots and English. They held their way all
together, and rode by night, so that they reached
the wood near Glentrool, where the king had
his quarters, without his knowing aught of their
coming.

He was now in great peril. Unless God by His
great might should save him, he must be taken
or slain; for they were six where he was one.

I have heard that when Sir Aymer with his
stalwart following came within a mile of the king,
he took counsel with his men in what manner they

should act. He told them the Bruce was lodged in so strait a place that horsemen could not attack him, and if footmen gave him battle he should be hard to vanquish if he were warned of their coming. "Therefore I counsel that we send a woman secretly to spy upon him. Let her be poorly dressed, and ask food for pity's sake, and see their whole arrangement, and how they lie, while we and our host are coming through the wood on foot, arrayed as we are. If we can so manage that we come upon them there, before they know of our coming, we shall find no stoppage in them."

This counsel they thought the best, and they straightway sent forward the woman who was to be their spy, and she quickly made her way to the lodges where the king, fearing no surprisal, went blithe and merry and unarmed.

Very soon he saw the woman, and knew her a stranger, and therefore looked at her the more carefully, and by her countenance bethought him that she was come for no good. Then he quickly made his men seize her, and she, fearing they should slay her, told them how Sir Aymer, with the Clifford and the flower of Northumberland in his company, were coming upon them, and at hand.

When the king heard these tidings he armed at once, as did all that were there, and they gathered in a close body, near three hundred in number, I believe. And when they were all come together the king caused his banner to be displayed, and set his men in good array.

They had stood but a little while when they saw, close to them, their enemies coming through the wood on foot, armed, spear in hand, and hastening with all their might.

The noise and outcry soon began, for the good king, who was foremost, made boldly at his foes, and snatched a bow and broad arrow out of a man's hand, who was going beside him, and hit the foremost enemy in the throat so that windpipe and weasand were split in two and he fell to the ground.

At that the others paused. Then at once the noble king took the banner from his standard-bearer, and cried, "Upon them, for they are vanquished all!" And with that word he swiftly swept out his sword, and ran so boldly upon them that all his company took hardihood from his bravery. Even some that at first had made off came again hastily to the fight, and met their foes so furiously that all the foremost were overthrown.

And when they that were behind saw the foremost borne back they turned and fled out of the wood. The king slew few of them, for they right soon made off. It altogether discom-

fited them to find the king and his company thus
fully armed to defend the place which they
thought to have won by stratagem without
fighting. This suddenly dismayed them, and
when he made at them so fiercely they ran with
the greatest speed out of the wood again to
the plain. By the failing of their purpose at
that time they were foully disgraced. Fifteen
hundred men and more were beaten by a hand-
ful, and they retreated shamefully.

For this reason there arose among them a
sudden and great debate and difference, each with
the other, regarding their mischance. Clifford
and Vaux came to strife. Clifford hit Vaux a
buffet, and the others drew to sides. But the
wise Sir Aymer, with much trouble, parted
them, and returned home to England. He knew
that if strife rose among them he should not
keep them together long. He returned to
England with more shame than he brought out
of it, seeing so many, of such renown, beheld
so few offer them battle, and were not bold
enough to make an attack.

BOOK VIII

THE BATTLE OF LOUDOUN HILL

AFTER Sir Aymer was gone the king gathered
followers, and left woods and mountains,
and held his way straight to the plains, for he
would fain make end of what he had begun, and
he knew well he could not bring it to good end
without an effort. First he went to Kyle, and
made all obedient to him, the men for the most
part coming to his peace. Next, ere he ceased,
he caused the greater part of Cunningham to
hold to his sovereignty.

Sir Aymer, then in Bothwell, was greatly vexed
in heart, because the men of Cunningham and
Kyle, who were lately obedient to him, left the
English fealty. Thereof he was fain to be
avenged, and sent Sir Philip the Mowbray with,
I have heard, a thousand men under his com-
mand, to Kyle, to make war on the noble king.
But James of Douglas, who had spies at all
times on every side, knew of their coming, and
that they would advance down Makyrnock's

Way.[1] He took with him privily the sixty men of his company, and went to a narrow place on Makyrnock's Way, called the Edryford, lying between marshes where no horse living could go. On the south side, where Douglas was, is an ascent, a narrow place, and on the north side is a difficult way.

Douglas and those with him made ambush and waited there. He could see the enemy coming a great way off, but they could see nothing of him. The Scots lay in ambush all night, and when the sun was shining brightly they saw the van of the English coming arrayed in a body, with banner displayed, and soon afterwards they saw the rest marching close behind.

They held themselves close and secret till the foremost of the enemy had entered the ford beside them. Then, with a cry, they rushed upon them, and with sharp weapons bore some backward into the ford, and with broad barbed arrows made such great martyrdom among others that they tried to draw back and leave the spot. But the way behind them was so blocked that they could not flee quickly, and this caused the

[1] This locality has always been obscure. Possibly it should be "Maich and Garnock way." These two streams, descending from Misty Law towards Kilbirnie Loch, traverse the ordinary route of the present day from Clydeside into Cunningham. If this be correct the ambush was probably set at the old ford crossing the Maich Water among the marshes by Kilbirnie Loch.

death of many. For they could escape on neither
side, but only by the road they came, unless they
made their way through their enemies. This
way, however, they all seemed to hate.

Douglas's men met them so sturdily, and con-
tinued the fight so boldly that they fell into
panic, and he who could flee first fled first. And
when the rearward saw them thus discomfited
and in flight they fled afar off, and made for
home. But Sir Philip the Mowbray, who was
riding with the foremost that entered the ford,
when he saw how he was placed, struck spurs
into his good steed, and by his great valour,
despite all his enemies, rode through the thickest
of them. He would have escaped without chal-
lenge, had not a man seized him by the brand.
But the good steed would not stand. It sprang
nimbly forward, and the man holding on
stalwartly, the sword-belt burst, and left belt
and sword both in his hand. And Sir Philip,
without his sword, rode his way right through
them. There he paused, but beholding how his
host fled, and how his foes cleared the ground
between himself and his men, he took his way to
Kilmarnock and Kilwinning and Ardrossan, then
through Largs to Inverkip, straight to the castle.
The stronghold was then filled with Englishmen,
and they received him with great respect; and
when they knew how he had ridden so far alone

through his enemies they honoured him greatly
and praised his exploit.

Thus Sir Philip escaped. Meanwhile Douglas
had slain sixty and more on the spot. The rest
foully turned their backs, and fled home again to
Bothwell. There Sir Aymer was nothing fain,
when he heard in what manner his host had
been discomfited. But when King Robert was
told how the good and bold Douglas had van-
quished so many men with so few, he was right
joyful in heart. All his men, too, were encouraged,
for they felt assured that since their enterprise
went so well they ought to fear their foes less.

The king lay in Galston, which is right opposite
Loudoun, and took the country to his peace.
When Sir Aymer and his following heard how
he ruled all the land, and how none durst with-
stand him, he was vexed in heart, and by one of
his company sent him word, saying if he durst
meet him in the open country, he, Sir Aymer,
should on the tenth of May come under Loudoun
Hill. "And if the Bruce would meet him there,"
he said, "the renown would be greater and more
knightly that was won in the open with hard
blows and in equal fight than was to be got with
far more trouble in skulking."

When the king heard this message he greatly
disliked Sir Aymer's haughtiness. Therefore he
answered seriously, and said to the messenger,

I

"Tell thy lord that if I be living he shall see
me that day very near, if he dare hold the way
he has said, for assuredly I shall meet him by
Loudoun Hill."

The messenger at once rode to his master, and
told his answer. Then was there no need to
make Sir Aymer glad, for he felt sure, by the
great strength and force of arms he possessed,
that, if the king dared appear to fight, he should
overthrow him beyond recovery.

On the other side the Bruce, ever wise and
prudent, rode to see and choose the ground. He
saw that the highway lay upon a fair field, even
and dry, but upon either side, a bowshot from
the road, was a great moss, broad and deep. The
place seemed to him all too wide for a stand to
be made there against cavalry. Therefore he cut
three ditches across, from each of the mosses to
the road. These were a bowshot and more apart
from each other, and so deep and steep that men
could not pass them without much trouble, even
though none withstood them. But he left gaps
at the road large enough for five hundred to ride
through abreast. There he determined to await
battle, and oppose the enemy, having no fear
that they could attack him on the flank or
rear, and feeling sure that in front he should be
defended against their strength.

He caused three deep trenches to be made so

that, if he could not manage to meet the enemy
at the first, he should have the second in his
power, and afterwards the third, if it so happened
that they passed the other two.

Thus he arranged. Then he assembled his host.
They were six hundred fighting men, besides
camp-followers as many or more. With all that
host he went, on the evening before the battle
was to take place, to Little Loudoun. There he
determined to wait, to see the coming of the
enemy, and then hasten forward with his men,
to be at the trench before them.

Sir Aymer, on the other side, gathered a great
force, nigh three thousand strong, well armed and
equipped, and then, in knightliest fashion, held
his way to the tryst. And when the set day
was come he sped fast towards the place that he
had named for the battle. The sun had risen,
shining brightly, and flashed on the broad shields,
as he advanced with his array in two squadrons.

Very early in the morning the king saw their
first squadron coming, well arrayed in close order,
and at its back, a little way off, he saw the second
following it. Their basnets were all burnished
bright, and flamed in the light of the sun, and
their shields, spears, and pennons lighted up all
the field. Their bright embroidered banners, and
horses caparisoned in many hues, and many-col-
oured coat-armour, and hauberks white as flour,

made them glitter like angels of the kingdom of heaven.

The king said, "Sirs, ye see now how yonder mighty men would slay us if they could, and how they appear for that end. But, since we know their cruelty, go we and meet them boldly, so that the stoutest of their host shall be discouraged at the encounter. For if the foremost be fiercely met ye shall see the hindmost suddenly discomfited. And though they be more in number than we, that need dismay us little, for when we come to the fighting there can no more meet us than ourselves. Therefore, sirs, let each be stout and valiant to uphold our honour here. Think what gladness awaits us if we can, as may befall, gain the victory here over our foes! For there will be none in all this land that we need fear."

Then said all that stood about, "Sir, please God, we shall act so that no blame shall be ours."

"Then go we forward," said the king; "and He that made all things of nothing, lead us and preserve us for His greatness' sake, and help us to keep our right!"

With that they sped upon their way. They were full six hundred strong, doughty and valiant, stalwart and stout, yet, were it not for their extraordinary valour, all too few, I promise, to stand in battle against so many.

Stoutly and in good array the noble king marched forth, and reached the foremost ditch, and took the field in the gap. The baggage-carriers and rabble, of no account in battle, he left halted behind, standing all together on the hill.

Sir Aymer saw the king and his men come proudly and boldly down from the hill to the plain, right willing, as it seemed to him, either to defend or attack any who should give them battle. Accordingly he encouraged his men, and bade them be strong and valiant, for if they could overcome the king and gain the victory, they should be right well rewarded, and add greatly to their renown.

With that, they were very near the king, and Sir Aymer stopped his exhortation, and caused the trumpets to sound the charge, and the foremost of his host seized their broad shields and rode together in close array. With heads stooping and level spears they rushed right at the king. And he met them with so much vigour that the best and bravest were brought to the ground at their meeting. There arose such a crashing and breaking of spears and such cries and shouts of the wounded as were dreadful to hear. For those that first encountered fenced and fought all sturdily, and kept up the noise and outcry.

Ah! mighty God! whoever had been there and
had seen the king's majesty and his brother
beside him bear themselves so hardily, and en-
courage their host by deeds of valour, and how
Douglas so manfully encouraged those beside
him, he should indeed say they desired to win
honour. The king's valiant men with their sharp
spears stabbed both riders and steeds till the red
blood poured from wounds. The wounded horses
lashed out, and overthrew the men about them,
so that the foremost were stabbed here and there
in troops.

The king seeing them thus overthrown and
reeling to and fro, ran upon them so keenly
and dealt blows at them so stoutly that he laid
low many of his enemies. The field was wellnigh
all covered with slain horses and men; for the
good king was followed by full five hundred
men-at-arms who spared their foes no whit.
They drove at them so doughtily that in a short
time a hundred and more of the enemy might
be seen lying on the ground. The rest were the
weaker for this, and began to fall back. And
when those in the rear saw their vanguard thus
overcome, they fled without waiting longer.

And when Sir Aymer saw his men all presently
in flight, ye may well know he was full sad.
But by no exhortation could he get any to turn
for him again. And when he saw he lost his

pains he drew his bridle, and fled. For the good king pressed them so that some were slain and some were taken and the rest were in flight.

The soldiery fled thus without stopping, and Sir Aymer went again to Bothwell, lamenting the hurt he had taken. And so ashamed was he to have been vanquished, that he went forthwith straight to King Edward in England, and greatly abased gave up his wardenship; nor ever afterwards on any account, save when he came with the king himself, did he return to make war in Scotland. Thus heavily did he take to heart that the Bruce, in set battle, with a few rabble-like followers, had vanquished him, who was renowned for his valour, and his great host. This was Sir Aymer's vexation.

Meanwhile the bold king Robert remained in the field till his men had quite left the pursuit, and, with the prisoners he had taken, they went again towards their quarters, praising God diligently for their welfare. Then might one have seen a folk glad and merry for their victory. And they had a lord so sweet and debonair, so courteous and of such fair demeanour, so blithe too, and so full of jest, and so strong in battle, so wise, and so prudent, that they had great cause to be glad. Thus blithe they were, without a doubt; and many that dwelt about them, after they saw the king so mend his fortunes, made their homage to him.

Then his power waxed more and more, and he determined to march across the Mounth[1] with his following to see who would be his friends. He trusted in Sir Alexander the Fraser and his brother Simon,[2] for they were his cousins. He had need indeed of more, for he had many foes. Sir John Comyn, Earl of Buchan, and Sir John the Mowbray, and stout Sir David of Brechin, with all the men at their command, were enemies to the noble king. And because he knew they were his enemies he took his journey northward, for he wished to see what end they would make of their menacing.

The king equipped himself and made ready to fare northwards with his men. He took with him his brother and Sir Gilbert de la Haye. The Earl of Lennox also was there, for he went everywhere with the king, as well as Sir Robert Boyd, and others beside.

The Bruce set forth, and left James of Douglas and all his men behind, to see whether he could recover his country. Douglas was left in great peril, but he wrought with such bravery that in a little while he brought to the king's peace the

---

[1] The North-Eastern Grampians.

[2] Barbour makes a slip here. Sir Simon Fraser was executed the year before.

whole forest of Selkirk, as well as Douglasdale and Jedburgh forest. Whoever should undertake with skill enough to tell his deeds of valour one by one would find many to tell. For in his time, I have been told, he was vanquished thirteen times and won seven and fifty victories. He seemed not to lie idle long, and was never at a loss for labours. Methinks men had reason to love him.

This James, when the king was gone, took his men all privily, and went again to Douglasdale, and secretly laid a plot for those in the castle. He made there a cunning ambush, and caused fourteen or more of his men to take sacks filled with grass, and lay them on their horses, and hold their way beyond the place of the ambush as if they would go to Lanark fair. And when those of the castle saw so many loads going in a row, they were wondrous pleased at the sight, and told it to their captain. He was named Sir John of Webton, and was young, stout, and fierce. Right festive too he was, and light of conduct, and because of certain love affairs would the more blithely sally forth.

He caused his men all to take their gear, and sally out to get that victual, for their victual was fast failing them. They issued all in disorder, and pricked forward with right good will to take the loads they saw passing by, till Douglas and his men were all between them and the castle.

The load-men, who saw them well, hastily cast down their burdens, and threw away the gowns that covered them, and with the utmost speed seized their horses, and with a shout rushed sturdily at their foes.

The men of the castle were greatly amazed when they saw those that before were lurking so low come so boldly upon them. They grew suddenly dismayed, and would have made for the castle, when on the other side they saw Douglas break from his ambush and come stoutly against them.

They knew not what to do or say. Their foes they saw at hand, who struck without sparing, and they could help themselves in no way, but fled to shelter where they might. But Douglas's men made so fiercely at them that not one of them all escaped. Sir John of Webton was slain, and when he was dead they found in his purse a letter sent him by a lady that he wooed with love-service. The letter spake in this manner. When he had as a good bachelor guarded for a year in war, and governed well in all ways, the adventurous castle of Douglas, that was so perilous to keep, then might he indeed ask a lady for her love and her love-reward. Thus spake the letter.

And when the men were thus slain, Douglas rode straight to the castle, and there made such an assault that he entered the stronghold. I know not the whole matter surely, whether it

was by force or stratagem, but he so wrought
that he took the constable and all the rest
within, both man and boy, and gave them money
to spend, and sent them home unharmed, to the
Clifford in their own country. And afterwards
he laboured busily till he had thrown down all
the wall and destroyed the whole house. Then
he held his way to the forest,[1] where many
a hard assault and many a fair point of war
befell. He who could rehearse and tell all these
exploits should set his name in great and lasting
renown.

[1] Lintalee above Jedburgh, in the ancient Jed Forest, is pointed
out by tradition as the spot where he took up his open-air quarters.

BOOK IX

THE TAKING OF PERTH

NOW in the forest leave we Douglas, who was
to have little rest till the country was
delivered from Englishmen and their might, and
turn we to the noble king who, with his fol-
lowers, had set forth right stoutly, and in good
array, towards the Mounth. There he was met
by Alexander Fraser and his brother Simon,
and all the folk they had with them. The king
made them good countenance and was right
glad of their coming. They told him all the
purpose of John Comyn, Earl of Buchan, who
had taken to help him Sir John Mowbray and
Sir David the Brechin, with all their following,
"and more than anything desire to take ven-
geance on you, Sir King, for the sake of Sir
John Comyn, who was slain in Dumfries."

"As Our Lord will forgive me," said the king,
"I had great cause for slaying him; but since
they take on hand to war against me because
of him, I shall wait a while, and see how they

show their strength, and if so be they seek to fight we must defend ourselves, and take the fortune God sends us."

After this speech the king hastened straight to Inverury, and there was seized with such a sickness as put him to the direst distress, and made him forbear both drink and meat. His men could get no medicine that helped him, and his strength so wholly failed him that he could neither ride nor walk. Then, ye may well believe, his men were sad, for there was none in that company who would have been half so grieved to see his own brother lying there dead before him as they all were for the king's sickness, for he was their whole encouragement. But good Sir Edward, his brother, the gallant and bold, stalwart and wise, strove with all his might to cheer them. And when the lords who were there saw that the sickness ever more and more troubled the king, they thought presently it was not expedient to lie in that place. For the country there was all plain, and they were but a small company to lie, without a stronghold, in the open. Therefore, till their captain recovered from his great malady, they resolved to make their way to some fastness.

Folk without a captain, unless they be the better men in a difficulty, shall not be wholly so stout of deed as if they had a lord to lead

them who dare put it to the touch boldly to
take the fortune God will send. When a leader
is of such heart and valour as to dare an
exploit, his men take example from his man-
hood and bravery, so that each one of them
becomes worth three others who have only a
sorry chief. A leader's cowardice, on the other
hand, so acts upon his men that they lose their
manliness through the unskilfulness of his leader-
ship. For when the lord who should lead them
is no better than a dead man, or flees the field,
trow ye not they shall be vanquished in their
hearts? Yea, indeed they shall, I trow, except
their hearts be so high that because of their
valour they will not flee. And some, though
they be of such nobleness, yet, when they see
the lord and his company flee, shall flee at a
pinch, for all men right gladly flee from death.

See what he does who thus so foully flees
because of his cowardice! Both he and his men
are vanquished, and his foes are set upper-
most. But he who, by reason of his great
nobility, devotes himself to dangers to encourage
his host, fills his men with such bravery that
many a time they bring unlikely ventures to a
right good end.

Thus did King Robert, of whom I tell. By
extraordinary manhood he so encouraged his
men that none knew fear where he was. They

desired not to fight while he was lying in such sickness, and so they laid him in a litter, and made their way to the Sliach,[1] and resolved to lie in that fastness till his malady was past.

But when the Earl of Buchan knew that they were gone thither, and learned that the king was so sick that men doubted his recovery, he sent hastily after his men, and assembled a great company. All his own men were there, and all his friends were with him, Sir John the Mowbray and his brother, I have heard, also Sir David of Brechin, and many in their following.

And when they were all come together they set out forthwith in full force, on the march to the Sliach to attack the sick king. This was after Martinmas, when snow had covered all the land.

As they came near the Sliach, in their best array, the king's men, who knew of their coming, armed themselves to make defence if they should be attacked. They did this notwithstanding that their enemies were two to their one.

The earl's men were coming close, blowing trumpets and making a great show. They made knights too when they were near. And the

[1] A fastness of the hills on the borders of the Garioch, sixteen miles north-west of Inverury.

king's men stood in the woodside in close array and determined to await the coming of their enemies boldly there. They would on no account issue forth to an attack till the king was recovered, but if the others should attack them they would make defence, help what might.

And when the earl's company saw they wrought so busily and prepared to defend that fastness, they sent forth their archers to skirmish with them as men of might. And Bruce's party sent archers against these, who skirmished so stoutly with them that the earl's skirmishers withdrew into their ranks.

Thus they lay there three days, and skirmished each day, and the earl's bowmen ever had the worst. And when the king's company saw the foes before them growing more in number each day, while they themselves were few and so placed that they had nothing to eat unless they toiled to get it, they took counsel and agreed to lie there no longer, but make their way to a place where they could get victual and meat for them and theirs.

They laid the king in a litter, and made ready, and set out, and all their foes could see each man armed in his degree to fight if they were assailed. They bore the king in their midst, and marched closely around him, and made no great haste.

The earl and his men saw them make ready to march, and beheld with how little fear they set forth with the king, and how they were ready to fight whoever might attack; and the hearts of the assailants failed, and they let the company go their way in peace, and themselves went home.

The earl made his way to Buchan, and Sir Edward the Bruce went straight to Strathbogie with the king, and made sojourn there till he began to recover and walk, then they returned to Inverury. For they wished to lie during the winter in the low country, where victual could not fail them.

The earl learned they were there, and gathered his scattered host. Brechin, Mowbray, and their men all gathered to him, and were a right great company bravely arrayed. They came to Old Meldrum, and quartered there, a thousand strong, on the night before Christmas Eve.[1] They all lodged there that night, and on the morrow, at daylight, Sir David, the lord of Brechin, went towards Inverury, to see whether he could in any manner do hurt to his enemies. So suddenly did he come riding into the end of Inverury that he slew some of the king's men, while the rest withdrew and fled towards the king, who, with most of his followers, was

[1] This was the Christmas Eve of 1307.

K

then lying in the further half of the place.
And when he was told the tidings how Sir David
had slain his men, Bruce asked quickly for his
horse, and bade his men make ready with the
greatest speed, since he would go to fight his
enemies. With that, though not yet fully re-
covered, he made ready to rise.

Then some of his servants said, "What! think
ye, Sir, thus to go and fight, and not yet
recovered of your sickness?

"Yea," said the king, "without a doubt, their
insolence has made me sound and whole. No
medicine could so soon have recovered me as
this has done. Therefore, as God sees me, I shall
either have them, or they me."

And when his men heard the king so wholly
set on fighting, they all rejoiced at his recovery,
and made ready for the battle.

The noble king and his host, which might be
very near seven hundred strong, set out for Old
Meldrum, where the earl and his company lay.
The scouts saw them coming, with banners wav-
ing to the wind, and they told it quickly to their
lord, and he caused his men to arm in haste, and
arrayed them for battle. Behind them they set
the rabble of their camp, and made a good show
for the fight.

The king came on in great strength, and the
earl's men stood their ground, making great show

till they were near joining battle. But when they saw the noble king come on stoutly and without check, they backed their steeds a little. And the Bruce, who knew right well that they were all well-nigh discomfited, pressed on them with his banner. Then they withdrew more and more, and when the small folk saw their lords thus retreat they all turned their backs, dispersed, and fled, scattered here and there. The lords, who still held together, saw their small folk flee and the king coming stoutly on, and were so dismayed that they, too, turned their backs and fled. A little space they held together, and then each man took his own way.

Never so foul mischance befell a host, after making so sturdy a show. For when the king's company saw they fled so cravenly, they chased them with all their might, and took some and slew others. The rest fled without pause. He whose horse was good got best away. The Earl of Buchan fled to England, and Sir John Mowbray went with him, and found refuge with King Edward. But they had both only a short respite, for they died soon afterwards. And Sir David of Brechin fled to Brechin, his own castle, and provisioned and armed it well. But David, son of the Earl of Atholl, who was in Kildrummy, came presently and besieged him there, and he, wishing to war and battle no more against the noble king, shortly, with fair treaty, became his man.[1]

Now go we again to the king. He was right glad of his victory, and caused his men to burn all Buchan from end to end, and spared none. He harried the region in such fashion that nigh fifty years afterwards men lamented the Ravage of Buchan. The Bruce then took the north country to his peace, and it humbly obeyed his sovereignty, so that north of the Mounth there was none that was not his man, and his rule waxed ever more and more. He made his way then towards Angus, and planned soon to free all the country north of the Scottish Sea.[2]

The castle of Forfar was then garrisoned with Englishmen, but Philip the Forester of Platane took his friends and ladders, and went secretly to the stronghold, and climbed the stone wall, and with little difficulty, by fault of the watch, took the place. He slew all whom he found, then yielded the castle to the king, who made him right good reward, and afterwards had the wall broken down and the castle and well destroyed.

When the castle of Forfar and all its towers were thrown down, the wise king, active and bold, went with all his rout to Perth, and beset

---

[1] According to Fordoun this battle occurred in 1308, and Lord Hailes in his *Annals* makes May 22 the date.

[2] The old name for the Firth of Forth.

the town and laid siege to it. But so long as
it had men and meat it could not be taken, except
with great trouble, for the walls were all of stone
with strong and high towers. At that time there
dwelt in it Moffat and Oliphant. These two had
the whole town in ward. The Earl of Strathearn
also was there, but his son and many of his men
were without in the king's host.

There was frequent skirmishing hard and
stubborn, and men were slain on each side, but
the good king, shrewd in every act, saw the
strength of the wall, and the defence the garrison
could make, and how hard the town was to take
by strength or force in open assault, and he
resolved to work by stratagem. All the time he
lay there he espied and cunningly caused discovery
to be made as to where the ditch was shallowest,
till at last he found a place which men might
wade to their shoulders. And when he had
found that place he caused his followers each
one to make ready. Six weeks of the siege
were then gone. They packed up their armour
altogether, and openly left the siege, and the
king marched away with all his folk as if he
would do no more to the place.

They that were within the town, when they
saw him make ready to march, shouted and
scoffed at him. And he rode forth on his way
as if he had no wish to return or make sojourn

beside them. But in eight days he had ladders made secretly, sufficient for his purpose, and then in a dark night went with his host towards the town. He left all the horses and grooms far from the place, and took the ladders, and went on foot secretly towards the walls.

No sentinels were heard to speak or cry, for the folk within, mayhap, as men that fear nothing, all slept. They had no dread of the king, for they had heard no tidings of him these three days and more, and so they were trusting and secure.

When the king heard nothing stir he was greatly pleased, and took his ladder in hand for an example to his men. Then, full arrayed in all his armour, he plunged into the ditch, and, testing with his spear, waded across. But the water stood to his throat.

There was at that time in his company a stout and active knight of France, and when he saw the king thus crossing in the water, and undauntedly carrying his ladder, he crossed himself at the marvel, and said, "Ah, Lord! what shall we say of our nobles of France who for ever stuff their paunch with sweet morsels, and think but to eat and drink and dance, when a knight so very valiant and renowned for feats of arms sets himself in such peril as this to win a wretched hamlet!"

With that he ran to the ditch and made his way across after the king.

And when the Bruce's followers saw their lord pass over, in a short space they crossed the ditch, and without further hindrance set their ladders to the wall, and pressed diligently to climb up. And the good king, I have heard, was the second man to take the wall.

He waited there till all his force was over. Still there rose neither noise nor outcry. But soon afterwards a noise was made by some that perceived them, and from that the alarm rose through the town. But the king, being ready with his men to attack, entered the town. He sent most of his force scattering through the place, but kept a large body with himself, so that he should be provided with defence, if he were attacked. Those, however, whom he sent through the town soon put their foes to great confusion, they being in bed or flying scattered here and there, and before the sun rose the enemy were every one discomfited and taken.

Both of the wardens were captured, and Malise of Strathearn went to his father, the Earl Malise, and took him by force, and all his people. Afterwards, for his son's sake, the noble king gave the earl his land to rule. The others of the king's party ran throughout the town, and seized for themselves in great abundance men, armour, merchandise, and other goods of sundry sort, till some who before were poor and bare became rich and mighty with the spoil. But there were few slain, for the king had given command, with great penalty, that his men should slay none who could be taken without much conflict. He considered they were natives of the country, and he had pity for them.[1]

Thus the town was taken. Then the king caused the towers and walls to be every one thrown down. He left no stone wall or tower standing about that town, but wholly destroyed them all. The prisoners he sent to safe keeping, and he took all the land to his peace. There was none then who durst withstand him. All north of the Scottish Sea obeyed his sovereignty except the Lord of Lorne and the people of Argyll who sided with him. That lord remained ever against the king, and hated him above all else. Yet, before all the play was done, the king was, I trow, to take vengeance on his great cruelty, and make him sore repent, when he could not mend the matter, that he ever persecuted the Bruce.

When the town was thus taken and cast down, the king's brother, the valiant Sir Edward, took with him a great company, and set out for

[1] According to Fordoun, Perth was captured January 8, 1312.

Galloway. For with his men he desired to try whether he could recover that country out of the hand of the English.

This Sir Edward, of a truth, I promise, was a noble knight of his hands, and in manner delightful and joyous. He was extraordinarily bold, and so high of courage that he never was dismayed by the number of his enemies. Because of this he often discomfited many with few, and was renowned above his peers. Of the rehearsal of all his deeds, his valour, and his manhood, many romances might be made. Though I take on hand to say something of him, it is nevertheless not the tenth part of his labours.

This good knight and all the folk with him very soon reached Galloway. There he made all his that he found, and greatly harried the country.

At that time there dwelt in Galloway Sir Ingraham Umphraville, renowned for high prowess and more than common valour. By reason of this, and for a sign that he was set in the highest rank of chivalry he caused ever to be borne before him a red bonnet on a spear. There was also Aymer de St. John. These two had the country in charge, and when they heard of the coming of Sir Edward, and how he so openly rode over the land, they in great haste

got together all their host. Twelve hundred, I
trow, they might be.

But with fewer men he met them beside the
Cree, and so boldly assailed them in hard battle
that he put them all to flight, and slew more
than two hundred of them. The chiefs fled to
Butel for safety, and though Sir Edward chased
them fast, both Sir Ingraham and Sir Aymer
at last reached the castle. The best of their
company, however, they left behind them dead
on the ground. And when Sir Edward saw
the chase had failed he secured the prey, and
carried off such a number of cattle as was a
wonder to see. From Butel tower they saw how
he made his men drive the prey with them, but
to this they could set no hindrance.

Galloway was vastly astonished by this chival-
rous feat of arms, and feared Sir Edward for
his valour. Some of the men of the country
came to his peace, and made oath to him.
But Sir Aymer, after the defeat, rode to
England, and procured there a great company
of armed men to avenge him of the disgrace
done him by the noble Sir Edward in the battle.
He got together fifteen hundred and more good
men of right fair renown, and set out privily
with that armed force to surprise Sir Edward,
if he could. He planned to attack him in open
battle before he could get away.

Now may ye hear of a great marvel, and of the highest feat of arms. Sir Edward was in the country near at hand with his company, and very early in the morning he heard a cry that the English were coming. Then without delay he armed himself, and leapt nimbly on his horse. He had fifty men in his rout, well mounted and armed, and he caused his small folk every one to withdraw to a strait place near by, and rode forth with his fifty.

A knight valiant and active, stalwart and stout, courteous and fair and of good repute, Sir Alan of Cathcart by name, who was then in his company, told me this tale as I shall tell it.

There fell that morning a great mist, so that men could not see a full bow-shot's distance for it. But it chanced that the little company found the trace of the route by which their enemies had passed. Sir Edward, who had at all times a great eagerness for valorous achievements, spurred with his whole rout upon the track. And before mid-morning the mist all suddenly cleared away, and he and his company saw themselves not a bow-shot from the enemy. Then with a shout they dashed upon them; for they saw that if they fled, not a fourth part should well get away, so Sir Edward took the risk of onset rather than of flight, and with a shout the little Scottish company dashed forward.

When the English host saw this band come so suddenly and dauntlessly upon them they were confounded with fear, and their assailants rode so boldly among them that at once they bore many to the earth. Sir Aymer's men were right greatly dismayed by the force of that first attack, and were put in great fear, and supposed, because they were so assailed, that the Scottish troop was larger by far. Then Sir Edward's company, having pierced quickly through the enemy, turned their horses' heads stoutly at them again, and at this charge a great number of their foes were borne down and slain. The English were then so much dismayed that they became greatly scattered. And when Sir Edward and his men saw them in such ill array they pricked on them the third time. And the enemy, seeing them come on so stoutly, were cast into such fear that all their rout, both greater and less, fled, scattering each one here and there. None among them was so bold as stay, but all in common fled for a place of safety.

Sir Edward, being eager to destroy them, gave chase, and took some and slew others. But Sir Aymer with much difficulty escaped, and went his way. His men were discomfited every one— some were taken, some were slain, some escaped. This was indeed a right fair feat of arms.

Lo, how a bold deed suddenly conceived, and forthwith driven sharply forward, may cause an unlikely enterprise to come to a right fair and good ending. Just so it fell out in this case, for boldness, without doubt, caused fifty to overcome fifteen hundred, though it was thirty to one, and two men are one man's master. But fate led the English in such a way that they were each one discomfited.

Sir Aymer made for home, right glad that he got so away. I trow he had no desire for many a day to harry the country where Sir Edward was. And Sir Edward dwelt from that time in Galloway, harrying those in rebellion, and carried on the warfare so that in a year he brought that region freely to the peace of his brother the king. It was a year of nought but hard fighting, and in that time there fell to him many a fair achievement which is not written here. I know of a truth that in that year he won by force thirteen castles, and overcame many a proud man. From this the truth about him may be judged. Had he been moderate in action I trow none worthier than he could have been found in his time, excepting only his brother, to whom, in fair feats of arms, I dare compare none then alive. For the king governed himself always with moderation, and managed his feats of arms always with such valour and wisdom that often he brought an unlikely enterprise to a right fortunate issue.

In all this time James of Douglas was wandering in the Forest,[1] and held it, by hardihood and stratagem, despite all the strength of his many foes, notwithstanding that they full often beset him with fierce attack. But, sometimes by wisdom and sometimes by bravery, he brought his purpose to a happy issue.

It happened that one night at that time, as he was journeying, and thought to lodge in a house on the Water of Lyne, when he came with his company near the place he listened and heard the words, every one, of those within. And by these he perceived that strangers were that night quartered there. It was as he thought, for Alexander Stewart, the Lord of Bonkyl,[2] was there, and others besides of great valour. Thomas Randolph, of great renown, was

[1] The remnant of the ancient Caledonian Forest about the springs of Ettrick and Tweed was for centuries known as *par excellence* The Forest. It was the haunt of the historic Merlin in the sixth century—his grave is still pointed out at Drummelzier within its bounds, and in the sixteenth century the Seventy of Selkirk who fell round James IV. at Flodden were lamented as the "Flowers o' the Forest."

[2] This was the son of Sir John Stewart of Bonkyl who fell while marshalling the Scottish archers at the Battle of Falkirk in 1298. That hero was the John of Gaunt of Scotland. A younger son of the fourth High Steward, he was ancestor of four Earls of Angus, the French Lords d'Aubigny, the Stewart Lords of Lorne and Earls of Atholl, the Stewarts of Appin, the Earls of Galloway, the Earls of Traquair, the Barons of Blantyre, and the Earls of Lennox, who finally ascended the throne in the person of James VI.

among them, and Adam of Gordon also. They had come thither with their company, and meant to lie in the Forest, and hold it by means of their great force, and with marching and stout fighting chase Douglas out of that country.

But otherwise altogether went the game. For when Douglas was aware that strangers had taken quarters in the place where he meant to lie, he went hastily to the house, and beset it all about. When those within heard such a noise around the walls they rose in haste, and hurriedly seized their weapons, and armed themselves, and rushed forth.

Their foes met them with bare weapons, and attacked right boldly, and they defended themselves doughtily with all their might, but at last they were pressed so hard that their folk all failed them. Thomas Randolph was taken, and Alexander Stewart was wounded in a place or two. Adam of Gordon alone, by dint of stratagem and force, escaped from the fight, with many of his men. Those who were seized were wondrous woful at their capture, but this of necessity it behoved them to be.

That night the good Lord of Douglas made right gladsome cheer to Sir Alexander, who was his uncle's son. So also assuredly he did to Thomas Randolph, since he was in near degree of blood to the Bruce, being his sister's son.

And on the morrow, without more ado, he rode towards the noble king, and carried both of these two with him.

The king was blithe at his coming, and thanked him many times for it. And to his nephew he said, "Thou hast a while denied thy faith, but must now be reconciled."

Then forthwith Randolph answered and said, "Ye reprove me, but ye have better need to be reproved, for seeing ye make war upon the king of England, ye should endeavour to make good your right in open battle, and not by stratagem and craft."

"Mayhap," said the king, "it shall come ere very long to such endeavour. But since thou speakest so royally, there is much reason to reprove thy proud words, till thou knowest what is right and bowest to it as thou oughtst."

Without more delay the king sent him to close keeping, where for a time he should not be altogether at his own disposal

BOOK X

THE CAPTURE OF CASTLES

WHEN Thomas Randolph was taken, in the way I here describe, and sent to safe keeping for the words he spake to the Bruce, the good king took thought of the hurt, the hatred, and the cruelty he had suffered from John of Lorne, and soon afterwards he gathered his host, and marched toward Lorne in good array.

Long before he arrived John of Lorne had knowledge of his coming, and gathered men from all sides, two thousand in number they might be, and sent them to stop the way by which the king behoved to march. This was in a difficult place, so strait and narrow that in some parts of the hillside two men could not ride abreast. The lower side was perilous, for a sheer crag, high and hideous, dropped from the path to the sea, and above rose a mountain so steep and difficult that it was hard to pass that way. Ben Cruachan was the name of the mountain.

L

I trow that in all Britain there is not a higher hill.[1]

There John of Lorne caused his host to lie in ambush above the road, and considered that if the king came that way he should soon be overthrown. He himself kept on the sea[2] near the pass, with his galleys.

But the king, wise and prudent in all his undertakings, perceived their cunning. He knew also that he must needs go that way. He parted his men in two bodies, and committed the archers to the good Lord of Douglas, in whom was all wisdom and valour. This good lord took with him the stout Sir Alexander Fraser, and William Wiseman, a good knight, as well as good Sir Andrew Gray. These with their following went forward, and nimbly climbed the hill, and, before they were perceived, had seized the high ground above their enemies. The king and his men marched on, and when they had entered the pass the men of Lorne raised a cry and rushed and began to throw down on them great

[1] The place where John of Lorne laid his ambush for Bruce is pointed out under Ben Cruachan at the foot of the Pass of Awe. Some funeral cairns still mark the scene of the struggle, near the old Bridge of Awe. Ben Cruachan, though 3689 feet, is not even the highest mountain in Argyllshire, that honour being held by Bidean nam Bean, 3766 feet, above Glencoe. Ben Nevis, the highest mountain in Britain, is 4408 feet.

[2] Loch Etive receives the waters of the Awe, a mile away.

and heavy stones. But these did not greatly hurt the king, for he had there in his following men light and nimble and lightly armed, and they boldly climbed the hill and prevented the enemy fulfilling most of their fell purpose. Also, on the other side came James of Douglas and his men, and rushed with a shout upon them, and wounded them sore with arrows, and at last dashed boldly among them with their swords.

Right manful, great, and active defence was made by the men of Lorne, but when they saw they were assailed thus upon two sides, and perceived that their enemies had all the best of the fight, they took flight in utmost haste. Bruce's men made a fierce pursuit, and slew all they could overtake. The fugitives made for a water that ran under the hillside, and was right strong, and both deep and wide, and could be crossed nowhere except at a bridge beneath that place. To that bridge they eagerly made their way, and strove diligently to break it down. But the pursuers, when they saw them pause, rushed instantly and boldly upon them and overcame them utterly, and held the bridge whole until the king and all his following passed it at their ease.

It must have displeased John of Lorne, I trow, when from his ships on the sea he saw his men slain and chased from the hill, while he could give them no help. For hearts that are good and valiant are vexed as greatly to see their foes accomplish their ends as they are to suffer hurt themselves.

In evil case were the men of Lorne, for many had lost their lives, and the rest were in flight. The king quickly caused the spoil of the whole land to be seized, and such an abundance of cattle was to be seen there as was a marvel to behold. Meanwhile the Bruce, bold, stark, and stout, passed suddenly to Dunstaffnage, and besieged it sturdily, and made assault to capture the castle.[1] And in a short time he brought the garrison to such distress that, despite their strength, he won the place. He set a good warden in it, and furnished him with both men and meat, so that he should be able to hold the castle a long time notwithstanding all the men of that country.

Sir Alexander of Argyll, seeing the Bruce altogether destroying his land, made treaty with him, and without delay became his man, and was received into his peace. But his son, John of

[1] Dunstaffnage, on its small peninsula at the mouth of Loch Etive, was the capital seat of the Scottish monarchy till 873, when Kenneth MacAlpine removed the Coronation Stone to Scone and the seat of government to Forteviot. It was afterwards a chief stronghold of the Lords of the Isles, and from Somerled, the great Lord of the Isles in the 12th century, it passed to his son Dugal and his descendants, the MacDougals of Argyll and Lorne of Bruce's time.

Lorne, still remained a rebel as before, and fled in his ships to sea. All those left on land, however, were obedient to the king, and he took homage of them all. Then he passed again to Perth to pleasure him in the open country.

Lothian was still against him, and at Linlithgow there was a peel great and strong, well garrisoned with Englishmen, which was a place of refuge for those going from Edinburgh to Stirling and back with arms and food, and which did great hurt to the country.

Now may ye hear, if ye will, episodes[1] and hazards of many kinds that were essayed for the taking of peels and castles. This Linlithgow was one of these places, and I shall tell how it was taken. In that countryside there dwelt a small farmer who with his cattle often led hay to the peel. William Bunnock was his name, and he was a stalwart man in a fight. He was greatly vexed and grieved to see the country so hard bested, and troubled beyond measure, through fortresses filled and commanded by Englishmen. He was a stout, strong carl, stubborn and bold himself, and he had friends dwelling near. To some of them he

---

[1] The word here used by Barbour is "interludys," which might go some way to suggest that even in the 14th century the stage was familiar with a style of entertainment which is not generally supposed to have been invented till a couple of centuries later

shewed his secret plan, and got them to agree
to make an ambush while he went with his
waggon to lead hay to the peel. His waggon
was to be well filled, for eight armed men were
to sit secretly in the body of it, covered about
with hay, while he himself, being hardy and
bold, went idly beside it, and an active stout
yeoman in front drove the waggon, and carried
a sharp-cutting hatchet under his belt. And when
the gate was opened, and they were at it, when
the yeoman heard him cry sturdily, "Call all!
call all!" then he was quickly to strike the
traces in two with the axe, and at once the
men within the waggon were to leap out and
give fight, while their fellows, who were to be
in ambush near, came to maintain the struggle.

This was in harvest time, when fields fair and
wide were filled with ripe corn, and the various
grains they bore waxed ready to be gathered for
the food of man, while the trees stood loaded
with fruits of sundry kinds. Now the men of the
peel had made hay, and had bespoken Bunnock,
as he was at hand, to lead it in, and he had agreed
without difficulty, and had said that in the
morning very early he should bring a load fairer
and greater and much more than any he had
yet brought that year. And assuredly he kept
his covenant with them, for that night he secretly
warned the men who were to go in the waggon,

and bade the ambush be made. And they sped so fast that before day they were ambushed very near the peel, where they could hear the cry as soon as any arose. There they kept themselves so secret, without movement, that none had knowledge of them. Meanwhile Bunnock took much pains to dress his company in the waggon, and some time before day he had them covered with hay. Then he set himself to yoke his cattle, till the sun could be seen shining.

Some of the garrison of the peel had come forth, to their own misfortune, to gather their harvest at hand. Then Bunnock, with the company enclosed in his waggon, without waiting longer, started and drove his load towards the peel. The porter, when he saw him very near, opened the gate. Thereupon Bunnock, without delay, caused the waggon to be driven rapidly, and when it was just between the cheeks of the entrance, so that the gate could in no way be closed, he cried, "Thief! call all! call all!" Then his man dropped his whip, and quickly hewed in two the trace. With that Bunnock nimbly dealt the porter a knock that dashed out both blood and brains. And they within the waggon leapt forth lightly and slew the men of the castle standing about. Then in a moment the cry arose, and the men in ambush leapt out with swords bare, and came and took the whole castle without trouble, and slew those within it. And when the men who had gone forth before, saw the castle utterly lost, they fled to and fro for refuge. Some made their escape to Edinburgh, and others to Stirling, and some were slain by the way.

Thus Bunnock with his waggon took the peel and slew its men. Then he hastened and delivered it to the king, who worthily rewarded him. Bruce caused it to be thrown down to the ground, then went over the country setting all the land at peace that was willing to obey him.

And when a little time was gone he sent after Thomas Randolph, and dealt so well with him that he promised to be his man, and the king soon forgave him, and to heighten his estate gave him Moray and made him earl of it, and gave him sundry other broad lands in heritage. He knew his valiant prowess and his great wisdom and prudence, his faithful heart and loyal service. Therefore he put trust in him, and made him rich in land and cattle, as was indeed right proper to do. If men speak truth, he was a knight courageous, wise, brave, and active, and of great and sovereign nobleness, and many great things can be told of him. Therefore I think to speak of him, and to show part of his achievement, and describe his appearance and something of his character. He was of middle stature, every way well formed, with broad visage, pleasant and fair, courteous at all points, debonair, and of right steadfast demeanour. Loyalty he loved above everything; falsehood, treason, and cruelty he constantly withstood. He esteemed honour and liberality, and ever upheld righteousness. He was agreeable in company, and amorous, and ever loved good knights. In truth he was full of all nobleness, and made of all virtues. I will commend him no more here, but ye shall assuredly hear furthermore how he, for his valiant deeds, was in truth to be sovereignly esteemed.

When the king was thus reconciled with him, and had bestowed great lordships on him, he waxed very wise and prudent. First he settled his own lands, then he sped to the war to help his uncle in his affairs. With the consent of the good king, but with small preparation, he hastened to Edinburgh with a company of trusty men, and laid siege to the castle. The stronghold was then wondrous well furnished with men and victual, so that it feared no man's might. Nevertheless this good Earl right boldly set his siege, and pressed the garrison so that none durst pass the gate. They might abide within and eat their victual while they had it, but I trow they were prevented getting more in the country outside.

At that time King Edward of England had given the keeping of the castle to Sir Piers Lumbard, a Gascon. And when the men of his garrison saw the siege so strongly set, they suspected him of treason, because he had spoken with the Bruce, and for that suspicion they took and put him in prison, and made one of their own nation constable, a leader right wary, wise, and active. This leader set skill, strength, and craft to keep the castle in his charge.

But of this siege I will now be silent, and speak a little while of the doughty Lord of Douglas. At that time he was in the Forest,[1] where he tried many a hazard and fair point of chivalry, both day and night, against the garrisons of Roxburgh and Jedburgh castles. Many of these exploits I will let pass, for I cannot rehearse them all, and though I tried ye may well believe I could not compass the task, so much should there be to describe. But those that I know certainly I shall, out of my knowledge, relate.

While, as I have said, the good Earl Thomas besieged Edinburgh, James of Douglas set all his wit to discover how, by any craft or

[1] The remains of the ancient Caledonian Forest extended about all the upland waters of Clyde and Tweed, Ettrick, Yarrow, Teviot and Jed. Douglas's camp is still pointed out at Lintalee in the old forest country above Jedburgh.

stratagem, Roxburgh could be taken. At length he caused Sim of the Leadhouse, a crafty and skilful man, to make ladders of hempen ropes with wooden steps, so bound that they should in no way break. They devised and made a hook of iron, strong and square, which if once fixed on a battlement, with the ladder straitly stretched from it, should hold securely.

As soon as this was devised and done, the Lord of Douglas, in secret, gathered trusty men— I trow there might be three score of them—and on Fastern's Even,[1] in the beginning of the night, took the road for the castle. They covered all the armour they wore with black frocks. Soon they came near the castle; then they sent all their horses back, and went along the path in single file on hands and feet, as if they were cows and oxen that had been left out unsecured.

It was very dark, without a doubt; nevertheless, one of the garrison, who lay on the wall, said to his fellow beside him, "This man," and he named a small farmer near the place, "thinks to make good cheer, for he has left all his oxen out." The other said, "No doubt it is so. He makes merry to-night, though they should be driven off by the Douglas."

They supposed the Douglas and his men were oxen because they went on hands and feet,

[1] It was Shrove Tuesday, February 27, 1313.

always one by one. Douglas took right good heed to all they said, but soon they passed indoors, talking as they went.

Douglas's men were glad at this, and sped swiftly to the wall, and soon set up their ladders. But one made a sound when the hook fastened hard in the battlement. This was clearly heard by one of the watchmen, and he instantly made for the spot. Leadhouse, who had made the ladder, hastened to be first to climb the wall, but, ere he had quite got up, the warder met him, and, thinking to throw him down, without noise, cry, or sound, dashed quickly at him. Then Leadhouse, who was in hazard of his life, made a leap at him and got him by the throat, and stabbed him upwards with a knife till he took the life in his hand. And when he saw him lie dead he went forthwith upon the wall, and cast the body down to his fellows, and said, "All goes as we wish; speed quickly up!"

This they hastened to do, but before they came up, a man came along and saw Leadhouse standing alone, and knew he was not of the garrison. This man rushed at him, and attacked him stoutly, but was quickly slain, for Leadhouse was armed and active, and the other had no armour and nothing to stop a stroke.

Thus Leadhouse did battle upon the wall till Douglas and his company were come up. Then

they went quickly into the tower. At that
moment the garrison were all in the hall, dancing,
singing, and otherwise at play, as is the joyous
and glad custom upon Fastern's Even among
folk in safety, as they believed themselves to be.
But, ere they knew, Douglas and all his men
poured into the hall, crying aloud, "Douglas!
Douglas!" And though they were more in number
than he, when they heard the dreadful shout of
"Douglas!" they were dismayed, and set up no
right defence. Douglas's men slew them without
mercy till they got the upper hand, and the
garrison, fearing death beyond measure, fled seek-
ing safety. The warden, Gylmyne de Fiennes,
saw how it went, and got into the great tower
with others of his company, and hastily closed
the gate. The rest, who were left outside, were
taken or slain, except some who leapt the wall.

That night Douglas held the hall, to the sorrow
of his enemies. His men kept going to and fro
throughout the castle all that night till daylight
on the morrow. The warden in the tower, Gyl-
myne de Fiennes, was a man of great valour,
and when he saw the castle altogether lost, he
set his force to defend the keep. Those without
sent arrows in upon him in such number that he
was greatly distressed; nevertheless, he held the
tower stubbornly till the next day. Then, in an
attack, he was wounded so badly in the face

that he feared for his life. For this reason he speedily made parley, and yielded the tower on condition that he and all with him should pass safely to England. Douglas kept good faith with them, and convoyed them to their own country, but De Fiennes lived there but a short time, for, by reason of the wound in his face, he soon died and was buried.

Douglas seized all the castle, which was then enclosed with a strong wall, and he sent Leadhouse to the king, who rewarded him greatly. Bruce at once sent thither his brother, the doughty Sir Edward, to cast down tower, castle, and dungeon, and the latter came with a great company, and so busily set to work that tower and wall were thrown down to the ground in little space. And he dwelt quietly there till Teviotdale came wholly to the king's peace, except Jedburgh and other places near the English bounds.

While Roxburgh was thus being won the Earl Thomas, who ever set high value upon sovereign valour, was lying with his company at the siege of Edinburgh, as I have already told. But when he heard how Roxburgh was taken by a stratagem, he set all his endeavour by skill and searching to compass some device that might help him, by stratagem and feat of arms, to win the castle wall. He knew well that no strength could take the place openly while the garrison within had men and meat. So he privily enquired whether any man was to be found who could show any bold way of secretly climbing the walls, and he should have his reward. For it was his intention to make the adventure, before the siege should miscarry for his fault.

There was one William Francis, active and brisk, wise and courteous, who in his youth had been in the castle. When he saw the Earl so specially set upon finding some subtle device or wile by which he might take the stronghold, he came to him in secret, and said, "Methinks ye would gladly find some bold plan for getting over the walls. If ye will indeed make the attempt in such a way, I undertake for my service to let you know how the wall may be climbed, and I shall go foremost of all. There is a place where with a short ladder of twelve foot we may easily climb the wall. And if ye will understand how I know this I shall freely tell you. In days past, when I was young, my father was keeper of yonder house, and I was somewhat giddy, and loved a wench here in the town; and in order that I might repair to her secretly without suspicion, I made a ladder of ropes, and therewith slipped over the wall. Then I went down a narrow way I had spied in the crag, and ofttimes came to my love. And

when it drew near day I went again that same
way, and ever came in without discovery. I
long used that way of going, so I can find the
road aright though the night be ever so dark.
If ye think ye will make the attempt to climb
up after me by that way I shall bring you up
to the wall. God keep us from being seen by
the watchers there! If it so fair befalls us that
we can set up our ladder, and if a man can
get upon the wall, he shall defend, if need be,
till the rest speed up."

The Earl was blithe at his words, and promised
him full fair reward, and undertook to go that
way. He bade him make his ladder soon, and
hold him privy till they could set a night for
their purpose.

Soon afterwards the ladder was made. Then
the Earl, without more delay, provided himself
on a night secretly with thirty active and bold
men. It was a dark night when they started,
and they set themselves a right bold attempt,
and put themselves assuredly in great peril. I
trow, could they have seen clearly, that path
had not been undertaken though there had been
no man to oppose them. For the crag was high
and dreadful, and the climbing right perilous,
and if any happened to slide or fall he must
at once have been broken in pieces.

The night was dark, I have heard say, and

they were soon come to the foot of the high, sheer crag. Then William Francis climbed before them in the crevices, and they followed at his back with much difficulty, sometimes near, sometimes at a distance. They climbed thus in the crannies till they had surmounted half the crag, and there they found a place so broad that they could just sit on it. They were breathless and weary, and tarried there to get their wind. And just as they were sitting so, above them, on the wall, the officers of the watch all came together.

Now help them, God, that can do all things! for in right great peril are they. Should they be seen, there should none escape out of that place alive. They must be stoned to death and could help themselves nothing.

But all the night was wondrous dark, so that the enemy had no sight of them. Nevertheless, there was one who threw down a stone, and said, "Away, I see you well!" But he saw them not a bit, and the stone flew over their heads, and they sat still, each one keeping quiet.

The watches, when they heard nothing stir, passed all in a body from that place, and moved far off, talking as they went. Then at once Earl Thomas and those who sat by him on the crag climbed hastily towards the wall, and reached it after much effort and with great difficulty and peril. From that point upwards the climb was

M

more grievous by far than the part beneath.
But, whatever were their difficulties, they came
at last right to the wall. It was very nigh
twelve foot in height, and without sight or
knowledge they set their ladder to it, and there,
before them all, Francis climbed up, and then
Sir Andrew Gray, and after him the Earl him-
self was the third man to take the wall.

When those below saw their lord climb up
thus upon the rampart, they all, like madmen,
climbed after him. But before they were all
come up the officers of the watch heard
moving and speaking and the clashing of arms,
and dashed full sturdily upon them. The Earl
and his men met them right boldly, and made
furious slaughter of them. Then the cry rose
through the castle, "Treason! treason!" and some
of the garrison were so terrified that they fled
and leapt over the wall. But to tell the truth,
not all of them fled; for the constable, a brave
man, rushed forth fully armed at the shout, and
many bold and stout men with him.

The Earl was still with all his company
fighting upon the wall, but he soon discomfited
all those against him. By that time all his
men had come up, and he made his way
forthwith down to the castle. He put himself
in great peril, for there were far more men
within it than with him, if they had been of

good heart; but they were dismayed. Nevertheless, with drawn weapons the constable and his company right boldly met him and his men. Then arose a great conflict, for with their weapons they struck at each other with all their might, till their fair, bright swords were all bloody to the hilts. And there began a dreadful uproar, for those that were felled or stabbed shouted and shrieked and made great noise.

The good Earl and his company fought so sturdily in that fight that all their foes were overthrown. The constable was slain on the spot, and when he fell the rest fled where they best could for refuge. They durst not stay nor fight more. The Earl was so hotly handled there, that had it not chanced that the constable was slain he had been in great peril; but at that the garrison fled, and there was no more to fear. Each man sought to save his life and live forth his days, and some slid down outside the wall. The Earl took the whole castle, for there was none durst withstand him.

Never in any land have I heard of a castle so boldly taken, excepting Tyre alone, when Alexander the Conqueror, who captured the Tower of Babylon, leapt from a tower to the wall, and there, among all his foes, right doughtily defended himself till his noble knights came with ladders over the walls. None of these knights turned back for death or fear, for after they were well assured that the king was in the town nothing could stop them, and they set all peril at nought. They climbed the walls, and Aristaeus came first to the good king. Alexander was defending himself with all his might, but was so hard beset that he was brought down on one knee. He had set his back to a tree for fear they should attack him behind. Then Aristaeus sped valiantly to the rescue, and dealt blows so doughtily on the enemy that the king was saved. For his men in sundry places climbed over the wall and sought their lord, and rescued him with hard fighting, and speedily took the town.

Except this capture alone I never heard in time past of a castle so stoutly taken. And of this capture that I describe, Saint Margaret, the good, holy queen, knew in her time through the revelation of Him who knows all things. Thereof, instead of prophecy, she left a right fair token. In her chapel she caused to be pictured a castle, a ladder standing up to the wall, and a man climbing on it, and wrote above him in French, as old men tell, "Gardez vous de François!" And because of this word which she caused to be written men believed the French should take it. But since Francis was the name of him who thus climbed secretly up, her writing proved prophetic. The thing fell out indeed just as she said, for the place was taken, and Francis led them up.

In this wise was Edinburgh stormed, all therein being taken or slain or leaping the wall. The Earl's men seized all their goods, and searched every one of the houses. Sir Piers Lumbard, who was made prisoner as I said before, they found sitting fettered with gyves in the dungeon. They brought him quickly to the Earl, and he at once caused them to loose him, and he became the king's man. Straightway then they sent word to the king, and told how the castle was taken; and he speedily went thither with many in his company, and caused them to undermine wholly both tower and wall, and cast them to the ground. Then he went over all the land taking the country to his peace. For this valiant deed the Earl was mightily praised. The king, seeing him so worthy, was blithe and joyous above the rest, and to maintain his state gave him rents and fair lands enough; and he drew to such great valour that all men spake of his great excellence. His foes he greatly dismayed, for he never fled because of force in battle. What shall I say more of his might! His great manhood and valour make him still renowned.

At the time that these hazardous enterprises were so boldly achieved, the valiant Sir Edward

the Bruce had won all Galloway and Nithsdale
to his pleasure, and thrown down all the castles,
tower and wall, into the ditch. He heard say
then, and was well aware, that there was a
peel tower in Rutherglen. Thither he went with
his company, and shortly took it. Then he set
out for Dundee, which was then held, I have
been told, against the king. Forthwith he laid
siege stoutly to it, and lay there till it was
yielded. Next he made his way to Stirling. There
good Sir Philip the Mowbray, right doughty in
attack, was warden, and had that castle of the
English king in his keeping. To it Sir Edward
laid strong siege. They skirmished sturdily and
often, but no great deed of arms was done. Sir
Edward, after the siege was set, lay before the
place a very long time; that is to say, from Lent
till before the mass of St. John. Then the English
folk within the castle began to find their victual
fail, and the doughty Sir Philip made a treaty
to which both sides agreed, that, if at midsummer
a year thence it was not rescued by battle, he
should without fail yield the castle freely. To
this covenant they firmly bound themselves.

BOOK XI

THE EVE OF BATTLE

WHEN this covenant was made Sir Philip rode into England, and told the king the whole tale, how, according to the treaty, he had a full twelve-month to rescue Stirling by battle. And when King Edward heard Sir Philip say that the Scots had set a day to fight, and that he had so much time to prepare, he was right glad, and said it was great presumption that urged them to such folly, for he intended before that time to be so provided, and in such array, that no force should withstand him.

And when the English lords heard that this day was openly set, they deemed it great foolishness, and thought to have all at their pleasure if the Scots met them in battle. But the fool's purpose often fails, and even wise men's aims come not always to such issue as they expect. A little stone often, they say, may overturn a great waggon. No man's strength can stand against the grace of God, who guides all things.

He knows whither all things tend, and disposes all things at His pleasure, according to His ordinance.

When Sir Edward, as I have said, had given this extraordinary time for the yielding or rescue of Stirling, he went forthwith to the Bruce, and told the treaty he had made, and the time he had given. The king, when he heard the time, said, "That was unwisely done indeed. Never have I heard so long a warning given to so mighty a king as the King of England. For he has now in his hand England, Ireland, Wales, and Aquitaine, with all under his seignory, and a great part of Scotland, and he is so provided with treasure that he can have plenty of paid soldiers. We are few against so many. God may deal us our destiny right well, but we are set in jeopardy to lose or win all at one throw."

"As God will judge me," said Sir Edward, "though the King of England and all he can lead come hither, we shall fight, were they twice as many."

When the Bruce heard his brother speak thus boldly as to the battle, he esteemed him greatly in his heart, and said, "Brother, since it so happens that this covenant has been made, let us prepare manfully for the struggle, and let all that love us and the freedom of this country make ready for that time with all the force

they can, so that if our foes attempt to rescue
Stirling by battle we may defeat their purpose."

To this all agreed, and all men were bid make
ready and be equipped in their best fashion
against that day. Then all in Scotland who were
valiant to fight set their whole strength to pre-
pare against that day. They made ready weapons
and armour, and all that pertains to war.

And the mighty King of England purveyed
himself so great an array as never yet was
heard of in that country. And when the time
was drawing near he gathered all his power,
and besides his own chivalry it was marvellous
great. He had with him good men of great
valour from many a far country. In his com-
pany was a valiant body of French knights. The
Earl of Hainault too was there, and with him
valiant men of Gascony and Germany. Edward
had also from the Duchy and from Brittany
active and well-favoured men completely armed
from head to foot. He had gathered so com-
pletely the whole knighthood of England, that
he left none that could wield weapons, or were
able to take the field in battle. From Wales
also and from Ireland he had a great following.
From Poitiers, Aquitaine, and Bayonne he had
full many of great renown. And from Scotland
besides he had a great following of men of
might.

When all these were gathered together he had a hundred thousand fighting men and more. Of these, forty thousand were horsemen, armed both head and hand, and of these, three thousand had their horses covered with complete mail, to make the front of the battle. He had also fifty thousand archers, with light-armed horsemen, and men on foot, besides camp-followers to look after harness and victual. He had so many, it was a marvel. A vast number of carts also went with them. Besides those that carried armour, and those that were loaded with tents and vessels, and furnishings of chamber and hall, and wine and wax, shot and victual, fourscore were loaded with fuel. They were so many as they rode, and their ranks were so broad, and such great space did their baggage train take up, that their vast host could be seen over-spreading the whole land.

There might be seen many a valiant and active man, and many a gaily armed knight, and many a sturdy, stirring steed, richly arrayed, and many helms and habergeons, shields and pennoned spears, and so many comely knights, it seemed indeed that they might vanquish the whole world in battle.

Why should I make my tale too long? They all came to Berwick, and some took quarters in the town, and some lodged without in tents and pavilions. And when King Edward saw his host so great, so gallant, and so complete, he was right joyful in heart, and deemed there was not indeed in the world a king that could withstand him. He thought to bring all into his power, and he liberally dealt the lands of Scotland among his host. He was liberal with other men's lands, and his followers menaced the Scots one and all with great words. Nevertheless, ere all came to pass as they expected, there were to be rents made in much whole cloth.

King Edward, by advice of his leaders, divided his men into ten battles. In each battle were fully ten thousand men, all determined to make a stout stand and bold fight, and leave nothing in their foes' power. He set leaders to each battle, known men of good generalship. And he gave the leading of the vanguard to two renowned earls, Gloucester and Hereford, with many captains under their command, in right great ordered array. Right brave were they, and believed if they came to battle no strength could withstand them. And when his followers were thus disposed, King Edward ordered his own battle, and arranged who should be at his bridle. Sir Giles d'Argentine he set upon one side to hold his rein, and, on the other, the valiant Sir Aymer de Valence; for above the rest he trusted in their sovereign great valour.

When the king in this fashion had arranged his battles and his leadership, he rose early one morning and set out from Berwick. The English covered hills and valleys, as their broad battles rode separate over the fields. The sun was shining bright and clear, and their newly burnished armour flashed in the light, while banners blazed brightly, and pennons waved to the wind, and the whole field was aflame. So many were their banners and pennons, and of such different device, that it would need great skill to describe them. Were I to tell all their show, their colour and bearings, I should be cumbered in the doing of it, even were it in my power.

King Edward, with all that great host, rode straight to Edinburgh. They were altogether too many to fight with the few folk of a harmless land. But where God helps, what can withstand?

When King Robert heard that the English had come into his country in such array and such number, he sent abroad a summons to his knights, and they all came right willingly to the Torwood, where he had ordained their meeting. The valiant Sir Edward Bruce came with a right great company of good men well armed and equipped, bold and strong for the battle. Walter, Steward of Scotland, too, who was but a beardless boy, came with a noble rout that all might know by their bearing. And the good Lord of Douglas brought with him men well used, I warrant, to battle. Such men were less likely to be dismayed in the press of the fight, and likely to see more quickly the chances of confounding the strength of their enemies, than men unused to war. The Earl of Moray came also with his men well arrayed, in good order for the strife, and determined to uphold their rights. Many other stout barons also, and knights of full great fame, came right valiantly with their men.

When the brave array had come together there were, I trow, thirty thousand and more of fighting men, besides baggage-carriers and camp-followers who tended harness and provender. The king then went over all the host, and noted their bearing, and saw that all were fully equipped. They were bold of carriage. The most timid among them seemed likely to do his part right well. The king noted all their looks as, at such a pass, he well knew how, and saw that they were all of bold and assured countenance, without dismay or fear. It greatly pleased his heart, and he was persuaded that men of such a mind, if they set their strength to it, must be indeed right hard to vanquish. Ever as he met them in the way he welcomed them in hearty manner, speaking brave words here and there ; and they, seeing their lord welcome them

so graciously, were right glad, and deemed they
might well put themselves to the touch of hard
fighting and stress of battle to uphold his honour.

When the valiant king saw his host all forth-
with assembled, eager with heart and mind to
do his pleasure and maintain their freedom, he
was glad in many ways, and called all his privy
council, and said, " Sirs, now ye see how the
English in great strength have disposed them-
selves for battle in order to rescue yonder strong-
hold. Therefore it is well we now ordain how
we shall hinder their purpose, and so close the
road to them that they pass not without great
obstacle. We have here at our command full
thirty thousand men. Of the whole number
make we four battles, and so arrange that when
our enemies come near we take our way to the
New Park.[1] There for certain they behove to
pass, unless they march beneath and go over the
morass. Thus we shall have them at advantage.
Methinks it most expedient that we go to this
battle on foot, arrayed only in light armour. Our
foes are in more strength and better horsed
than we, and should we fight mounted we must

[1] The New Park, or King's Park, was the old royal hunting
ground of Stirling. It was formerly of much greater extent than
now, and stretched from the King's Knot, or Round Table, under
the castle walls, southward to the Bannockburn, three miles away,
and beyond.

be in great peril. But if we fight on foot, it
is certain we shall always have the advantage,
for in the Park among the trees the horsemen
must always be cumbered, and the ditches below
must also throw them into confusion."

All agreed to what he said, and in a little
space they ordered their four battles. The king
gave the leading of the vanguard to the Earl
Thomas, for all had full assurance and trust in
his noble leadership and high courage. To uphold
his banner, lords of great valour with their fol-
lowings were assigned to his division. The leader-
ship of the second battle was given to the
valiant Sir Edward, doughty in deed and famous
for his great feats of arms. I trow that, how-
soever the game might go, his enemies were
likely to have cause to mourn. The king gave
the third battle to Walter Stewart to lead, and
to the doughty Douglas. They were cousins in
near degree; therefore Stewart, being young, was
given to Douglas in charge. Nevertheless, I trow
the young leader was to do his duty so man-
fully and bear himself so well, that he was to
need no guardianship. The command of the
fourth battle the noble king took to himself,
and had in his company all the men of Carrick,
and of Argyll, Kintyre, and the Isles, among
whom were Sir Angus of Islay and Bute, and
all his following. He had also a great host of

armed men of the lowlands. His division, which was strong and formidable, he said should form the rearguard, and straight in front of him should go the vanguard, and behind it, a little space apart on either hand, should march the other battles. So the king, being behind, should see where most need was, and bring his banner to the relief.

Thus the Bruce, in every way wise and active and right valiant, and above everything bold, ordered his men for the battle. And on the morrow, which was Saturday, he heard from his scouts that the English, in great strength, had lain that night at Edinburgh. Accordingly, without more delay, he set out with his whole host, and quartered in the New Park. And in an open field, where he thought the English must needs pass if they held their way through the Park to the castle, he caused many pits to be dug, of a foot's breadth and the depth of a man's knee. So thickly were they dug that they might be likened to the wax comb of a hive. He toiled all that night, so that before day he had made these pits, and had covered them with sticks and green grass, that they might not easily be seen.

On Sunday, in the morning, very soon after sunrise, the Scots most reverently heard mass, and many shrived themselves devoutly, determined to die in that struggle or make their country free. They prayed to God for their cause. None of them dined that day, but all fasted on bread and water for the Vigil of St. John.

The king, whenever mass was done, went to the pits, and saw they had been made as he desired. On either side the road a full broad space was honey-combed as I have described. If their foes advanced on horseback in that direction, I trow they could not well escape without overthrow. Then he caused the cry to go forth throughout the host, that all should arm at once, and make ready in their best fashion. And when they were all assembled he had them arrayed for the battle. Next, along all the line he caused it to be cried aloud, that whatsoever man found his heart not assured to stand and win all, and to maintain that mighty struggle or die with honour, should betimes leave the field, and that none should remain but those who would stand by him to the end, and take the fortune God sent. Then all answered with a shout, and with one voice cried that none should fail him for fear of death till the battle was won.

When the good king heard his men so boldly make answer, and declare that neither death nor fear could daunt them, or bring them to avoid the battle, he rejoiced greatly in his heart. He felt sure that men of such a mind, so stout, so bold, and so trusty, must hold their own well in

battle against the strongest enemies. Then he
sent all the small folk and camp-followers, and
all the harness and victual that were in the Park,
a great way from him, and made them leave
the field of battle. They took their departure as
he ordered, to the number of nigh twenty thou-
sand, and made their way to a hollow ground.
Nevertheless, the king was left with a complete
host of thirty thousand men. I trow they were
to make a stalwart stand, and do their duty as
they ought. They stood then in rank, all ready
to abide any attack.

The king made them all arm themselves, since
he knew for a certainty that the enemy had lain
that night at Falkirk, and were marching straight
upon him in strong and great array. He bade
his nephew, the Earl of Moray, keep the road
beside the kirk[1] with his host, so that no man
should pass that way to the castle without fight-
ing. He himself, he said, with his division, should
keep the approach through the Park if any
sought to attack there. At the same time his
brother, Sir Edward, and young Walter the
Steward, with the Lord Douglas and their host,
should take good heed which of them had need
of help, and should help them that had need.
He then sent James of Douglas and Sir Robert
of Keith, marshal of all the feudal host, to spy

[1] The church of St. Ninian's, between Bannockburn and Stirling.

the English advance. They mounted and rode forth with well-horsed followers, and soon beheld the great array coming on, with shields shining clear, and basnets burnished full brightly, flashing back the strong beams of the sun. They saw so many braided banners, standards, and spear pennons, and so many mounted knights all flaming in gay attire, and so many broad battles taking such vast space as they rode, as might, by their number and battle array, have dismayed the greatest and boldest and best host in Christendom.

When the scouts had had sight of the enemy they made their way to the king, and told him in great privacy the multitude and splendour of their foes, and the breadth of their array, and the great strength they had. And the king bade them give no sign of these things, but declare throughout the host that the enemy were coming in ill array, and thus encourage his men. For ofttimes a single word may cause discouragement and damage, and in the same way a word may bring about the courage and hardihood that make men succeed. Thus it happened here; the courage and good cheer of the scouts so greatly raised the spirits of the host that the least bold was, by his looks, most forward to begin the great struggle.

In this fashion the noble king, by the bold

countenance and cheer that he so bravely made, gave courage to all his men. It seemed to them that no great mischance could happen while he was their leader, and no danger befall that his valour could not avert. His bravery and carriage so encouraged them that the most faint-hearted became bold.

On the other hand, the English approached in their battles with their banners waving to the wind in such right stalwart array as I have already described. And when they were come so near, that but two miles lay between the hosts, they chose a doughty company of men-at-arms, active and stout, on fair full-armed steeds. Three bannerets of right great might were captains of that company, and the stout Lord Clifford was their chief leader. They were, I trow, eight hundred armed men. They were all young and gay and eager to do feats of arms, the best of all the host in bearing and array, the fairest company in such number to be found. They thought to make their way to the castle, and they deemed, if they could reach it, it should be held relieved. This host rode forward, and took the way towards Stirling. They avoided the New Park altogether, for they knew well the king was there, and they kept the lower ground all in a body till they were below the kirk.

The stout Earl Thomas, when he saw them thus take the field, made for them with the greatest speed at the head of only five hundred men. He was grieved and troubled in heart that they had so far passed him, for the king had said to him roughly that a rose of his chaplet had fallen, since these men had passed where he was set to keep the way. Because of this he made double haste, and in short space came with his following to the open field, for he meant to amend his fault or end his life.

When the English saw him come on without doubt or fear, and so boldly take the plain, they sped against him, spurring their steeds, and riding straight and bold and swift. And the Earl, seeing that host coming so stoutly, said to his men, "Be not dismayed because of their din, but set your spears before you, and keep all back to back with the spear-points out. Thus shall we best defend us if we be surrounded."

They did as he bade, and forthwith the enemy came on. Before them all came pricking a knight bold of heart and hand, a great lord at home, Sir William Dayncourt by name. He spurred on them so hardily, and they met him so stubbornly, that both he and his horse were borne down and slain beyond recovery on the spot. Greatly were he and his valour lamented by the English that day.

The rest came on them sturdily, but none rushed
among them so boldly as did he. Riding far
more cautiously, they gathered all in a body,
and surrounded the Scottish company, attacking
them on every side. But the Earl's men with
their spears gave wide wounds to the horses that
came near, and the riders when they lost their
seats lost their lives. Many spears, darts, knives,
and weapons of all sorts were cast among the
Scots, but they defended themselves so skilfully
that the English were filled with wonder. For
some would dash out of their company and stab
the steeds, and throw down men among their
assailants. So fiercely did the English throw
swords and maces among the Scots, that a mound
of the weapons cast there arose in their midst.

The Earl and his men were fighting thus at
great disadvantage, for they were fewer by far
than their enemies, and were wholly surrounded.
Many a blow was dealt, and their enemies harassed
them most straitly and mercilessly. In two ways
were they hard beset, by the heat of fighting and
the heat of the sun, and all their flesh was
drenched with sweat. There rose above them
such a mist of the breathing of horses and men,
and of dust, that it made a darkness in the air
wondrous to see, and put them to great per-
plexity. Making great endeavour, they manfully
defended themselves, and set will and skill and

strength to overthrow the foes so fiercely harassing them. Nevertheless, except God helped them quickly, they were like to have their fill of fighting.

But when the king and the lords beside him saw the Earl recklessly take the open field, James of Douglas came up to the Bruce and said, " Ah, sir, by Saint Mary, the Earl of Moray takes the plain field openly with his following. He is in peril unless he be helped soon, for his enemies are more than he, and horsed well besides. With your leave I will speed to help him at his need, for he is surrounded with foes."

" As our Lord sees me," said the king, "thou shalt not stir a foot towards him. Let him take the fortune that falls to him; whether he happen to win or lose, I shall not break my battle plan for him."

" Of a surety," said Douglas, " I will in no wise see him overwhelmed by his foes when I can bring him help. With your leave I will assuredly help him, or die in the endeavour."

" Do so then," said the king, "and speed thee soon again."

So Douglas set forth. If he should arrive in time, I trow he was like to help the Earl in a fashion that his foes should feel.

BOOK XII

THE FIRST STROKE OF THE FIGHT.

NOW as Douglas set forth it chanced that the King of England, having come with his great host near to the place where the Scots were arrayed, caused a halt of his whole division to be made, in order to take council whether they should pitch their camp that night, or at once join battle. But the vanguard knew nothing of this halt and delay, and rode in good array, without stopping, straight to the Park. And when the Bruce knew they were come so near in full order of battle, he set his men in array. He rode upon a grey palfrey, small and spirited, ordering his ranks, with an axe in his hand. On his basnet he wore everywhere a hard leather hat, and on it, for a sign that he was king, a high crown.

Gloucester and Hereford with their hosts were approaching near, and before them all there came riding, with helm on head and spear in hand, the gallant Sir Henry de Bohun. He was a good and bold knight, cousin to the Earl of Hereford, and was clad in strong fine armour. He came on his steed a mark-shot before all the rest, and knew the king by his arraying his men and by reason of the crown on his basnet, and he spurred at him.

When the Bruce saw him come on so openly before all his comrades he turned his horse towards him. And when Sir Henry saw the king come fearlessly on, he rode at him with the utmost speed. He thought he should right easily vanquish and overpower him since he saw him mounted so ill. They dashed together in straight career, but Sir Henry missed the king, and the Bruce, standing in his stirrups, with his keen strong axe dealt him such a mighty blow as neither hat nor helmet could withstand. The heavy stroke that he gave clove skull and brain; the axe-handle shivered in two; and De Bohun crashed helpless to the earth. This deed, performed so doughtily, was the first stroke of the battle.

When the king's men saw him so stoutly, at the first encounter, without fear or hesitation, slay a knight thus at a single stroke, they were seized with courage and came hardily on. And when the English saw them so stoutly advance they were greatly daunted, more especially because the king had so speedily slain that good knight. They every one drew back, and so much feared the king's might that they durst not abide the battle. And when the king's men saw them thus withdraw in a body, they made a great dash at them. The English in haste took flight, and their pursuers overtook and slew some of them. But, to tell the truth, the slain were few; their horses' feet got most of them away. But though so few died there, they were heavily repulsed, and galloped off with the greatest disgrace.

When the king had stopped the pursuit and returned, the lords of his company blamed him greatly—as much as they durst—for putting himself to the hazard of meeting so strong and sturdy a knight in such array as they saw him in. It might indeed, they said, have been the ruin of them all. The king made them no answer, but lamented his axe-handle thus with one stroke broken in two.

The Earl Thomas was still fighting with foes on every side. He slew many of them, and though his men and he were weary, they nevertheless stubbornly and manfully defended themselves with their weapons till the Lord Douglas, making the utmost speed, drew near. The English, as they fought, when they saw the Douglas at hand, gave way and made an opening. Sir James, by their wavering, knew they were nigh discomfited, and bade those with him stand still and press no further.

"Those fighting yonder, he said, "are of such great valour that by their own strength, though no man help them, they shall right soon discomfit their enemies. Were we now, when they are at the point of victory, to come into the battle, it would be said that we had overthrown the enemy, and they who have stood the brunt with great labour and hard fighting should lose part of their praise. It were a sin to lessen the honour of one of such sovereign nobleness, when by plain, hard fighting he has achieved here an unlikely thing. He shall have what he has won."

When the Earl and those fighting with him saw the enemy thus fall into confusion, they fell upon them with haste, and pressed them with strokes wondrous many and heavy, till at last they fled and durst abide no more. Their slain, both men and horses, they left on the spot, and made off with the utmost speed. They did not hold together, but fled singly, and those that were overtaken were slain. The others returned to their host sad and sorry for their loss.

Having thus acquitted himself, the Earl, and his men as well, being weary and hot and all covered with sweat, took off their basnets to air themselves. They looked, I vow, like men who had indeed put their foes to the proof in battle, and this right doughtily they had done. They found that of all their company there was but

one yeoman slain, and they praised God and were
right glad and joyous that they had so escaped.
Then they set out towards the king, and soon
drew nigh to him. He asked them of their
welfare, and made gladsome cheer to them because
they had borne themselves so well. And all ran
in great joy to see the Earl of Moray, everyone
eager to do him honour for his high worth and
valour. So eagerly did they run to see him then
that nigh all the knights were gathered together.
And when the good king saw them thus assem-
bled, blithe and glad that their enemies were
repulsed, he held him silent a little while, then
in this wise spoke to them:

"Sirs," he said, "we should praise Almighty
God who sits above, for sending us so fair a
beginning. It is great discouragement to our
foes to have been twice repulsed thus early in the
struggle. For when the others of their host shall
hear and know for certain in what fashion their
vanguard, which was so strong, and afterwards
yonder other pretty rout, that I trow was of the
best men they could get, have been so suddenly
put to flight, I am full well assured that many a
heart shall waver that seemed erstwhile of mighty
valour. And if the heart be dismayed, the body
is not worth a mite. I trow, therefore, that a
good ending shall follow this beginning. Never-
theless, I say not this to you in order that ye

should follow my desire to fight; for with you shall rest the whole matter. If ye think it expedient that we fight, we shall fight; and if ye will that we depart, your desire shall be fulfilled. I shall consent to do in either fashion right as ye shall decide. Therefore speak plainly your desire."

At that they all cried with one voice, "Good king, without more delay, to-morrow, as soon as ye see light, ordain you wholly for the battle. We shall not fail you for fear of death, nor shall any effort be wanting till we have made our country free."

When the king heard them so manfully and boldly declare for battle, saying that neither life nor death should so discourage them as lead them to eschew the fight, he was greatly rejoiced in heart, and in great gladness said, "Sirs, since ye will it so, make ready in the morning, so that by sunrise we shall have heard mass; and be well prepared, each man in his own squadron, before the tents, in battle order, with banners displayed. See to it that ye nowise break array, and, as ye love me, I pray you let each man for his own honour provide himself a good banner-bearer, and, when it comes to the fight, set his heart and strength to break the mighty pride of our foes. They will come in horse array, and ride upon you at the greatest speed: meet them with spears boldly, and wreak on them the mighty

ill that they and theirs have done to us, and
have yet the will to do if only they have the
strength.

"And, certes, methinks that we may well be
undismayed, valiant, and of great prowess, for
we have three great vantages. First, we have
right on our side, and every man should do
battle for the right. Next, they are come here,
trusting in their great strength, to seek us in
our own land, and have brought, right to our
hand, riches in such great plenty that if we win,
as may well befall, the poorest of you shall be
made therewith both rich and mighty. The third
advantage is that we are constrained to stand
in battle for our lives, our children, our wives,
and the freedom of our country, while they are
made to fight only because of their mightiness,
and because they esteem us lightly, and because
they seek to destroy us all. It may happen yet
that they shall rue their fighting.

"And, certes, I warn you of one thing. If it
happen, as God forbid! that in action they find
us cowards, and thus openly overcome us, they
will have no mercy on us. Now, since we know
their cruel intent, methinks it should accord with
sense that we set stubbornness against cruelty,
and so make bold endeavour. Wherefore I require
and pray you that, with all the strength ye have,
ye strive without cowardice or dismay, so stoutly

to meet those that first come to the encounter, that the hindmost of them shall tremble. Think on your great manhood, your valour, and your doughty deeds, and of the joy that awaits you if it falls to us, as may well happen, to win the battle. In your hands, without fail, ye carry honour, praise, riches, freedom, welfare, and great gladness, if ye bear yourselves manfully; and the contrary altogether shall befall if ye let cowardice and weakness surprise your hearts. Ye might have lived in thraldom, but because ye yearned to be free ye are come together with me here. To gain your end it is needful that ye be valiant and strong and undismayed.

"I warn you well of one more thing—that no greater harm can befall us than to be taken by their hand, for right well I know they would slay us as they did my brother Neil. But when I think on your valour and the many great deeds of prowess ye have so gallantly done, I trust, and believe of a surety, that we shall have full victory in this battle. Though our enemies have great might, they are on the side of wrong and presumption, and are moved by nothing more than hunger for dominion. The strength of this place, as ye see, shall keep us from being surrounded. And I especially pray you all further, both greater and less, that none of you by reason of greed, have an eye to seize their riches, nor yet to take prisoners, till ye see them so far defeated that the field is plainly ours. Then, at your pleasure, ye may take all the wealth there is. If ye work in this wise ye shall for certain have the victory.

"I know not what more to say. Ye know well what honour is. Bear yourselves in such fashion as to keep your honour. And I promise here, upon my honour, that if any die in this battle, his heir, be he ever so young in age, shall possess his land from the first day without guardian's due, or fee to overlord.

"Now make ye ready for the fight. Almighty God be our help! I counsel ye to lie all night armed, prepared for battle, that we be at any moment ready to meet our foes."

Then answered they all with one voice, "As you direct it shall be done!" And they went straightway to their quarters, and ordered them for the battle. Afterwards, in the evening, they came together for the attack, and remained thus all the night, till it was daylight on the morrow.

When, as I have told, the Clifford and all his host were repulsed, and the great vanguard of the English also was constrained to flee, they of the vanguard told their fellows of their repulse, and how the Bruce had slain at one stroke so openly the best of their knights, and how the whole of the king's host and Sir Edward Bruce's

had made right stoutly to attack them when
they gave back, and how they had lost men;
and Clifford further told how Thomas Randolph
had taken the open field with a small follow-
ing, and had slain the valiant Sir William
Dayncourt, and how manfully the Earl had
fought, causing his host, like a hedgehog, to set
out spears all around, and how the English
horse had been driven back, and many brave
men among the riders slain; at the tidings the
English were seized with dismay and fear
and in five hundred places and more they could
be seen whispering together, and saying, "Our
lords ever will battle by might against the right,
but whoso wrongfully makes war tries God all
too greatly, and perchance comes to grief, and
it may hap that we shall do so here."

And when their lords saw their discourage-
ment, and the whispering they held together,
two and two, they sent heralds forthwith
throughout the host, to proclaim that it should
be no whit discouraged, since in skirmishes it
was the common happening at times to win and
at times to lose, but that in the great battle they
could by no means fail, and that when the Scots
fled full amends should indeed be made. There-
fore they urged them to be most valorous and
stout, and to stand strong in the battle, and
take amends at their hand.

The lords might urge as they pleased, and the men might promise to fulfil all their behest with stalwart strokes; nevertheless, I trow they remained fearful in their hearts.

King Edward took the advice of his privy council that he should not fight before the morrow, unless he were attacked. The host therefore quartered that night in the Carse, and made all ready, and got their gear in order against the battle. Because of the pools in the Carse they broke down houses and thatch, and carried them to make bridges that they might pass over. And some say yet that, when night fell, nigh all the Castle garrison, knowing their evil case, went forth and carried doors and windows with them, so that before day they had bridged the pools, and the host had all passed over, and with their horses occupied the firm ground, and, arrayed in their gear, stood ready to give battle.

The Scots, when it was day, devoutly heard mass, then took a slight meal, and made themselves ready. And when all were come together, and ranged in their divisions, with broad banners displayed, they made knights, as the custom is among those of the craft of war. The king knighted Walter Stewart and the stalwart James of Douglas, and others also of great nobleness, each in his degree. When this was done they all went forth in brave array, and openly took the field. Many an active man, stout and bold and valorous, was there.

On the other side the English could be seen in their hosts, shining bright as angels. But they were not arrayed in the same fashion as the Scots, for all their divisions were together in one mass. Whether it was through the exceeding straitness of the ground on which they were arrayed to abide the battle, or whether through lack of courage, I know not; but it seemed they were one and all in a single mass, except only the vanguard, which, a right great company, was arrayed by itself, and made ready for the battle. That company covered a huge broad field, and many a shining shield and many a piece of armour burnished clear, and many a man of mighty valour, and many a banner bright and glorious, might be seen in that great host.

And when the King of England saw the Scots venture to take the field so openly on foot, he marvelled and said, "What! will yonder Scots fight?"

"Yea, for a surety, sir," said a knight. It was Sir Ingraham de Umphraville, and he added, "Of a truth, sir, now I see the most marvellous sight by far that ever I beheld—Scotsmen undertaking to fight against the great might of England, and to give battle in the hard open field. But if ye will trust my counsel ye shall discomfit them with ease. Ye shall withdraw hence suddenly, with host, banners, and pennons, till we have passed our tents, and ye shall forthwith see that, despite their lords, they shall break array, and scatter to seize our gear. And when we see them thus scattered, spur we boldly on them, and we shall have them right easily, for none shall then be in close array to withstand our great strength."

"By my faith," said the king, "I will not do so; for there shall no man say that I avoided the battle, or withdrew me because of any such rabble."

As this was said the Scots all most devoutly knelt down, and made a short prayer to God to help them in that fight. And when the English king saw them kneeling, he quickly said, "Yonder folk kneel to ask mercy!"

"Ye say truth now," said Sir Ingraham; "they ask mercy, but not at you. They cry to God for forgiveness. I tell you one thing for certain, yonder men will win all or die. None there shall flee for fear of death."

"Now so be it," said the king, "we shall see presently."

He caused the trumpets to sound the assembly, and on either side could be seen full many active and valiant men all ready to do deeds of chivalry.

Thus they were ready on either side, when with great pomp the English vanguard made straight for the division ordered and led by Sir Edward Bruce. They spurred their steeds, and rode sturdily upon the Scots, and Sir Edward's host met them right boldly, and at their encounter there was a crashing of spears that could be heard a long way off.

At their meeting, of a surety, many a steed was stabbed, and many a good man borne down and slain, while many a deed of valour was doughtily and boldly achieved. They struck at each other with different weapons, and though some of the horses that were stabbed reared and bore back most madly, the others, notwithstanding, who could come to the encounter, made no stopping for that hindrance, but right boldly rushed to battle. And the Scots met them most stubbornly with spears sharpened for cutting, and well-ground axes, wherewith they dealt full many a stroke.

The fight at that place was fierce and stubborn, and many valiant and active men, overthrown in the onset, were never able to rise again. The Scots made diligent endeavour to overthrow the vast might of their foes. I trow they were to shirk no pain or peril till their enemies were brought to hard perplexity.

When the Earl of Moray saw the English

vanguard advance bold and straight against Sir
Edward, and the Scots meet them with full great
might, he made, with his banner, towards the
great rout where the nine divisions were together.
These were so broad, and had so many banners,
and such number of men, that they were a
wonder to see. The good Earl made his way
towards them with his division in stout array,
and joined battle most boldly with a great crash
of breaking spears. For the enemy attacked
without ceasing, spurring haughtily on horse-
back as if they would over-ride the Earl and all
his company.

But the Scots met them so sturdily that they
bore many of them to the ground. Many a steed
was stabbed there, and many a brave man felled
under foot with no power to rise again. There
a stern battle was to be seen, some attacking
and some making defence, and many a great
and rude blow was struck upon either side, till
blood burst through the coats of mail, and
streamed to the earth.

The Earl of Moray and his men so stoutly bore
themselves that they gained ground ever more
and more upon their enemies, though, of a truth,
these were ten to one, or more. It seemed,
indeed, as if the Scots were lost among so great
a host, like men plunged in the sea.

And when the English saw the Earl and all

his men fight so stoutly and fearlessly and un-
dismayed, they charged with all their might
And the Scots, with spears and bright swords
and axes that cut sharply, met them face to face.
A mighty struggle took place there, and many
men of great valour, with spears, maces, knives,
and other weapons, exchanged their lives. Many
fell dead, and the grass grew red with blood.
The active and valiant Earl and his men fought
so manfully that whosoever had seen them that
day must have said they did their duty well
upon their foes.

BOOK XIII

THE BATTLE OF BANNOCKBURN

WHEN the two first divisions of the Scots had joined battle, as I have said, Walter the Steward and the good Lord of Douglas, seeing the Earl with his company so stoutly, without doubt or fear, attack the whole host, set forth with their division in brave array to help him, and joined battle so boldly a little way from the Earl that the enemy were made well aware of their coming; for they drove at them with strong weapons of steel and with all their might.

Their enemies received them well, I promise, with swords, maces, and spears. The battle there was most fierce, and so mighty was the spilling of blood that it stood in pools on the ground. The Scots bore themselves so well, and made so great a slaughter, and reft the lives from so many, that all the field was left bloody. At that time the three Scottish divisions were fighting well-nigh side by side. There one might hear right many a stroke, and weapons striking on armour, and see knights and steeds go down, and many a rich and splendid garment fouled roughly under foot. Some kept their feet, some lost their lives.

A long while thus they fought without shout or cry being heard. No sounds came forth but those of groans and blows that struck fire like steel on flint. So keenly they fought, each one, that they made neither noise nor cry, but drove at each other with all their might with their bright burnished weapons. The arrows, too, flew so thick that those who saw them have said they in truth made a dreadful shower; for where they fell I warrant they left after them tokens that called for the leech.

The English archers shot so fast that had their shower lasted it had gone hard with the Scots. But King Robert, who knew well that the archers were dangerous, and their shooting right grievous and hard, had, before the battle, ordained his marshal, with a great host—five hundred well armed in steel, and well mounted on light horses —to charge among the archers, and attack them with spears, so that they should have no leisure to shoot.

This marshal, Sir Robert of Keith, when he saw the hosts come together, and join battle, and saw the archers shooting stoutly, forthwith rode at them with all his company, and took them in the flank. He charged fiercely among them,

striking them mercilessly, and bearing down and
slaying numbers of them without ransom. And
they every one scattered, and from that time
forth none came together to make such shooting.

When the Scottish bowmen saw the English
archers thus overwhelmed they waxed bold, and
shot quickly with all their might among the
charging horsemen, and made great wounds among
them, and slew of them a right great number.
These bowmen bore themselves boldly and well;
for now that their archer foes, who were far
more than they in number, were scattered, and
they had nothing to fear from their shooting, it
seemed to them they should set all their enemies
at nought.

Meanwhile, among the English archers, the
Marshal and his company, wherever they rode,
made room with their spears, and slew all whom
they could overtake. Right easily could they do
this, having neither to stop a stroke nor with-
stand a blow; for unarmed men are little able
to fight against men in armour. In such fashion
Sir Robert scattered these archers that some
withdrew with the utmost speed to their great
battles, and some fled altogether.

But the English who had been behind the
archers, and who had had no room by reason of
their own host to come yet to the encounter,
dashed quickly into the battle. The archers whom

they met fleeing were by that time become
altogether cowards. They had clean lost heart,
and I trow were not likely to hurt the Scots
greatly with their shooting that day.

And when the good King Robert, who was ever
full of the greatest nobleness, saw how boldly his
three battles made encounter, and how well they
bore themselves in the strife, and how hard and
undauntedly they drove at their foes, and how
the English archers were scattered, he was right
blithe, and said to his men, "Sirs, look now that
ye be valiant and bold and of good guidance at
this encounter, and join battle so stoutly that
nothing shall stand before you. So freshly are
our men fighting, and so greatly have they
harassed their foes, that I warrant, if the enemy
be pressed a little harder, ye shall see them
presently discomfited. Let us now drive at them
so boldly, and so doughtily lay on our strokes,
that they may feel at our coming that we hate
them to the uttermost. Great cause have they
given us to hate them. Our broad lands they
seized, and brought all to subjection. Your whole
goods they made their own. Our kin and friends,
for defending their own possessions, they have
mercilessly hanged and drawn. And they would
destroy us if they could. But God in his foresight
has this day, I trow, granted us his grace to
wreak our wrongs upon them."

At these words the Bruce's men set forward
and joined battle so stoutly on the enemies' flank
that at their coming their foes were driven back
a great way. There men could be seen fighting
freshly, and valiant and active knights doing
many a noble deed of prowess. They fought as
they were mad. At these places especially where
the Scots saw their enemies most stubborn against
them, they laid on with all their might and
main, like men out of their minds. Where their
blows fell full and straight no armour could
stop the strokes. They charged against all they
could reach, and with their axes gave blows that
clave helmets and heads.

Their enemies met them right boldly, and dealt
blows doughtily with strong weapons of steel.
Well was the battle stricken in that place.
Mighty was the din of blows, as weapons struck
upon armour, and great was the crashing of
spears, with turning and thrusting, grunting and
groaning and mighty noise, as they laid on each
other. They called their battle-cries on every side
as they gave and took wide wounds, and the
uproar was horrid to hear, as the four strong
battles fought all together in one front.

God Almighty! most doughtily Sir Edward the
Bruce and his men bore themselves there among
their foes. They were so bold and stout, and
fought so skilfully and to such purpose, that the

vanguard of the enemy was overthrown, and, despite its leaders, left the ground. The English made for refuge to their great host. But that host itself had weighty business in hand and was itself dismayed. For the Scots now all in a single body assailed it hard.

He who chanced to fall in that fight never, I trow, rose again. There men might see brave deeds of many kinds doughtily achieved, and many men who had been active and bold lying all dead under foot, and the field all red with blood. Their badges and coats of arms were so defiled with blood that they could not be discerned.

Ah, mighty God! if one could have seen Walter the Steward, and his rout, and Douglas the stout and brave, as they fought in the strong battle, he must have declared them worthy of all honour. So hard in that fight did they press upon the strength of their foes that they overthrew them wherever they went. Many a steed was to be seen there fleeing astray without a rider.

Ah, Lord! it was a sight to see how the brave Earl of Moray and his men dealt great blows, and fought in that hard strife. They underwent such labour and toil, and did such battle, that wherever they came they made themselves a way. There could be heard the shouting of battle-cries, and the Scots calling boldly, "On them! on them! on them! they fail!"

With that they made a most bold attack, and slew all they could come at, and the Scottish archers also shot boldly among the enemy, and harassed them greatly. Then, what with their adversaries dealing them mighty blows and pressing them eagerly, and what with the arrows making many great and cruel wounds and slaying their horses, the English host gave way a little space, and came so greatly into fear of death that their condition grew ever worse. For the Scots fighting with them set hardihood and strength and will, as well as heart and courage, and all their might and main, to put them to foul flight.

At this moment, when the battle was in this fashion being fought, and either side was struggling right manfully, the yeomen, swains, and camp-followers who had been left in the Park to mind the victual, knowing for certain that their lords had joined battle and were in dire conflict with their foes, made one of themselves captain, and fastened broad sheets for banners upon long poles and spears, and said they would see the fight, and help their lords to their utmost. When all were agreed to this, and were come together in a body, they were fifteen thousand and more. Then they hastened forward all in a rout with their banners, like men strong and stout. They came with their whole host to a place where they could see the battle. Then all at once they gave a shout, "Upon them! on them boldly!" and therewith they all came on.

But they were yet a long way off when the English, who were being driven back by force of battle as I have said, saw coming towards them with a shout a company which seemed full as great as the host they were fighting, and which they had not seen before. Then, be assured, they were vastly dismayed, and without doubt the best and boldest in the host that day would, had honour allowed, have been away.

By their reeling King Robert saw they were near discomfiture. He shouted loudly his battle-cry, then with his company pressed his foes so hard that they were thrown into great affright, and ever more and more left the ground. Then all the Scots, when they saw them avoid the fight, drove at them with all their strength, so that they scattered in separate troops, and were near defeat, and some of them openly fled. Still some who were active and bold, whom shame kept from taking flight, at great cost maintained the battle, and stood firm in the storm.

When the King of England saw his men in sundry places flee, and saw the host of his foes become strong and bold, and the English array altogether defeated and without strength to with-stand its enemies, he was so vastly dismayed

that, with all his company, five hundred armed
cap-a-pie, in utter disorder, he took to flight,
and made for the castle. Some say, however,
that Sir Aymer De Valence, when he saw the
field nigh lost, took the king's rein and led him
away from the fighting against his will.

And when Sir Giles De Argentine saw Edward
and his host thus make so speedily to flee, he
came forthwith close to the king, and said, "Sir,
since so be that thus ye go your way, farewell,
for I will again to the battle. Never yet, of a
surety, have I fled, and I choose rather here to
abide and die than to flee shamefully and live."

Forthwith then he turned his steed, and rode
against the foe. And, as if he had no whit of
fear, crying "De Argentine!" he pricked on the
strong and bold Sir Edward Bruce's host. They
met him with their spears, and so many set upon
him that he and his steed were overborne, and
both went to the earth, and in that place he was
slain. There was right great sorrow for his
death. He was the third best knight, of a truth,
known to be living in his time.[1] Many a fair feat
of arms he achieved. Thrice had he done battle
on the Saracen, and in each attack had vanquished
two of his foes. But his great valour came here
to an end.

[1] The others, according to Lord Hailes, were the Emperor Henry
and King Robert the Bruce.

After Sir Aymer had fled with the king, there durst none remain; but all fled, scattering on every side. Their foes pressed them hard, and they were all, to speak truth, terrified. In such great terror they fled that a very great body of them, fleeing towards the Forth, were most part drowned. The Bannockburn between its banks was so filled with men and horses that men could pass over dryshod upon the drowned bodies. Lads, hinds, and camp-followers, when they saw the battle won, ran among the fallen, and slew those who could make no defence, in fashion that was piteous to see. Nowhere have I heard in any land of folk so grievously bested. On one side were their foes, who slew them without mercy, and on the other side was the Bannock-burn, deep and full of mud, so that none could ride across it. Against their will they behoved to abide, and some were slain, some drowned, and none escaped that came there.

Nevertheless, many who fled elsewhere got away. King Edward and those with him rode in a body to the castle, and sought to be taken in, for they knew not where to escape. But Philip the Mowbray said to him, "The castle, sir, is at your will, but should ye come into it ye should presently see yourself besieged, and there shall none in all England undertake to bring you succour. Without succour can no castle be long

P

held, as well ye know; therefore take courage, and rally your men right straitly about you, and take the way round the Park. Keep as close array as ye can, and I trow that none who follow shall have force enough to fight so many."

They did as he counselled. Beneath the castle forthwith they held their way, close by the Round Table,[1] then compassed the Park, and held in haste towards Linlithgow. But I trow they were speedily to have convoy of a kind they could have suffered away. For Sir James, Lord of Douglas, came to the Bruce and asked leave to chase, and he gave him leave forthwith. Douglas's horse were all too few; he had no more than sixty in his rout; nevertheless he sped hastily after the English king. Now leave we him on his way, and afterwards we shall tell fully what befel in the pursuit.

In the great battle thus decided there were thirty thousand slain or drowned, while some were taken prisoner, and others fled.

The Earl of Hereford left the strife, with a great host, and made his way straight to Both-well, which was then in the English fealty, and

---

[1] This curious relic, now known as the King's Knot, under the walls on the south side of Stirling Castle, is believed by many to be the actual Round Table of Arthurian times, and to date from the reign of that famous British monarch, who had his chief stronghold at Stirling in the sixth century. See Nennius, *Historia Britonum*, and Skene's *Celtic Scotland*.

held as a place of war. Sir Walter Gilbertston was captain there, and had it in keeping. Thitherward sped the Earl, and was taken in over the wall, with fifty of his men, and separately housed in such fashion that they had no mastery of the place. The rest went towards England. Of that rout I warrant three-fourths were taken or slain, and the others reached home with great difficulty.

Sir Maurice De Barclay set forth from the great battle with a great host of Welshmen. Wherever they went they could be known by reason that they were well-nigh wholly naked, or had only linen clothes. They marched with the greatest speed, but ere they were come to England many of their company were taken and many slain.

The English fled also by many other ways. But to the castle of Stirling at hand fled such a host as was a marvel to behold. The crags about the castle were all covered here and there with those who, because of the strength of that place, fled thitherward for refuge. And because the number thus fled under the castle was so great, King Robert prudently kept his good men ever near him, out of fear that the English should rise again. It was by reason of this, indeed, that the King of England escaped to his own country.

When the field was so cleared of the English that none remained, the Scots forthwith took possession of all spoils of the enemy that they could find, such as silver, gold, clothing, and armour, with plate, and all things else that they could lay hands upon. Such vast riches they found there that many a man was made great by the wealth he got.

When this was done the king sent a strong company up to the crag to attack those that were fled from the great battle, and these yielded themselves without struggle, and were speedily seized and carried to the king.

The Scots, after an end was made of the fighting, spent that whole day in spoiling and taking gear; and when all who had been slain in the battle had been spoiled of their arms it was of a truth a wondrous sight to see so many lying dead together. Seven hundred pairs of red spurs were taken from dead knights. There among the dead lay the Earl of Gloucester, whom men called Sir Gilbert of Clare, also Sir Giles d'Argentine and Sir Payn Tybetot, with others beside whose names I cannot recount.

And on the side of the Scots were slain two worthy knights, Sir William Vipont and Sir Walter the Ross, whom Sir Edward, the king's brother, loved as himself, and held in high esteem. When Sir Edward knew that this knight was dead he was so sorrowful and distressed that he said, making full evil cheer, he had rather the day had been lost than that Sir Walter were slain. Besides him it was not seen that Sir Edward made moan for any man. The reason of this affection was that he loved the sister of Ross as a paramour, and held his own wife, Dame Isobel, in great dislike. For this cause a great distance had fallen betwixt him and the Earl David of Atholl, brother of this lady; and upon Sir John's Eve, when the two kings were ready to fight, the Earl seized the Bruce's victual at Cambuskenneth, and heavily attacked and slew Sir William of Airth and many with him. Wherefore afterwards he was banished to England, and all his land was seized and forfeited to the king, who did therewith at his pleasure.

When the field was spoiled and left all bare, as I have said, the Bruce and all his company, joyful and blithe and merry over the grace that had befallen them, betook them to their quarters to rest, for they were weary. But the king grieved somewhat for the Earl Gilbert of Clare slain in the battle, for he was near kin[1] to himself. He caused him to be carried to a church, and guarded all that night.

[1] It was the Earl of Gloucester who sent Bruce a pair of spurs at the court of Edward I., and by this hint to flee saved his life.

And on the morrow, when it was light, the
king rose as his custom was. Then it happened
that an English knight went hither and thither,
no man laying hands on him. He had hid his
armour in a coppice, and waited till, early in the
morning, he saw the king come forth. Then he
hastened to him. Sir Marmaduke de Twenge he
was called, and he reached the near presence of
the king, and greeted him upon his knee.

"Welcome, Sir Marmaduke," said the Bruce, "to
what man art thou prisoner?"

"To none," he said, "but here to you I yield,
to be at your pleasure."

"And I receive thee, sir," said the king. Then
he caused him to be courteously treated, and
Sir Marmaduke dwelt long in his company, and
afterwards the king sent him to England arrayed
well and ransom free and with great gifts beside.
A worthy man who should do thus might make
himself greatly praised.

When Sir Marmaduke in this wise had yielded
himself, Sir Philip the Mowbray came and yielded
the castle to the king. He had kept his covenant
well, and the king so dealt with him that he
became of his household, and kept his faith
loyally to the last day of his life.

Now shall we tell of the Lord Douglas, how
he followed the chase. He had few in his com-
pany, but he sped with right great haste, and as

he fared by the Torwood he met, riding on the moor, Sir Laurence of Abernethy, who with fourscore in his company was come to help the English, for he was still English then. But when he heard how the day stood, he left the English peace and swore to the Lord Douglas right there to be loyal and true. Then they both followed the chase.

And ere the King of England had passed Linlithgow the Scots came so near with all their followers that they could well nigh have charged among them. But they deemed themselves too few to fight with the great rout of the English, for these were five hundred armed men. The English rode together in close order with drawn bridle, and were right shrewdly managed, appearing ever ready to defend themselves to the utmost if they were attacked. The Lord Douglas judged he should not then attempt to fight openly with them. But he convoyed them so narrowly that constantly he took the hindmost. None could be behind his fellows a stone-cast but at once he was either taken or slain, and none could bring him succour though he loved him ever so much.

In this fashion he convoyed them till King Edward and his host were come to Winchburgh. There the English all lighted down to bait their weary horses; and Douglas and his company baited also close beside them. They were so

many, and so fully armed, and so constantly
arrayed for battle, and he so few, and without
support, that he would not attack them in open
fight, but rode ever by them, constantly waiting
his chance.

They baited there a little while, then mounted
and fared forward, and he was always close by
them. He let them have not so much leisure as
to relieve themselves; and if any were so bested,
and were left any space behind, forthwith he was
made captive.

In this fashion Douglas convoyed them till the
king and his rout were come to the Castle of
Dunbar. There he and some of his men were
right well received; for still at that time the
Earl Patrick was an Englishman.[1] He caused
them to be well refreshed with meat and drink,
and afterwards procured a boat, and sent the
king by sea to Bamborough in his own country.
Their horses they left to go astray, but I trow
they were taken possession of soon enough.

The rest, who were left without the castle,
arrayed themselves in a body, and made straight
towards Berwick. To say truth, they lost part
of their rout ere they came thither. Neverthe-
less they came at last to Berwick, and were

[1] The Earls of March claimed direct descent from the ancient
Kings of Northumbria. They are represented to-day by the
Dunbars of Mochrum.

there received into the town, else mischance had befallen them. And when the Lord Douglas saw that he had lost his pains he went again to the Bruce.

Thus King Edward escaped. Lo! what changes there are in fortune! Now she will smile upon a man, and another time will thrust a knife into him. At no time does she stand stable. This mighty King of England she had set high on her wheel when with so marvellous a host of men-at-arms and archers, and men on foot and men on horse-back, he came riding out of his country, as I have already described. And afterwards, in a night and a day, she set him in so hard a strait that with seventeen in a boat he was fain to make his way home.

But King Robert had no need to make lament of the turning of this same wheel, for by the turn of the wheel his side vanquished its foes, and was made great in might.

Two opposites ye may well perceive set against each other on a wheel. When one is high the other is low; and if it befall that fortune turn the wheel about, that which was erst above is perforce downmost sped, while that which erst was wondrous low must leap aloft. So fared it with these two kings; when King Robert was bested in his time of evil fortune, the other was in royal estate; and when King Edward's might was brought low, King Robert's leapt on high; and now it was his fortune to be exalted and achieve his desire.

While he still lay at Stirling he caused the great lords whom he found dead in the field to be buried honourably in holy ground. The other dead were buried afterwards in great pits. Then he caused the castle and towers to be mined and thrown down. Next he sent Sir Edward with a great host to Bothwell, for word reached him from that place that the rich Earl of Hereford and other mighty men were there. Sir Edward soon made treaty with Sir Walter Gilbertston, so that he gave the Earl and castle, and all else, into his hand. Sir Edward sent the Earl to the king, and he caused him to be warded right well, till at last they made treaty that he should return to England ransom free, and that for him there should be exchanged Bishop Robert,[1] who had become blind, with the queen, and her daughter the Lady Marjory, whom the English held in prison. The Earl was exchanged for these three.

And when they were come home, the king's daughter, a fair maid, who was his apparent heir, was wedded with Walter Stewart, and they

---

[1] Bishop Wishart of Glasgow, who absolved the Bruce and robed him for his coronation, had become blind in prison. Several of his letters in Rymer's *Foedera* refer to this fact.

presently, by our Lord's grace, begat a boy child, who was called Robert after his brave grand-father, and later, after his worthy uncle David, who reigned two and forty years, he became king, and had the land in government.

At the time of the compiling of this book this Robert was king, and five years of his reign were past. It was the year of grace 1375, and the sixtieth of his age, and six and forty winters after the good King Robert's life was brought to an end. God grant that they who are come of his offspring shall uphold the land, and keep the people in all safety, and maintain right and loyalty as well as the Bruce did in his time!

King Robert was now full at his fortune's height, for each day his strength grew greater. His people were rich, and his country abounded greatly in corn and cattle, and all other kinds of wealth. Mirth, comfort, and gladness were every-where in the land, for each man was blithe and festive.

After the great day of battle the king, by advice of his privy council, caused it to be publicly proclaimed in different towns that whoso claimed the right to hold land or fee in Scotland should, within a twelvemonth, come and claim it, and do therefor the service pertaining to the king. And they must take note that, if they came not within the year, of a certainty none should thereafter be heard.

Soon after this was done, the king, being of great valour and activity, caused a host to be summoned, and went into England, and over-rode all Northumberland, and burnt and plundered, and then came home again. I pass this shortly by, for in that riding was done no deed of approved chivalry that need be narrated here. The king went often in this manner into England to enrich his men, for that country abounded then in wealth.

BOOK XIV

EDWARD BRUCE IN IRELAND

SIR EDWARD BRUCE, the Earl of Carrick, who was bolder than a leopard, and had no desire to be at peace, thought Scotland too small for his brother and himself; therefore he set his purpose to be King of Ireland. To this end he entered into treaty with the Irish, and they on their honour undertook to make him king, provided that he, by hard fighting, could overcome the English then dwelling in the country; and they promised to help him with all their might.

When he heard this promise he had great joy in his heart, and with consent of the king gathered to him men of great valour, and taking ship at Ayr in the next month of May, sailed straight to Ireland.

He had in his company the valiant Earl Thomas, and good Sir Philip the Mowbray, trusty in hard assault, Sir John Soulis, a good knight, and the doughty Sir John Stewart, as well as the Ramsay

of Auchterhouse, right able and chivalrous, with
Sir Fergus of Ardrossan, and many another
knight.

They arrived safely in Wavering Firth[1] with-
out skirmish or attack, and sent their ships every
one home. It was a great enterprise they under-
took, when, few as they were, being no more
than six thousand men, they set out to attack
all Ireland, where many thousands were ready
armed to fight them. But though they were few,
they were valiant, and without doubt or fear
they set forth in two battles towards Carrick-
fergus, to spy it.

But the lords of that country, Mandeville,
Bysset, and Logan, assembled their men every
one. De Savage also was there. Their whole
gathering was wellnigh twenty thousand men.

When they knew that the Scottish host had
arrived in their country, they hastened towards
it with all their following. And when Sir Edward
knew of a certainty that they were coming near
him, he set his men in their strongest array. The
Earl Thomas had the vanguard, and the rear-
guard was under Sir Edward.

Their enemies drew near to battle, and they
met them without flinching. Then was to be seen
a great melee. Earl Thomas and his host drove
so doughtily at their foes, that in a short time

[1] Now Lough Larne

a hundred were to be seen lying all bloody. The Irish horses, when they were stabbed, reared and flung, and made great room, and threw their riders. Sir Edward's company then stoutly joined the battle, and all their enemies were driven back. If a man happened to fall in that fight, it was a perilous chance if he rose again. The Scots bore themselves so boldly and well in the encounter that their foes were overwhelmed, and altogether took flight. In that battle were taken or slain the whole flower of Ulster. The Earl of Moray won great praise there, for his right valiant feats of arms encouraged his whole company.

That was a right fair beginning; for being but newly arrived, Sir Edward's host defeated in open battle enemies who were four for their one. Afterwards they went to Carrickfergus, and took quarters in the town. The castle was at that time well and newly furnished with victual and men, and the Scots forthwith set siege to it. Many a bold sally was made while the siege lasted, till at length they made a truce.

When the folk of Ulster came wholly to his peace, and Sir Edward undertook to raid the land further, there came to him some ten or twelve of the chiefs of that country, and gave him their fealty. They kept faith with him, however, only a short while; for two of them, one MacCoolechan and another MacArthy, beset a place on his way where he must needs pass.

Two thousand spearmen were got together there and as many archers; and all the cattle of the country were drawn thither for safety. Men call that place Endwillane;[1] in all Ireland there is none more strait. There the Irish kept watch for Sir Edward, believing he should not escape. But he soon set forth and went straight towards the spot.

Sir Thomas, Earl of Moray, who ever put himself first in attack, alighted on foot with his company, and boldly assailed the fastness. The Irish chiefs of whom I spoke, and all the folk with them, met him right stubbornly; but he with his host made such an attack, that despite their efforts he won the place. Many of the Irish were slain there, and the Scots chased them throughout the wood, and seized an abundance of prey. So great was this that all the Scottish host was refreshed well for a week and more.

Sir Edward lay at Kilnasagart, and there presently he heard that at Dundalk the lords of that country were assembled for war. There was, first, Sir Richard of Clare, lieutenant of all Ireland for the King of England.[2] The Earl of Desmond also

---

[1] Probably the Moiry Pass, in Killevy parish, Armagh.

[2] Edmund Butler was really the Justiciary or Lord-Lieutenant of Ireland at the time, though Richard of Clare was a conspicuous figure.

was there, and the Earl of Kildare as well, with De Bermingham and Verdon, lords of great renown. Butler also was with them, and Sir Maurice FitzThomas. These were come thither with their men, and were in truth a right great host.

And when Sir Edward knew of a surety that there was such a knightly company, he forthwith arrayed his force and set out thither, and took quarters near the town. But because he knew full well that a great host was in the town, he arrayed his men, and kept in battle order, to meet the enemy if they should attack.

And when Sir Richard of Clare, and the other lords in that place, knew that the Scottish battles were come so near, they took counsel and agreed not to fight that night, because it was late, but determined that on the morrow, immediately after sunrise, they should sally forth with their whole force. Accordingly that night they did no more, but each side kept its quarters.

That night the Scottish company kept right careful watch, all in order, and on the morrow at daylight they arrayed themselves in two battles, and stood with banners all displayed, ready prepared for the fight.

Those within the town, when the sun was risen and shining clear, sent forth fifty of their number to spy the order and advance of the Scots. These

Q

rode forth and soon saw them; then came again without delay. And when they were alighted together they told their lords that the Scots seemed to be valiant and of right great nobleness. "But of a surety," they said, "they are not half a dinner for us here!"

The lords at these tidings were greatly rejoiced and reassured, and caused the order to go throughout the city that all should quickly arm themselves. And when they were armed and ready and all arrayed for the fight, they went forth in good order.

They soon came in touch with their foes, who were watching for them right boldly. Then a fierce battle began, for either side set all its strength to overwhelm its foes in the fight, and each charged the other with all its force. The furious struggle lasted long, while none could see or know who was likely to be uppermost. From soon after sunrise till after midday the fighting lasted thus doubtful; but at length the stout Sir Edward, with the whole of his company, rushed so furiously upon the enemy that they could no longer endure the battle. With broken ranks they all took flight, followed right keenly by the Scots. Mixed all together the two hosts entered the town. There a cruel slaughter was to be seen, for the right noble Earl Thomas followed the chase with his host, and made such a butchery in the place, and such fierce slaughter, that the streets were all bloody with slain men. But the English lords got all away.

When the town, as I have told, was stormed, and all their foes were fled or slain, the Scots quartered in the place. There was in it such plenty of victual, and such great abundance of wine, that the good Earl feared greatly lest his men should be drunken, and in their drunkenness come to blows; therefore he appointed a free gift of wine to be paid to each man, and of a surety they had all enough. That night they were right well at ease, and right glad of the great renown begotten by their valour.

After this fight they sojourned there in Dundalk three days and more, then they set forth southward. The Earl Thomas ever rode in front, and as they marched through the country they could see upon the hills a marvellous number of men. But when the Earl would sturdily make towards them with his banner, they would flee, all that were there, and none abide to fight.

The Scots rode southward till they came to a great forest, Kilross it was called, and they all took their quarters there.

Meantime Richard of Clare, the English king's lieutenant over all the baronage of Ireland, had got together a great host. There were five battles great and broad, and they sought Sir Edward and his men, and were by this time come very near him.

He soon got knowledge that they were coming upon him, and were so near, and he led his men against them, and boldly took the open field. Then the Earl rode forward to espy, and he sent Sir Philip the Mowbray and Sir John Stewart forward to discover the way the English were taking. Soon they saw the host coming at hand. They were, at a guess, fifty thousand strong. Then the knights rode back to Sir Edward, and said the enemy were right many.

"The more they be," he answered, "the more honour altogether have we, if we bear us manfully. We are set here at bay, and to win honour or die. We are too far from home to flee; therefore let each man be valiant. Yonder host are the scourings of the country, and if they be manfully assailed they shall easily, I trow, be made to flee."

All then said they should do well. With that the English battles, ten thousand strong, approached near, ready to fight, and the Scots met them with great force. The Scots were all on foot, and their enemies on steeds well equipped, some covered wholly with iron and steel. But the Scots at the encounter pierced the English armour with spears, and stabbed the horses, and bore down the men. A fierce battle then took

place. I cannot tell all their strokes, nor who
caused his enemy to fall in the battle; but in a
short time, I warrant, the English were so over-
whelmed that they durst no more abide, but
scattered all of them and fled, leaving dead on
the battlefield very many of their good men. The
field was all strewn with weapons, armour, and
dead men.

That great host was fiercely overthrown, but
Sir Edward let no man pursue. With the
prisoners they had captured the Scots went
again to the wood, where their harness was left,
and that night they made merry cheer, and
praised God earnestly for His grace.

This good knight, who was so valiant, might
well be likened in that fight to Judas Maccabæus.
No number of enemies caused him to retreat so
long as he had one man against ten.

Thus was Richard of Clare repulsed with his
great host. Nevertheless he kept diligently
gathering men about him, for he thought still
to recover his overthrow. It grieved him won-
drous much that he had been twice discomfited
in battle by a small company.

And the Scots, who had ridden into the forest
to take rest, lay there two nights, and made
themselves mirth, solace, and play. Then they
rode to meet O'Dempsy, an Irish chief who had
made oath of fealty to Sir Edward; for previously

he had prayed him to visit his country, and had promised that no victual nor anything that could help should be lacking to the Scottish host.

Sir Edward trusted in his promise, and rode straight thither with his rout. O'Dempsy caused him to cross a great river, and in a right fair place, low by a lough edge,[1] he made them take their quarters, and said he would go and have victual brought to them. He departed without more delay, for his plan was to betray them. He had brought them to a place from which all the cattle had been withdrawn full two days' journey and more, so that in all that country they could get nothing sufficient to eat. His plan was to weaken them with hunger, then bring their enemies upon them.

This false traitor had caused his men to dam the outlet of a lough a little above the place where he had quartered Sir Edward and the Scots, and in the night he let it out. The water then came down on Sir Edward's men with such force that they were in peril of being drowned ere they knew they were in the midst of a flood. With great difficulty they got away, and by God's grace kept their lives, but much of their armour was lost there.

[1] Professor Skeat conclusively shows the "great river" to have been the Blackwater, and the lough edge the western shore of Lough Neagh.

Of a truth O'Dempsy made them no brave feast, nevertheless they had enough. For though they lacked meat, I warrant they had plenty to drink. They were bested there in great distress, for they had great want of victual, being set between two rivers, and able to cross none of them. The Bann, which is an arm of the sea, and cannot be crossed with horses, was betwixt them and Ulster. They had been in great peril there, were it not for a rover of the sea, Thomas of Down he was called. He heard that the host was thus straitly bested, and he sailed up the Bann till he came very near the place where they lay. They knew him well, and were glad. With four ships that he had seized he set them every one across the Bann; and when they came to inhabited land they found victual and meat enough, and quartered themselves in a wood. None of the Irish knew where the Scots lay, and Sir Edward's men took their ease, and made good cheer.

At that time Richard of Clare and the great chiefs of Ireland were quartered with a vast host on a forest side near the Scots. Each day they sent riders to bring victual of many kinds from the town of Connor, full ten Irish miles away. Each day, as these riders came and went, they passed within two miles of the Scottish host. And when Earl Thomas had knowledge of their coming and their gathering, he got him a good

company of three hundred active and bold horse-
men. There were Sir Philip the Mowbray, and
also for certain Sir John Stewart, with Sir Allan
Stewart, Sir Gilbert Boyd, and others. They rode
to meet the victuallers, who were making their
way with the provisions from Connor to their
host, and so suddenly dashed on them that they
were wholly discomfited, and let fall all their
weapons, and piteously cried for mercy. There-
upon the Scots gave them quarter, but made such
clean capture that not one of them all escaped.

The Earl learned from them that a part of
their host would come out in the evening at the
woodside, and ride towards their victual. He
thought then upon an exploit. He caused his
whole following to dress themselves in the pri-
soners' array. Their pennons also they took with
them, and waited till it was near night, and then
rode towards the English host. Some of the host
saw them coming, and fully supposed they were
their victuallers. Therefore they rode in disorder
towards them, having no suspicion that they
were their enemies, and being sore hungered
besides. For that reason they came on recklessly.
And when they were near, the Earl and all who
were with him rushed upon them at great speed
with bare weapons, shouting their battle-cries.
And the English, seeing their foes thus suddenly
drive at them, were affrighted, and had no heart

to help themselves, but made off towards their host.

The Scots made chase and slew many, so that all the field was strewn with them, more than a thousand being slain. They chased them right up to their host, and then again went their way. In this fashion the victual was seized, and many of the English were slain. Then the Earl and his company brought the prisoners and provisions to Sir Edward, who was blithe of their coming. That night the Scots made merry cheer, being all then fully at their ease, and guarded securely.

Their enemies, on the other hand, when they heard how their men had been slain, and their victual all seized, took counsel, and determined to set out towards Connor and take quarters in the city. They did this in great haste, and rode to the city by night. There they found provisions in great plenty, and made good and merry cheer, for all trusted in the town where they were.

Upon the morrow they sent to espy where the Scots had taken quarters. But the spies were all met and seized, and brought to the Scottish host. The Earl of Moray quietly asked one of their company where their host was, and what they planned to do, telling him if he found that he told him the truth he should go home ransom free.

"Of a truth," the man said, "I shall tell you.
Their plan is, to-morrow at daybreak, to seek
you with their whole host if they can get
knowledge where ye be. They have sent word
throughout the country that all the men of this
region, on right cruel pain of their lives, betake
themselves this night to the city. Of a truth
there shall be so many that ye shall in no wise
cope with them."

"Par Dieu," said the Earl, "that may be so!"

With that he went to Sir Edward and told
him the whole tale. Then they took counsel all
together, and determined to ride to the city that
same night, so as to lie with all their host
between the town and those outside. They did
as they devised; they came presently before the
town, and rested but half a mile from it.

And when daylight dawned, fifty Irish on active
ponies came to a little hill a short space from the
town, and saw Sir Edward's place of quartering.
They marvelled at the sight, how so few durst
in any wise undertake so high an enterprise as
to come thus boldly upon the whole great chivalry
of Ireland to do battle. This was the truth
without fail, for opposed to them were gathered
there with the warden, Richard of Clare, the
Butler, and the two Earls, of Desmond and
Kildare, with Bermingham, Verdon, and Fitz-
Warenne, as well as Sir Pascal, a Florentine,

and knight of Lombardy, renowned for feats of arms. The Mandevilles were also there, the Byssetts, Logans, and others besides, the Savages as well, and one called Sir Nicol of Kilkenan. And with these lords were so many men that, I trow, for one of the Scots they were five or more.

When the scouts had thus seen the Scottish host, they went in haste, and told their lords all plainly how the Scots were come near, so that there was no need to go far to seek them.

And when the Earl Thomas saw that these men had been on the hill, he took with him a good company of horsemen—there might be a hundred of them—and made his way to the hill. They made an ambush in a hollow place, and in a short time they saw a company of scouts come riding from the city. At that they were blithe, and kept themselves secret till the scouts were come near. Then with a rush all who were there dashed boldly upon them.

The scouts, seeing them thus suddenly come on, were dismayed. Some of them kept their ground stoutly to make fight, while the others fled; but in a right short time those who made halt were overcome so that they altogether turned their backs. The Scots pursued right to the gate, and slew a great number, then went again to their host.

BOOK XV

KING ROBERT IN THE ISLES

WHEN the Irish within the town saw their men thus slain and chased home again, they were all downcast, and in great haste called loudly to arms. All armed themselves and made ready for the battle, and they marched forth all in fair array, with banners displayed, ready in their best fashion to attack their enemies.

And when Sir Philip the Mowbray saw them come forth in such brave array, he went to Sir Edward the Bruce, and said, "Sir, it is good that we devise some stratagem which may avail to help us in this great battle. Our men are few, but their will is greater than their power. Therefore, I counsel that our baggage, without man or page, be arrayed by itself, and it shall seem a host far more in number than we. Set we our banners in its front, and yonder folk who come out of Connor, when they see them, shall believe that we for certain are there, and shall charge thither. Let us then come on their flank, and we

shall have the advantage, for if they be entered
among our baggage they shall be entangled, and
then we with all our strength may lay on and
do all we can."

They did as he proposed, and the host that
came out of Connor made at the banners, and,
spurring their steeds, dashed at full speed amongst
the baggage. The water carts there greatly cum-
bered the riders. Then the Earl came upon them
with his battle, and made grievous attack. Sir
Edward also, a little way off, joined battle right
boldly, and many foes fell under foot. The field
soon grew all wet with blood. Both sides fought
with great fierceness, and dealt mighty blows
and thrusts, dashing forward and drawing back,
as either side beat the other. It was dreadful to
see how they kept up that great struggle in
knightly fashion upon either side, giving and
taking wide wounds. It was past prime before
it could be seen which were to be uppermost.
But soon after prime the Scots drove on so
desperately, and charged so recklessly, each man
like a champion, that all their foes took flight.
None was able to stand by his comrade, but each
fled his different way, most making for the town.

The Earl Thomas and his host so eagerly chased
them with naked swords, that, being all mingled
among them, they came together with them into
the place. There the slaughter was so fierce that

all the streets ran with blood. Those the Scots took they put all to death, so that well nigh as many were slain in the town as in the field of battle. Fitz-Warenne was taken; but so affrighted was Richard of Clare that he made for the south country. All that month, I trow, he was to have no great stomach for fighting. Sir John Stewart, a noble knight, was wounded with a spear that pierced him sharply right through the body. He went to Montpelier, and lay there long in healing, and at last recovered.

Then Sir Edward, with his host, took quarters in the town. That night they were blithe and jolly over the victory they had got. And forthwith, on the morrow, Sir Edward set men to discover what provisions were in the city. And they found in it such abundance of corn and flour, wax and wine, that they marvelled greatly. Sir Edward caused the whole to be carted to Carrickfergus. And he went thither with his men, and set close and vigorous siege to the castle till Palm Sunday was past. Then a truce was made on either side till the Tuesday in Easter week,[1] so that they might spend that holy time in penance and prayer.

But upon Easter Eve, during the night, there arrived safely at the castle fifteen ships from Dublin loaded with armed men. Four thousand

[1] *I.e.* till April 13th, 1316.

all told, I trow, they were, and they all privily entered the castle. Old Sir Thomas the Mandeville was captain of that host.

They had espied that many of Sir Edward's men were scattered over the country, and they planned to sally forth in the morning, without waiting longer, and suddenly surprise the Scots, who, they believed, would be lying trustfully because of the truce. But I trow falseness shall ever have foul and evil result.

Sir Edward knew nothing of this, for he had no thought of treason; but he ceased not because of the truce to set watches upon the castle. Each night he caused men to watch it well, and that night Neil Fleming kept guard with sixty valiant and active men.

As soon as the day became clear those within the castle, having armed themselves and made ready, let down the draw-bridge, and sallied forth in great number. And when Neil Fleming saw them he sent a messenger to the king[1] in haste, and said to those beside him, "Now I warrant shall men see who dares to die for his lord's sake! Bear ye yourselves well, for of a surety I will fight with all this host. We shall hold them in battle till our master be armed."

With that they joined battle. They were, of a

[1] Barbour here forestalls the fact. Edward Bruce was crowned king May 2nd, 1316, three weeks later.

truth, altogether too few to fight with such a great host. Nevertheless, they drove at them boldly with all their might, and their foes marvelled greatly that they were of such manhood, and had no dread of death. But their fierce enemies attacked in such number that no valour could avail them, and they were every man slain, and none at all escaped.

Meanwhile the man who went to the king to warn him of the Irish coming out, apprised him in the greatest haste. Sir Edward, then commonly called the King of Ireland, when he heard of such pressing business on hand, in right great haste got his gear. Twelve active men were in his chamber, and they armed themselves with the greatest speed. Then boldly, with his banners, he took the middle of the town.

With that his enemies were drawing near. They had divided their whole host in three parts. The Mandeville, with a great following, held his way right through the town. The rest went on either side of the place to intercept those that should flee. They planned that all whom they found there should die without ransom.

But otherwise went the game; for Sir Edward, with his banner and the men of whom I have spoken, made such bold attack on that host as was a marvel to see. In front of him went Gib Harper, the doughtiest of deed then living in his degree, and with an axe made room before him. He felled the foremost to the ground, and afterwards, in a little space, he knew the Mandeville by his armour, and dealt him such a swinging blow that he went headlong to the earth. Sir Edward, who was near by, turned him over, and with a dagger took his life on the spot.

With that Fergus of Ardrossan, who was a right courageous knight, joined the battle with sixty men and more. Then they pressed their foes right hard, and they, seeing their lord slain, lost heart, and would have drawn back. But ever as fast as the Scots could arm they came to the melee, and they drove so at their foes that these altogether turned their backs. The Scots chased them to the gate, and a hard fight and great struggle took place there. There, with his own hand, Sir Edward slew a knight who was called the best and most valorous in all Ireland. His surname was Mandeville, his proper name I cannot tell. The assault then waxed so hard that those in the donjon durst neither open gate nor let down bridge. Sir Edward so fiercely pursued those that fled there for refuge that, for certain, of all who sallied forth against him on that day never a one escaped. They were all either taken or slain. MacNicol then joined the fight with two hundred good spearmen, who slew all they could reach. This same MacNicol, by stratagem, took

four or five of the English ships, and slew the
whole crews.

When an end was made of this fighting, Neil
Fleming was still alive, and Sir Edward went to
see him. About him, all in a heap on either hand,
lay his followers slain, and he himself was in the
throes of death. Sir Edward pitied him and
mourned him greatly, and lamented his great man-
hood and his valour and doughty deeds. So
greatly did he make lament that his men mar-
velled, for he was not wont to lament for anything,
nor would he hear men make lament. He stood
by till Fleming was dead, then had him to a holy
place, and caused him to be buried with honour
and great solemnity.

In this wise Mandeville sallied forth. But of
a surety, as was well seen by his sallying, false-
hood and guile shall ever have an evil end. The
English made their attack in time of truce, and
on Easter day, the day on which God rose to
save mankind from the stain of old Adam's sin.
For this reason this great misfortune befell them,
each and all, as I have said, being taken or slain.
Those in the castle were thrown into such affright
forthwith, seeing not where any succour could
come to them, that they presently made treaty,
and, to save their lives, yielded the stronghold
freely to Sir Edward. He kept his covenant
with them to the utmost. He took the castle

and victualled it well, and set in it a good warden to keep it, and rested there for a time.

Of him we shall relate no more at present, but go to King Robert, whom we have left long unspoken of.

When he had convoyed to the sea his brother Edward and his host, the king made ready with his ships to fare into the Isles. He took with him Walter Stewart, his kinsman, and a great host, with other men of great nobleness. They made their way to Tarbert in galleys prepared for their voyage. There they had to draw their ships. Between the seas lay a mile of land sheltered all with trees. There the king caused his ships to be drawn across, and since the wind blew strong behind them as they went, he had ropes and masts set up in the ships, and sails fastened to the tops, and caused men to go drawing alongside. The wind that was blowing helped them, so that in a little space the whole fleet was safely drawn across.[1]

And when the men of the Isles heard tell how the good king had caused ships with sails to go between the two Tarberts, they were all utterly dismayed. For they knew by ancient prophecy that whoever should thus make ships go with

---

[1] Fifty years earlier the same feat was done at Tarbert by Hakon of Norway, and two centuries earlier still, Magnus Barefoot drew his galleys across the isthmus.

sails between the seas should have the dominion
of the Isles, and that no man's strength should
stand against him. Therefore they all came to
the king. None refused him obedience except only
John of Lorne. But very soon afterwards he was
taken and brought to the Bruce; and those of his
men who had broken faith with the king were
all slain and destroyed.

The king took this John of Lorne, and presently
sent him to Dunbarton, where he was kept in
prison for a time. Afterwards he was sent to
Loch Leven, and was long there in captivity, and
there I trow he died. The king, when all the
Isles, greater and less, were brought to his pleasure,
spent the rest of that season in hunting and games
and sport.

While the Bruce in this fashion subdued the
Isles, the good Sir James of Douglas was living
in the Forest, valiantly defending the country. At
that time there dwelt in Berwick Sir Eumond de
Calion, a Gascon knight of great renown. In
his own land of Gascony he was lord of a great
domain.[1] He had the keeping of Berwick, and he
made a secret gathering, and got him a great
company of men active and bravely armed. He

---

[1] There is some uncertainty about this name. Skeat suggests
a connection with a place called Caloy, on the Adour, in Gascony.
The name resembles the Scottish Colquhoun, but the Colquhoun
family claim an earlier native origin.

ravaged all the lower end of Teviotdale, and a great part of the Merse, then hastened towards Berwick.

Sir Adam of Gordon, who was then become a Scotsman, saw the English driving away the cattle, and supposed they must be few, for he saw only the fleeing skirmishers, and them that seized the prey. He sped in hot haste to Sir James of Douglas, and told how the English had seized spoil and gone towards Berwick with the cattle. He said they were few, and that if Douglas would make speed he should full easily overcome them, and rescue all the herds. Sir James immediately agreed to follow them, and went forth with only the men he had in that place and those that met him by the way.

They followed the English at the utmost speed, and quickly came up with them. Before they could fully see them they came close up to their host. Then the foragers and the skirmishers gathered into a close squadron, and made a right fair company. The cattle they caused to be driven before them by boys and countrymen, who had no strength to stand in a field of fight. The rest kept behind in scattered order. The Douglas saw their whole intent, and their good tactics, and saw besides that their number was twice that of his own men.

" Sirs," he said, " seeing we have thus made chase,

and are now come so near that we cannot eschew the fight except we foully flee, let each man think on his love, and how many a time he has been in great peril, and come safe away. Believe that we shall do the same this day. Let us take advantage of the ford at hand, for forthwith they shall come on us to fight. And let us set will and strength and force to the matter, and encounter them right boldly."

At that word full speedily he displayed his banner, for his enemies were drawing near. And when they saw his company so few they deemed they should soon make an end of it, and attacked the Scots vigorously. Then began a dire fight and most fierce melee, with many strokes given and taken.

Douglas was right sore bested; but his great hardihood so encouraged his men that none thought on cowardice. They fought so stoutly with all their might that they slew many of their foes; and though these foes were more by far than themselves, yet fortune so guided them that Sir Eumond de Calion was slain on the spot. When he was down all the rest were soon openly discomfited. Thereupon the Scots made chase, and slew some, and turned back the whole of the prey.

Of a truth this was the hardest fight that ever the good Lord of Douglas was in, by reason of his small following. Had it not been for his great

valour, and his slaying of the English captain
in the fight, his men had been all done to death.
It was his custom ever, when he found himself
hard pressed, to strive to slay the leader of his
enemies. And many a time it happened that the
doing of this got him the victory.

When Sir Eumond in this wise was slain, the
good Lord of Douglas took his way to the Forest.
His foes feared him greatly. Word of this exploit
spread far and wide, and in England near thereby
men still speak commonly of it.

Sir Robert de Neville at that time dwelt at
Berwick, near beside the marches where the Lord
Douglas had his abode in the Forest, and he had
a mighty envy of him because he saw him ever
more and more widen his bounds. He heard the
people round him speak of the might of the Lord
Douglas, of his force in battle, and the good
fortune that oft befell him. At this he presently
became enraged, and said, "Think ye there is none
valiant but him alone? Judge ye him to be with-
out a peer? I vow here before you that if ever
he come into this land he shall find me at his
throat. If ever I see his banner displayed for
war, I shall set on him, never fear, although ye
deem him never so stout."

News of this boast was soon brought to Sir
James of Douglas, and he said, "If he will keep
his promise I shall look to it that ere very long he

shall yet have sight of me and my company near enough."

He then gathered his retinue, good men of valour, and on a night set out in brave array for the marches. In the morning early he and all his company were before Berwick. There he displayed his broad banner, and sent some of his following to burn two or three towns. He bade them speed to him soon again, so that, if need were, they should be at hand ready for the fight.

The Neville had a great host there, for all the best of that country were then with him, and in number they were many more than the Scots. Now perceiving that of a certainty Douglas was come near, and seeing his banner stand displayed, he made his way to a hill, and said, "Sirs, I could wish to make an end of the great hurt that Douglas does us day by day. But methinks it expedient that we wait till his men be scattered throughout the country to plunder. Then may we fiercely dash upon him, and we shall have him at our pleasure." All present agreed, and lay waiting on the hill, and the men of the land gathered, and drew to him with the greatest speed.

The valiant Douglas then, deeming it folly to wait longer, rode towards the hill. And when the Neville saw that the Scots would not scatter to the plundering, but made to attack him with all their might, he knew well that they meant battle. To his host he said, "Sirs, now launch we forth. Here with us we have the flower of this country, and we are, besides, more in number than they. Let us therefore join battle boldly, for, by my faith, Douglas, with yonder yeomanry, shall have no strength against us."

At that they charged, and joined battle.

Then could be heard the crashing of spears, as men drove fast at each other, and blood burst out at wide wounds. They fought with ardour on either side, each party striving hard to drive the enemy back.

In the heart of the struggle, when the fighting was at its fiercest, the Lords of Neville and Douglas met. Then between them a great combat took place. They fought fiercely with all their might, dealing great strokes one upon the other. But Douglas, I promise, was the starker man, and was besides more used to fighting; and he set heart and will to deliver himself of his enemy, till at last by sheer main strength Neville was slain.

Then Douglas shouted aloud his battle-cry, and with all his company charged so boldly on the rest, that shortly his enemies could be seen taking flight. The Scots gave chase with all their might, and in the pursuit Sir Ralph the Neville and the Baron of Hilton were taken, while other men of might, who had been of honour in their time, were slain in the field.

And when the field was wholly cleared, and their foes were every one slain or taken or chased away, Douglas ravaged the whole land, and seized all he found, and burnt all the towns, and afterwards came home whole and well. Forthwith he dealt the spoil among his followers after their deserts, keeping nothing for his own behoof.

Deeds like these cause men to love their lord, and of a surety this was done by Douglas's men. He ever treated them so wisely and with so great affection, and set such countenance on their exploits, that he made the most fearful of them stronger than a leopard. Thus with his kindliness he made his men strong and of great valour.

When Neville thus and Sir Eumond of Calion were brought to the ground, the terror and renown of the Lord Douglas spread throughout the English border, so that all who dwelt there feared him like the Devil. Often to this day have I heard tell how greatly he was feared, and how women when they wished to threaten their children would, with a right angry face, commit them to the Black Douglas. By their account he was more fierce than any devil in hell. His great bravery and valour made him so dreaded by his foes that they shuddered to hear his name. He could now dwell in ease at home for a time, for I trow he was not likely for long to be sought out by his enemies. Now we shall leave him in the Forest, and speak of him no more for a space, but take up the tale of the brave Sir Edward, who, with all his valiant chivalry, was still lying at Carrickfergus.

BOOK XVI

KING ROBERT IN IRELAND

WHEN Sir Edward by his valiant prowess had three times defeated Richard of Clare and the whole baronage of Ireland, and afterwards, with all his men of might, was come again to Carrickfergus, Thomas, the good Earl of Moray, took his leave to pass into Scotland. Sir Edward gave him leave reluctantly, and charged him especially to pray the king to come to see him in Ireland, for were they both in that country, he said, none should withstand them.

The Earl took his departure and went to his ships, and passing over sea soon arrived in Scotland. Forthwith he went to the king, who received him gladly, and inquired how his brother fared and of his doings in Ireland; and the Earl told him truly all that had taken place.

When the king had done asking, the Earl gave him his message, and the Bruce said he would gladly see his brother, and also all belonging to that country and the war there. He then gathered a great host, and appointed two lords of great valour, Walter Stewart and James of Douglas, to be wardens in his absence, and to defend the country. Then he set out for the sea, and at Lochryan in Galloway took ship with all his following, and soon came to Carrickfergus.

Sir Edward was blithe at his coming, and went swiftly down to meet him, and welcomed him with gladsome cheer. He did the same to all who were with the king, and especially his nephew Thomas, Earl of Moray. And they went to the castle, and he made them much feasting and good fare. They sojourned there for three days in great mirth and royal state.

In this wise King Robert arrived in Ireland, and when he had sojourned with his men three days in Carrickfergus, they took counsel, and determined to make their way with their whole host through all Ireland from one end to the other.

Sir Edward, the king's brother, rode in front with the vanguard. The king himself had the rearguard, and in his company had the valiant Earl Thomas. They took their way forth, and soon passed Endwillane. It was the month of May, when birds on the bough sing many a different note for the softness of that sweet season, when the branches are covered with leaves and bright blossoms, the fields are gay with sweet-smelling many-coloured flowers, and all things become blithe and glad. At that season the good king rode forth.[1]

The warden, Richard of Clare, knew that the king had arrived, and learned that he purposed to march towards the south country. He gathered to him out of all Ireland a right great armed host of squires, burghers, and yeomanry, to the number of nigh forty thousand. Yet he would not venture to fight his enemies all together in open field, but bethought him of a stratagem. He planned that he, with all that great host, should privily make ambush in a wood by the way side, where the Scots must march, and that they should let the vanguard pass to a distance, and then fall boldly with all their men upon the rearguard.

They did as he devised, and took ambush in a wood. The Scottish van rode past them close at hand, while the Irish made no showing of themselves. Sir Edward rode a long way to the front with his host, taking no heed to the rearguard. And when Sir Edward had passed by, Sir Richard of Clare sent active yeomen who could shoot well to skirmish on foot with the rearguard. Now, two of the men sent out skirmished at the woodside, and shot arrows among the Scots.

[1] According to Hailes, King Robert's Irish campaign took place in the autumn and early spring of 1316-17.

The king had with him five thousand active and bold men, and when he saw these two come so nigh, and recklessly shoot among them, he judged right well that of a certainty they had support very near. Accordingly he gave order that no man should be so reckless as ride at them, but that all should keep close together, and ride ever in battle order, ready to make defence if they should be attacked, "For we shall soon, I warrant, have to deal with more of them."

But Sir Colin Campbell,[1] who was near by the place where these two yeomen were boldly shooting, spurred on them at full speed, and soon overtook one and slew him with his spear. The other turned, and shot again, and slew Sir Colin's horse. With that the Bruce came hastily, and, in great displeasure, with a truncheon that was in his hand, gave Sir Colin a stroke that sent him crashing down on his saddle-bow. Then he bade them quickly pull him down; but other lords who were there in some measure appeased the king.

"Disobedience," said the Bruce, "might bring about our discomfiture. Think ye yonder rascals durst assail us so near our host unless they had support at hand? Right well am I assured that we shall have enough to do presently; therefore let each man look to it that he be ready."

[1] The king's nephew, son of Lady Mary Bruce and Sir Neil Campbell, Bruce's early adherent, ancestor of the house of Argyll.

With that some thirty bowmen came and skir-
mished, and hurt a number of the king's men;
till the Bruce caused his archers to drive them
back with arrows. By this time the Scots entered
an open field, and saw forty thousand men arrayed
in four battles against them.

"Now, sirs," said the king, "let us see who
shall prove valiant in this fight! On them forth-
with!"

So stoutly then did the Scots ride at them, and
so hardily did they join battle, that a great
number of their foes were brought to the ground
at the first encounter. Then was heard a dreadful
breaking of spears, and mighty noise of onset, as
each side rode against the other. Horses came
crashing head against head, so that many fell
lifeless to the ground. Many an active and valiant
man, as one ran upon the other, was stricken dead
to the earth. The red blood poured from many
a wound in such great quantity that the streams
ran with it. Both sides, filled with rage and hate,
drove at each other boldly with their bare flashing
weapons, and many a strong man was slain on
the spot. For those that were bold and active
pressed to be foremost, and fight face to face
with their foes. There, I warrant, many a cruel
conflict and stern battle was to be seen.

In all the Irish war was no such hard fighting
known. In less than three years Sir Edward won

nineteen great victories, and in sundry of these
battles he vanquished twenty thousand men and
more, with horses mailed to the feet. But at
all these times he had at least one against five.
In this struggle the king had always eight enemies
to one of his own men. But he so bore himself
that his brave feats and his valour encouraged all
his host, and the most faint-hearted was made
bold. Wherever he saw the battle thickest he
rode most boldly into it, and ever made room
about him, slaying all he could overtake, and
furiously driving them back.

The valiant Earl Thomas was at all times near
him, and fought as if he were mad. From the
prowess of these two their men took mighty hardi-
hood. They shunned no danger, but demeaned
themselves most stoutly, and so boldly drove at
the enemy that their foes were all dismayed.
Then the Scots, seeing by their looks that the
enemy somewhat avoided the fight, dashed against
them with all their strength, and pressed them so
hard with blows, that at last they gave way. And
now, seeing them take flight, they charged them
with all their force, and slew many as they fled.

The king's men so pursued them that they were
every one scattered. Richard of Clare made his
way at the utmost speed to Dublin, with other
lords that fled beside him. There they garrisoned
both the castle and the towns in their possession.

S

So desperately were they daunted that I trow
Richard of Clare had no desire to prove his
strength in battle or skirmish while King Robert
and his host tarried in that country. They kept
within garrison in this fashion.

And the king, who was so much to be prized,
saw in the field right many slain. And one of
the prisoners, who was bravely arrayed, he saw
weep wondrous tenderly. He asked him why he
made such cheer, and the prisoner answered, "Sir,
of a surety it is no marvel that I weep. I see
here stricken under foot the flower of all the
North of Ireland, boldest of heart and hand, and
most doughty in fierce attack."

"By my faith," said the king, "thou art wrong.
Thou hast more cause to make mirth, since thou
hast thus escaped death."

In this fashion Richard of Clare and all his
following were overthrown by a slender host.
And when the bold Edward Bruce knew that the
king had fought thus with so great a host and
he away, there could have been seen no more
wrathful man. But the good king told him the
fault lay in his own folly, by reason that he rode
so heedlessly and far ahead, and made no vanguard
to them of the rear. "In war," he said, "those
who ride in the van should at no time press far
from sight of the rear, else great peril may
befall."

Of this battle we shall speak no more. The king and all who were with him rode forward in better array and nearer together than they did before. They rode openly through all the land, but found none to say them nay. They rode even before Drogheda and before Dublin, but found none to give battle. Then they went further inland, and held their way south to Limerick, which is the southmost town in Ireland. There they lay for two or three days, and got ready again for the march.

And when they were all ready the king heard a woman's cry, and forthwith asked what that was.

"Sir," said some one, "it is a laundress who just now has been seized with labour, and whom we must leave here behind us. For this reason she makes yonder evil cheer."

"Certes," said the king, "it were shame that she should be left in that strait! Of a surety he is no man I trow who will not pity a woman then."

At that he halted his whole host, and caused a tent to be pitched, and made her go into it, and bade other women stay beside her till her child was born, and gave order before he left how she should be carried with the host. Then he rode forward on his way. It was a right sovereign courtesy for so great and so mighty a king to cause his men to tarry in this fashion for a poor humble laundress.

They marched northward again, and passed athwart all Ireland, through Munster and Connaught right to Dublin, and through all Meath and Uriel,[1] as well as Leinster, and afterwards through the whole of Ulster to Carrickfergus. They fought no battle in all that march, for there was none that durst attack them. And all the Irish chiefs, except one or two, came to Sir Edward and did homage to him. Then they each went home again to their own districts, undertaking to do in everything the bidding of Sir Edward, whom they called their king.

He was now well on the way to conquer the whole land, for he had the Irish and Ulster on his side, and he was so far advanced in his war that he had passed with force of arms through all Ireland from end to end. Could he have governed himself with reason, and not followed his impulses too fast, but have been moderate in his actions, it seems almost certain that he should have conquered the whole country of Ireland. But his extravagant pride and his wilfulness, which was more than boldness, prevented his intent, as I shall hereafter describe.

Here now we leave the noble king at his ease and pleasure, and speak of the Lord Douglas,

[1] Now the counties of Louth and Monaghan.

who was left to keep the marches. He had crafty wrights brought, and caused them to make a fair manor in the meadow of Lintalee,[1] and when the houses were built he brought thither ample provision, for he meant to have a house-warming, and make good cheer to his men.

There was then dwelling at Richmond an Earl called Sir Thomas.[2] Moved with envy at Douglas, he said that if his banner could be seen displayed in the field he should soon attack it. He heard how Douglas intended to make a feast at Lintalee, and he had full knowledge also that the king, with Thomas, Earl of Moray, and a great host, were out of the country. For this reason he thought Scotland scant of men to withstand a strong attack, and he himself had at that time the government and command of the Border. He gathered a force till he had nigh ten thousand men, and he took wood-axes with him, for his plan was to make his men hew down the whole of Jedwood forest, so that no tree should be seen there.

They set out on their march; but the good Lord of Douglas had spies constantly out on every side,

[1] The spot, which has been already referred to, is still pointed out in the old Jed Forest, a few miles to the south of Jedburgh.

[2] The expedition here described was in reality led by the Earl of Arundel; Sir Thomas of Richmond, who was slain by Douglas, was not its leader, nor was he an earl. He was a knight of Yorkshire.

and was well aware that they meant to ride and
come suddenly upon him. In the utmost haste
he gathered those that he could of his following.
I trow he had then with him fifty who were
valiant and active, well armed and equipped in
all points. He had also with him a great host of
archers.

There was a place on the way where he knew
well the English must pass. It had forest upon
either side; the entrance was right large and
wide, and like a shield it narrowed ever till at
one place the way was not a quoit-throw broad.
The Lord of Douglas went thither when he knew
the enemy were coming near, and in a hollow
on one side he placed all his archers in ambush.
He bade them keep themselves secret till they
heard him raise his battle-cry; then they were to
shoot boldly among their foes, and keep them
there till he passed through; afterwards they were
to march forth with him. On either side of the
pass were birch trees growing young and thick.
Those he twisted together in such fashion that men
could not easily ride through them. When this
was done he waited upon the other side of the
passing place.

Richmond came riding in the first battle in brave
array. The Lord Douglas saw everything, and
caused his men to keep still till the enemy came
close at hand and entered the narrow way. Then

with a shout, crying aloud, "Douglas! Douglas!"
the Scots dashed upon them.

When Richmond, who was right valiant, heard
the cry thus rise, and plainly saw the banner of
Douglas, he made with speed to the spot. But
the Scots came on so boldly that they made
themselves good passage through the midst of their
foes, bearing down to the ground all they met.
Richmond was borne down there. Douglas paused
above him, and turned him over, and with a dagger
took his life on the spot. On his helmet Richmond
wore a hat. This Douglas took with him for a
token, for it was of fur. Then he made haste
out of the way and returned again to the Forest.

In that attack the archers bore their part well,
for they shot well and boldly, and the English host
was set in great panic. Then, before they knew,
Douglas suddenly, with all his company, was
among them, and pierced them wellnigh through
and through, and had almost finished his exploit
before they could take heed to help themselves.

And when they saw their lord was slain they
took him up and retreated, to withdraw them-
selves from the shot. They gathered together in
an open place, and because their lord was dead
they made ready to take quarters in that spot
for the night.

The doughty Douglas got knowledge that a clerk
Ellis, with nigh three hundred of the enemy, had

gone straight to Lintalee and taken quarters there. He hastened thither with all his company, and found clerk Ellis at meat, and all his rout set down about him. The Scots came boldly upon him, and with sharp swords right quickly did his carving. The English were so wholly cut to pieces there that wellnigh none escaped. The Scots carved for them to such purpose, with shearing swords and daggers, that wellnigh all lost their lives. It was a dire side-dish they got, a bellyful more than enough.

Those who by chance escaped made their way to their host, and told how their men were slain and how hardly one had escaped. And when the English heard how Douglas had done, slaying their harbingers and driving themselves back, and slaying their lord in the midst of his host, there was none of them all so bold as desire further to attack the Douglas. Accordingly they held a council, and determined to march homeward. They took their departure, and made such haste that they soon reached England. The Forest they left standing; they had no desire to hew it down at that time, especially while the Douglas was so near a neighbour to them.

When Douglas saw them retreat he perceived their lord was indeed slain. He knew this also by the hat he had taken, for one of the prisoners said to him that for a truth Richmond commonly was wont to wear that fur hat. Douglas at this was blither than before, for he was assured that Richmond, his cruel foe, was brought to destruction.

In this wise Sir James of Douglas, with valour and great daring, gallantly defended the land. This action, I warrant, was boldly undertaken and right stoutly achieved, for with no more than fifty armed men he overthrew a host full ten thousand strong.

There were two other exploits well achieved with fifty men, and sovereignly esteemed above all other deeds of war done in their time.

This was the first of three that was boldly accomplished with fifty men. The second befell in Galloway, when, as ye formerly heard me tell, Sir Edward the Bruce with fifty followers overthrew Sir Aymer of St. John and fifteen hundred men all told. The third happened in Eskdale, when Sir John de Soulis was governor of that region. With fifty men he beset the march of Sir Andrew Hardclay, who had in his company three hundred excellently mounted men. Sir John by his hardihood and sovereign valour vanquished them sturdily, every one, in plain battle, and captured Sir Andrew. The whole manner of the exploit I will not rehearse, for whoso likes may hear young women sing it among them every day as they amuse themselves.

These were three valiant exploits which I
trow shall evermore be esteemed in the memory
of men. It is without question most just that
the names of those who were so valiant in their
time, and of whose courage and worth men still
take pleasure to hear, should endure in praise
for evermore. May He who is the King of heaven
take them up to heaven's bliss, where prayer is
everlasting.

At the time when Richmond was in this fashion
brought to the ground the men of the English
coast near the Humber gathered a great force,
and taking ship, sailed for Scotland, and came
suddenly into the Firth. They thought to have
everything at their pleasure, knowing full well
that the king and many of great valour were
then far out of the country. Therefore they came
into the Firth, and held their way in a straight
course to its western shore, beside Inverkeithing,
near Dunfermline. There they landed and began
busily to ravage.

The Earl of Fife and the Sheriff saw ships
approaching their coast, and gathered a force to
defend their country. And ever, as the ships
sailed up the coast, they marched over against
them, intending to prevent the landing of the
enemy. When the shipmen saw them show such
array they said among themselves that the Scots
should not hinder their landing. Then they

hastened to the land, and reached it very speedily, and right boldly came ashore.

The Scots saw them coming, and were dismayed, and all in a body rode away and let them land without hindrance. Though near five hundred in number they durst not fight, but all together withdrew. But while they were thus riding away without beginning a defence, the good Bishop of Dunkeld, William Sinclair by name, came in brave fashion with a host of some sixty horsemen. He himself was fully armed, and rode upon a stalwart steed, wearing a loose gown above his armour, to cover his array; and his men were as well armed as he. He met the Earl and the Sheriff retreating with their great host, and forthwith asked them what pressing business made them turn so suddenly. They said their foes had landed by main force and in such number that they deemed them too many, and themselves too few to deal with them.

When the Bishop heard this he said, "The king ought to make much of you, who so finely take on hand to defend the country in his absence! Certes, if he served you rightly he should forthwith have the gilt spurs hewed from your heels. Thus should cowards be rightly served. Let him who loves his king and his country turn smartly now again with me!"

With that he cast off his bishop's robe, and took

in his hand a strong spear, and rode with speed towards the enemy. All the Scots turned with him, for he had so reproved them that none of them all went from him. He rode before them sturdily, and they followed him in close array till they came near the foes who had landed.

Some of the English were massed together in good order, and some had set out to the foray.

When the good Bishop saw them he said, "Sirs, without doubt or fear prick we boldly upon them, and we shall have them full easily. If they see us come without dismay and without stopping they shall right soon be discomfited. Now fight well, and men shall see who loves the honour of the king to-day."

Then all together in good order they spurred sturdily upon the enemy. The Bishop, who was right bold and big and stark, rode ever in front. They joined battle with a crash, and at the first meeting the English felt so sorely the pricking of their spears that they gave way and made off. They made in haste towards their ships, and the Scots pursued fiercely, and slew so many that all the fields were strewn with English slain, while those that survived hastened to the sea. In the chase the Scots slew all they could overtake; and some that fled, in their haste to reach their ships, went too many on board some of the barges because of the Scots pursuing them, and, the boats capsizing, the men in them were all drowned.

There it was, I have heard tell, that an Englishman did a right great feat of strength. When he was chased to the boat he seized by the two arms a Scotsman who had laid hands upon him, and, whether he would or not, threw him across his back, and, despite all his struggles, carried him to the boat and cast him in. This methinks was a right great feat.

The English who escaped hastened to their ships, and sailed home vexed and sorrowful that they had been thus overwhelmed.

When the shipmen were in this wise discomfited nearly five hundred English lay dead, besides those that were drowned, and the Bishop who had borne himself so well and encouraged all who were there remained on the scene of the fight. And not till the field was plundered bare did the Scots all go home. High honour befell the Bishop who by his enterprise and valour achieved this great feat of arms. On account of it the king ever from that day loved, honoured, and prized him, holding him in such esteem that he called him "his own Bishop."

Thus they defended the country upon both sides of the Scottish Sea while the king was away.

Meanwhile the Bruce had made his way through all Ireland, and come again to Carrickfergus.

And when Sir Edward, in royal fashion, had all
the Irish at his bidding, and all Ulster as well, the
king made ready to return home. A great number
of his men, the boldest and most approved in
feats of war, he left with his brother. Then
he passed to the beach, and when their leaves
were taken on either side, he went on board,
carrying the Earl Thomas with him, and, setting
sail forthwith, arrived without mishap in Galloway.

BOOK XVII

THE SIEGE OF BERWICK

THE Scottish lords were glad when they knew the king was come again. They made great haste to meet him, and he received them right blithely, and made a feast and gladsome cheer. They were more wondrously rejoiced at his coming than tongue can tell, and they entertained him with great feasting and honour. Wherever he rode the whole country gathered in delight to see him, and great gladness was in the land. The whole country from the Reidswyre[1] to the Orkney was now won to his hand. No part of Scotland was outside his rule except Berwick alone.

The captain of the town at that time was one who held all Scots in suspicion, and treated them most evilly. He had them ever in ill-will, and made diligence ever to keep them down. But at

[1] The Reidswyre was the high pass at the source of the Reid where the road between Jedburgh and Newcastle crossed the border. More than one border skirmish took place there. One of these skirmishes, fought July 7th, 1576, is still remembered in a wellknown ballad, "The Raid of the Reidswair."

last one day a burgher, Sym of Spalding, bethought him it was a right vexatious matter to be constantly rebuffed in such fashion. Accordingly he determined in his heart secretly to make a covenant with the marshal, whose cousin he had married, and he did forthwith what he planned. He sent letters to the marshal with speed and secrecy by a trusty man, and set him a time to come at night privily to the Cowport with ladders and stout active men. He bade him keep faith truly, and promised to meet him at the wall, where his watch should fall that night.

When the marshal saw the letter he took thought for a short space, for he knew that by himself he had not might or power enough to achieve so great an enterprise, and if he asked any to help him the other Scottish leaders would be made jealous. Therefore he went straight to the king, and showed him, between themselves, the letter and the business.

When the king heard the plot thus word by word described, it appeared to him to be without deceit, and he said to the marshal, "Certes, thou hast done wisely to disclose the matter first to me, for if thou hadst discovered it to my nephew, the Earl Thomas, thou hadst displeased the Lord Douglas, and the same the other way about. But I shall work in such fashion that thou shalt gain thy purpose, and have despite of none of them.

Thou shalt keep truly to thy day, and with the
men whom thou canst procure thou shalt make
an ambush in Duns Park. Only, be secret. And
I shall cause the Earl Thomas, and also the
Lord of Douglas, each with a small body of men,
to be there and do as thou shalt direct."

The marshal then at once took leave and went
his way, and kept what was said private and
secret till the appointed time. Then he took
with him to his tryst the best men of Lothian,
for he was sheriff of that district. All privily
with his following he came in the evening to
Duns Park. Soon afterwards the Earl Thomas
came with a good company, having met with the
Lord Douglas. They were a right fair host when
they were met together there.

Then the marshal told the covenant line by
line to the two lords, and they went their way
forward. They left their horses far from the
town, and, to make the tale short, they so wrought
that, without any man seeing them, except only
Sym of Spalding, who caused the enterprise to
be undertaken, they set their ladders to the wall,
and all came up. They kept in a secret nook
till the night should be past, and arranged that
most of their men should go in a body with their
lords, and keep a fixed stance, while the rest
should all scatter through the town, and take
and slay the men they could come at.

T

But they soon broke their arrangement, for whenever day dawned two thirds and more of the men scattered through the town. So greedy were they for the spoil that they ran as if they were mad, and seized houses and slew men. The English, seeing their foes thus so suddenly come upon them, raised the cry throughout the town, and rushed together here and there, and ever as they came together would stand and make fight. Had they been warned I am well assured they should have sold their lives dear; for they were brave men, and were far more in number than those who attacked them. But they were so scattered that they could in no wise be got together.

There were two or three great melees, but the Scots bore themselves so well that their foes were ever driven back, and at last were so overwhelmed that they altogether fled. Some reached the castle, but not all, and some slid over the wall, and some were taken prisoner, and some were slain in the strife.

In this way matters went till it was near noonday. Then those that were in the castle, and the others who had fled to them there, being a right great company, saw the Scottish banner standing little defended, and protected by few, and they opened their gates suddenly, and made a bold sally on the Scots.

Then the valiant Earl Thomas and the good

Lord of Douglas, with the few followers who were with them, met them stoutly with their various weapons. There, had one been at hand, he might have seen men demean themselves boldly and sturdily. The English fought fiercely, and laboured with all their might to drive the Scots back again, and I trow of a truth they would have done this, for the Scots were fewer far than they, if it had not been for a new-made knight, Sir William of Keith and of Galston (for he had different surnames). Sir William bore himself right well that day, and made most bold assault, and dealt mighty strokes about him. Where he saw the throng thickest he charged with all his strength, and fought with such force that he made way for his following. Those that were near him drove so boldly at their foes that at last the English altogether turned their backs and made for the castle.

They entered it at great cost, for they were pressed so hard there that they lost many of the rearmost. Nevertheless those that entered sparred their gates hastily, and ran quickly to the walls, for they were not then all secure.

In this wise, by dint of great valour and high enterprise, was the town taken.[1] All the spoil there was quickly seized by the Scots. They found

[1] The town of Berwick was taken on March 28, 1318, the castle five days later.

victual in great abundance, and all pertaining
to the provisioning of a town. This they saved
from destruction. Then they sent word to the
king, and he was blithe, and sped thither right
swiftly. And as he rode through the country
men gathered to him till he had a great and
valiant following. The people of the Merse and
Teviotdale, and the men of the Forest and the
eastern part of Lothian, went to Berwick in
strong force before the coming of the king, so
that none dwelling beyond the Tweed durst well
appear at that time.

When the men in the castle saw their enemies
gather before them in such number, and saw no
hope of rescue, they were greatly dismayed.
Nevertheless they held the castle stubbornly for
five days. Then on the sixth day they yielded
it, and went to their own country.

Thus were castle and town brought into pos-
session of the Scots. And soon afterwards the
king came riding to Berwick with his host, and
quartered fair and well, and all his great lords
beside him, in the castle. The rest all in common
quartered in the town.

The king then took counsel and decided not to
break down the wall, but to provide castle and
town well with men and with victual and all
kinds of gear useful or necessary for their keeping
in time of war.

Walter, Steward of Scotland, who was then
young and handsome and the king's son-in-law,
had such great desire and yearning to be near
the border that he took Berwick into his keeping,
and received from the king, town, castle, and
donjon. Bruce sent men of great renown into
England to drive a prey, and they brought out
a great abundance of cattle. And he treated with
certain countrymen for victual, and brought it
quickly in great abundance to the place, so that
both town and castle were well provisioned for
a year or more. The good Steward of Scotland
then sent for his friends and followers till he
had with him, besides archers, burghers, and
cross-bowmen, five hundred active and valiant
followers who bore ancestral arms. He had also
John Crab, a Fleming of great skill in the making
of gear for the defence and attack of castle or
town. None more skilful was to be found. He
caused engines and cranes to be made, and pro-
cured Greek fire, with springalds and shot of
different kinds pertaining to the defence of a
castle. He made provision in right great quantity,
but he had no cannon, for up to that time these
had not been seen in use in Scotland.

And when the town was garrisoned in this
fashion the noble king set forth and rode towards
Lothian, leaving the stout Walter Steward and
his host in Berwick, with diligent order to prepare

gear for the defence of the place if it should
be attacked.

When the king of England was told how
Berwick had been taken by force, and furnished
with men and victual and munition of war, he
was vastly vexed. He called his council hastily,
and determined to lead his host thither, and,
with all the force he could gather, lay siege to
the town, and entrench his army strongly, so that
so long as they chose to lie there they should
be altogether secure. And if the Scots should
attack them, the English, doing battle at their
trenches, should have great advantage. He felt
the more assured, for it would be a great folly
to make open attack on so strong a force in its
entrenchments.

When his plan was thus shaped, he caused his
whole host to be gathered from far and near.
He had then a great multitude with him. The
Earl Thomas of Lancaster, who, they say, was
afterwards made a saint, was there, and all the
other earls and mighty barons of England able
to fight. All these he took with him to the siege,
and he caused his ships to bring by sea shot and
other gear, with great store of victual.

He came to Berwick with all this host victu-
alled and arrayed, and to each of his great lords
separately he appointed a field for their quarters.
There presently were to be seen pavilions of

sundry kinds set up in such number that they
formed a town greater than Berwick and its
castle. Then, on the other side, by sea, came so
many ships, with victual, armour, and men, that
all the harbour was filled.

And when those in the town saw their enemies
come in such strength and number by land and sea,
they, like able and right valiant men, made ready
to defend the place. They were prepared either
to die or drive back their foes; for their captain
treated them very graciously, and most of those
who bore arms with him were of his blood and
his near kin, or else were his allies. They were
of high courage and right noble bearing, being
none of them dismayed. By day they kept in
full array, and by night they set good watch.

For full six days they remained thus without
any great struggle. During that time the English
had so enclosed their host with trenches that
they were strongly fortified. Then with all hands
they busily got ready their gear to attack the
town. And on the Eve of the Nativity of the
Virgin, early in the morning, the English host
armed, and boldly displayed its banners, and
gathered to its standards, with engines of many
kinds, such as scaffolds, ladders, and coverings,
pikes, hoes, and staff-slings. To each lord and
his battle was appointed a place where he should
attack.

And when those within the town saw the English host thus range themselves in order, they hastened to their posts. These were right strongly provided with stones, shot, and everything needed for defence. There the Scots waited the attack of the enemy.

When the English were all ready the trumpets sharply sounded the advance, and each man with his gear, in his appointed place, went to the assault. To each battlement archers were assigned to shoot. All things being thus ready, they hastened towards the town, and quickly filled the ditches, and boldly advanced with their ladders to the walls.

But those above upon the wall made stout defence, and the ladders and men upon them they threw flat on the ground. Then in a little space were to be seen men boldly making assault, some doughtily setting up their ladders, and some on ladders pressing up, while those on the wall risked every danger till their enemies were thrown down. At great disadvantage they defended their town, for, if the truth must be said, the walls were then so low that a man on the ground could, with a spear, strike another on the wall in the face. The arrows also flew so thick that it was a wonder to see them.

Walter Stewart rode ever about with a company to see where help was most needed, and where

the enemy pressed most he gave succour to his
men. The great multitude outside had so sur-
rounded the town that no part of it was free
from them. Everywhere the assailants could be
seen giving themselves boldly to the attack, and
the defenders striving doughtily with all their
might to thrust them back again.

Thus they bore themselves till noon was past.
Then they in the ships with great endeavour
prepared a vessel to come with all her gear right
to the wall to make an attack. They drew their
boat, full of armed men, up to the middle of the
mast, and they had a bridge to let fall from the
boat to the battlement. They rowed the ship
with barges alongside, and pressed hard, and set
all their intent to tow her past the bridge-house
to the wall. They brought her till she came very
near. Then men could be seen greatly busied,
some attacking and some making defence in many
ways and with great labour.

Those in the town bore themselves well, and
the shipmen were so handled that they could by
no means bring their vessel near enough the
wall to let their fall-bridge reach it. But they
remained fighting so long that the ebb left the
ship aground. Then in a little space those on
board were in more evil plight by far than before.
When the tide ebbed, so that men could go to
the ship dry foot, there sallied forth to her from

the town a right great company, and presently they
set her on fire. Within a short time they burnt
her up, some of those within her being slain and
some having fled and escaped. The Scots captured
there an engineer known far and near as the
most cunning of his craft; then they returned
into the town.

It was a happy chance indeed that they got
in so quickly; for when the English saw the ship
on fire, there came a great company of them at
the utmost speed up by the sea. But before they
came the Scots had passed in and barred the
gate, and made it fast.

The English host made diligent attack that
day, and those within defended themselves ever
in such fashion that their assailants with all
their force could in no way effect their purpose.
And when the time of evensong was near, the
host outside, being weary, and some of them right
cruelly wounded, looked at the defenders, and
saw it was not to be easy to take the town while
such defence was made by its captains. They
beheld their ship burnt and many of those in
it lost, and their people wounded and weary, and
they caused the retreat to be blown.

After the shipmen were repulsed the other
vessels made no more attack; for by means of
this ship they had everyone thought that the
town should easily be taken. Some say that

more than one ship tried at that time to reach the town; but since no more than one was burnt, and it was in it the engineer was captured, I have here made mention of one ship alone.

When they had blown the retreat, the English, having endured great hardships, withdrew altogether from the wall, and abandoned the whole attack. And those within, being weary, and many of them sore wounded, were blithe and glad when they saw their enemies thus withdraw. And when they knew for certain that the English had gone to their tents they set good watches on the wall, and went all to their quarters, and took their ease for their weariness. Others who were sore wounded had the service of good leeches, who helped them as they best could. On both sides they were weary. That night they did no more; and for five days thereafter they lay still, neither doing the other much hurt.

Now leave we these folk lying here at rest, and turn the course of our tale to the doughty King Robert.

When he knew for certain that the King of England had with a strong force laid siege to Berwick, where Walter Stewart lay with his men, he gathered a host from far and near and formed a plan. He determined not to attack the King of England in battle, especially at his trenches, for such an attack might easily prove folly. But he ordered two lords, the Earl of Moray and the Lord Douglas, to pass with fifteen thousand men into England, and burn and slay and make great harrying there. So that when those besieging the town heard of the destruction being made in England, they should be so fearful and so anxious for the lives of their wives and children, and for the loss of their goods, that they should hasten to leave the siege, and march quickly to rescue their gear, their friends, and their land.

To this intent Bruce sent forth these lords, and they set out hastily, and, passing into England, burned and slew, and laid waste the country. They wrought hurt pitiful for those that wished it any good to see, for they destroyed everything as they went. They passed to and fro destroying thus till they reached Ripon, and they wholly destroyed that town, and took their quarters at Boroughbridge and Mitton close by.

And when the men of that district saw their land so destroyed they came together with the greatest speed, archers, burghers, and yeomanry, priests, clerks, monks, and friars, farmers, and men of all crafts, till there were gathered together full twenty thousand of them. Right good armour and enough they had. The Archbishop of York they made their captain; and they took counsel and determined, since the Scots were far fewer than themselves, to attack them in open battle.

The Archbishop displayed his banner; other Bishops who were there did the same; and they set forth all in a body by the nearest way towards Mitton.

And when the Scots heard that the enemy were coming near, they made ready after their best fashion, and divided themselves into two battles. Douglas took the vanguard and the Earl Thomas the rear, for he was chieftain of the host; and thus ordered, in good array, they set out towards their foes.

When each caught sight of the other they pressed forward on both sides to fight. The English came on in good order, with brave and hardy bearing, in one straight front, with a banner, till they were so near that each side could easily see the other's faces. Three spear lengths I trow might be the space between them, when such panic seized the English host that, without more ado, they turned, showed their backs, and fled.

When the Scots saw them thus all flee in dismay, they dashed upon them with great speed, and slew and took a vast number. The rest fled in the utmost fear to seek refuge as they best could. They were chased so closely that a full thousand perished. Of these, three hundred were priests: for this reason the skirmish was called the Chapter of Mitton.[1] When this host was

[1] The Chapter of Mitton was fought Sept. 20, 1319.

overthrown, and pursuit ended, the Scots marched throughout the land, slaying, destroying, and burning.

Meanwhile, the English who lay at the siege of Berwick, before the fifth day was past, had made sundry engines to go again to the attack. Among great devices they made a sow that had a strong covering without and many armed men within. They also made tools for mining, and they had sundry scaffolds higher than the wall, and arranged also that the town should be strongly attacked by sea.

And those within, seeing them prepare such mighty engines, by the cunning counsel of Crab set up a high crane running on wheels, which they could bring where most need was. They also took pitch and tar, with lint and hards and brimstone, and dry sticks that would burn easily, and mixed them together, and made of them great faggots girded with broad bands of iron. Of these faggots they might have a great tun full. They planned to use them in a blazing bundle by means of their crane, and if the sow came to the wall, to let them fall burning upon her, and with a strong chain keep her there till all were burnt who were within. They also prepared engines for throwing stones, and made ready diligently, and appointed each man to his place of guard. Sir Walter, the brave Steward, was to ride

about with armed men, and watch where there was
most to be feared, and give succour there with
his company.

And when both sides had thus fully made
ready for the attack, on the Rood Eve at dawn
the English host blew the assault. Then, with its
many engines, that great host came stoutly on.
They quickly surrounded the town, and attacked
with good will, and set all their strength to it,
and pressed the garrison hard.

But the Scots, exposing themselves to wounds
and death, defended themselves right well. They
cast the ladders to the ground, and drove at their
foes with catapult stones so diligently that they
laid many low, some swooning, some hurt, and
some slain. The English foot soldiers, however,
drew the wounded nimbly away, and retreated
no whit on that account, but kept stoutly at
the assault. At the same time the defenders
above assailed them so hard and constantly,
and wounded so many, and made such great
defence, that they kept back the onset of their
foes.

In such fashion they fought till near noon.
Then the besiegers in great array pushed their
sow towards the wall. At that, those within
brought up the engineer who had been captured,
and laid great threats upon him, and swore he
should die unless he used his craft upon the sow,

and broke her to pieces. And he, seeing clearly that his end was near unless he could accomplish their desire, determined to do all he could. In great haste the catapult was got ready, and aimed at the sow. He drew the trigger, and smartly hurled out the stone. It went straight over the sow, and fell a little way behind her.

Then those within her shouted aloud, "Forward to the wall! without doubt all is ours!"

Then the engineer nimbly bent the catapult again, and the stone was smartly hurled out. It flew forth with a whizz and a roar, and fell right in front of the sow. The hearts of the assailants then began to quake, but still, with all their strength, they pushed the sow towards the wall, and brought her close up to it.

The engineer then quickly bent his catapult once more, and hurled forth the stone. It went straight towards the sky, and with great weight in a furious rush drove down right by the wall, and hit the sow in such fashion that it broke in sunder with its dint the main beam, which was the strongest to resist a stroke. The men within the sow ran out with the greatest speed, and the men on the walls called out that "The sow had farrowed there!"

John Crab then, having his gear all ready, set fire to his faggots, and hurled them over the wall, and burnt the sow to bare firebrands.

While all this was going on, the English host
was making fierce and diligent attack, and the
Scots, in great risk of death, were manfully and
with great strength defending the place. The
shipmen brought their ships with great engines
to the assault. Their top-castles were furnished
well with active men in armour of steel, and
their boats were drawn up and made fast high
upon their masts. Thus mightily prepared they
pressed towards the wall. But the engineer staved
in a long-boat with a stone, and the men in her
fell down, turning over and over, some of them
stunned, and some dead. Thenceforth none of
the ships durst undertake to attack the wall.

But the rest kept up the attack on every side
so eagerly that of a truth it was great marvel
that the Scots held them back. The garrison
were at great disadvantage, as I have already
told, because their walls were then so low that
a man could very easily with a spear strike up
in the defender's face. Many of them were sore
wounded, and the rest were labouring so hard
that none of them had time to take rest. Their
adversaries assailed so stoutly, and they within
were so straitly beset, that their warden, who
with a hundred armed men, active and bold, rode
about to see where his people were hardest pressed,
and to relieve those that had need, came at sundry
times upon places where the defenders were all

dead, or all sore wounded. There he had to leave part of his company, so that by the time he had made one circuit, of all his men there was only one remaining. He had left them all to relieve where he saw need.

The English attacking at the Marygate hewed down the barrier, and made a fire at the drawbridge, and burnt it down, and thronged in great numbers right to the gate to set it on fire. Those within sent a messenger quickly to the warden, to tell him how hard they were beset. And when Sir Walter Stewart heard how their enemies strove so straitly with them, he caused all the armed men in the castle to come out, seeing that no assault was made there that day. With that company he hastened to the Marygate, and ascended the wall, and saw the whole danger. Forthwith he was convinced that unless help were given at once the English would burn the gate with the fire they had put to it. Therefore he determined upon a sudden and bold manœuvre. He caused the gate to be thrown wide, and with a force of men scattered the fire he found thereat.

He set himself a right difficult feat, for the assailants attacked him with their naked weapons. He made defence with all his might, and it was a fierce sight to behold the stabbing, thrusting, and striking. But the Scots made sturdy defence, and with a great force of men kept the gate, and stood at it despite their foes till night caused both sides to give up the struggle.

When night fell the English host all withdrew from the attack, wounded, weary, and hard stricken. With evil cheer they left the assault, and went to their quarters, and set their watches. They took their ease as they best could, for they had great need of rest.

That night they spoke all in common of those within the town, and marvelled that they had made such stout defence against the great assault. Those within, on the other hand, when they saw their foes withdraw so completely, were all blithe, and quickly appointed watches, and went to their quarters. Few of them were slain, but many were cruelly wounded, and the rest beyond measure weary.

It was in truth a hard assault, and of a certainty I never heard tell of a few men so hard assailed making better defence. Of one thing that befell there I marvel; that is, that during all that day, when the enemy made their greatest attack, and the shot fell thickest, women and little children gathered up arrows in armfuls, and carried them to the men on the walls, and not one of them was slain or even wounded. It was a miracle of God Almighty; to nothing else can I attribute it.

All remained quiet that night on either side, but on the morrow there came tidings out of

England to the English host telling how their men were slain and overthrown at Boroughbridge and Mitton, and how the Scots still rode throughout the land, burning and destroying.

And when King Edward heard this news he gathered his whole council to decide whether it were better to remain about the town and assail it till it were taken, or to march into England and rescue his land and men.

His council warmly disagreed, for the men of the south wished him to remain till he had won the town and castle, but the men of the north would have none of this. They feared to lose their friends and goods through the ravage of the Scots, and they would that he left the siege and rode to rescue the land.

The Earl Thomas of Lancaster was one of those who counselled the king to go home, and because Edward inclined more to the desire of the men of the south than to that of the north countrymen, he took it so ill that he had his gear packed up in haste, and with his whole battle, which was near a third part of the host, took his way home to England. He made off home without leave, and thereafter befell a difference between him and the king which lasted till Andrew Hardclay was set upon the Earl by Edward. Hardclay took him at Pontefract, and on the hill beside the town struck off his head without redemption.

He was also hanged and drawn, and along with him a right fair following. It was said afterwards that this Thomas, who in this wise was made a martyr, became a saint, and did miracles, and that envy caused these to be hidden. But whether he was a holy man or no, he was slain in this fashion at Pontefract.

When the king of England saw him dare to depart so openly, he deemed it perilous to lie there with the rest of his host, and he had his harness packed up, and fared home to England.

The Scots destroying in England soon heard tidings of the breaking up of this great siege, and they set out westward and passed home by Carlisle with prisoners and plunder of many kinds. The lords went to the king, and the rest went their ways, each man to his own dwelling.

The king, of a surety, was wondrous glad that they were come home whole and sound, and had discomfited their foes. Without loss of men they had succoured the garrison besieged in Berwick when it was in the greatest danger, and when the English attack had made its way right to the wall. And when the king had asked tidings as to how they had fared in England, and the progress and success of their march, and when they had told him all their adventure, and how the English had been discomfited, he was right blithe in his heart, and entertained them with games and sport.

In this way were Berwick and those within it rescued. He was worthy to be a prince who by his valour and craft could conceive so excellent a strategy, and without loss bring it to a good ending.

To Berwick then he took his way, and when he heard there how boldly the place had been defended he greatly praised the garrison. Above the rest, he commended Walter Stewart's great valour for the right great defence he made at the gate, when the bridge had been burnt. And of a surety praise was rightly due to one who so stoutly, in plain fight, made defence at an open gate. Could he have lived till he was of perfect age, without question his renown must have spread far. But death, who watches ever with all her might to despoil the weak and the strong, had great envy of his worth, and in the flower of his youth she made an end of all his doughty deeds, as I shall tell in another place.

When the king had dwelt there some time he sent far and near for masons, the most cunning of their craft, and caused them to raise the wall ten feet round all his town of Berwick. Soon afterwards he took his way with all his host towards Lothian, and presently he gave order for both men-at-arms and yeomanry to pass into Ireland and bring his brother help.

BOOK XVIII

THE BATTLE OF BYLAND

SIR EDWARD BRUCE, ever irking at rest, and eager to be at work, a day before the succours arrived that had been sent him by the king, and despite the counsel of all who were with him, set forth upon the march. Besides the Irish chiefs, who rode with him in great bands, he had not in all in the country at that time, I trow, two thousand men.

He set out towards Dundalk. And when Richard of Clare heard that he marched with a small following, he gathered together out of the whole of Ireland all the armed men he could. Thus he had with him at that time twenty thousand equipped horsemen, besides a host of men on foot, and he set out towards the north.

When Sir Edward heard that he was come near, he sent out as scouts the Soulis and the Stewart and Sir Philip the Mowbray, and when these three had seen the enemy's advance, they returned and told the king that their foes were in right great number. Sir Edward made answer quickly, and said he should fight that day though the enemy were three times or four times as many.

"Of a surety," said Sir John Stewart, "I council ye, fight not in such haste. They say my brother is coming, and near at hand, with fifteen hundred men. Were they joined with you ye could with more confidence abide the battle."

Sir Edward looked right wrathful, "What sayest thou?" he asked Soulis.

"I' faith, sir," said he, "I say as my friend has said."

The king then asked Sir Philip, and he answered, "Sir, as our Lord sees me, methinks it no foolishness to await your friends, who make speed to ride hither. We are few; our foes are many. God may grant us good fortune, it is true, but it were a miracle if our strength should overcome so many in battle."

"Alas," said Sir Edward, in great wrath, "I never thought to hear that from thee! Now, help who will, assuredly without longer tarrying I will fight this day. While I live, no man shall say that any force made me flee. God save us from the charge of fouling our fair name!"

"So be it then," said they, "we shall take what God sends."

When the Irish chiefs heard what had passed,

and knew for certain that their king, with his small following, would fight against so great and mighty a host, they came to him with the utmost speed, and counselled him most earnestly to await his friends. They would, they said, keep the enemy engaged all that day, and the morrow as well, with their attacks.

But no counsel could prevail; the king's mind was set always upon the battle. And when they saw he was so stubbornly set to fight, they said, "Ye may indeed go to battle with yonder great host, but we account ourselves free utterly, and none of us will stand to fight. Set no store, therefore, by our strength. For our custom in this country is to follow and fight, and to fight fleeing, and not to stand in open battle till one side be discomfited."

"Since that is your custom," he said, "I ask of you no more than this, that ye and your host stand all together in battle array at a distance, without leaving the field, and see our fight and our ending."

They said of a surety they should do this; then they withdrew to their men, who were well-nigh forty thousand strong.

The king and those about him, not two thousand in all, arrayed themselves stalwartly to do battle with forty thousand and more. Sir Edward that day would not put on his coat armour,

but Gib Harper, whom men held without peer
in his estate, wore the whole of Sir Edward's
array.

In this wise they awaited the battle, and, their
enemies coming at great speed all ready for the
encounter, right boldly they met them. So
few were the Scots, of a truth, that they were
overwhelmed by their foes. Those of them that
endeavoured most to make a stand were cut down,
and the rest fled for succour to the Irish host.
Sir Edward, despite his valour, was slain, and
Sir John Stewart as well, with Sir John de
Soulis, and others besides of their company. So
suddenly were they overcome that few were
slain on the spot; the rest made their way to
the Irish chiefs who, in battle order, were waiting
at hand.

John Thomasson, leader of the men of Carrick
in the host, when he saw the discomfiture, with-
drew to an Irish chief of his acquaintance, who
received him loyally. And when he was come
to that chief he saw being led away from the
battle the stout Sir Philip the Mowbray. He
had been stunned in the fight, and was led by
the arms by two men on the causeway that
stretched in a long straight line between the
place of battle and the town. They held their
way towards the town; but when they were
midway on the road Sir Philip overcame his

dizziness, and perceived he was seized and led
away by two of the enemy. In a moment he
hurled from him first the one and then the
other, then swiftly drew his sword and set out
along the causeway towards the fight. The road
was full of a multitude of men going towards
the town, and he as he met them dealt such
blows that against their will he made a full
hundred leave the causeway. This was told for a
certainty by John Thomasson, who saw the whole
achievement.

Mowbray went straight towards the battle,
but Thomasson, taking certain heed that the
Scots were all completely overthrown, called
hastily to him, and said, "Come here, for there
is none alive; they are every one slain."

Then Sir Philip stood still awhile, and saw
that his friends were all done to death, and
he came and joined company with him.

This John Thomasson afterwards wrought so
shrewdly that all who had fled to the Irish host,
though they had lost part of their weapons,
reached Carrickfergus safe and whole. Meanwhile
the English who had been in the battle sought
among the dead to find Sir Edward, to get his
head, and they found Gib Harper in his coat of
mail. Then, because of the arms he wore, they
struck off his head, and salted it in a bucket,
and sent it afterwards to England as a present

to King Edward. They supposed it Sir Edward's head, but were deceived because of the splendour of the armour. Nevertheless Sir Edward died there.

In this wise through wilfulness were all these nobles at that time lost, which was afterwards a great regret. Had their extraordinary valour been guided with sense and moderation, unless the greater misfortune befell them, it should have been a right hard task to bring them to disaster. But great and extravagant pride caused them all to pay dear for their bravery.

Those who fled from the battle sped in haste towards the sea-coast, and came to Carrickfergus. And those on the way from King Robert to Sir Edward, when they heard of the discomfiture, returned to the same place. This retreat was not made without difficulty, for many times that day the Irish attacked them; but they held together in close order, defending themselves cautiously, and, sometimes by force, sometimes by craft, and sometimes giving bribes to be allowed to pass scatheless, they made their escape. Then in boats and ships they set forth and arrived all safely in Scotland.

When the people of Scotland had knowledge of Sir Edward's overthrow, the whole land mourned full tenderly for him and for those who were slain with him.

After Edward the Bruce had been discomfited
in the manner I have described, and the field
had been entirely cleared, so that no resisters
were to be seen, the warden, Richard of Clare,
and all the hosts with him set out towards
Dundalk. They made no direct encounter at that
time with the Irish, but hastened to the town.
Then they sent oversea to the King of England
Gib Harper's head in a bucket. John Maupas
carried it to the king, who received it with great
delight, and was right blithe at the gift, being
full glad to be delivered of so fierce a foe. His
heart was so filled with pride because of this
that he formed a plan to ride with a great host
into Scotland, to avenge himself with a strong
hand for the vexation, trouble, and harm that
he had suffered there. He gathered a vast host,
and sent his ships by sea with great abundance
of victual. On that occasion he thought to destroy
the whole of Scotland so utterly that none should
be left alive therein, and with his people in great
array he set forth towards the North.[1]

When King Robert knew that he was coming
upon him with such a host, he gathered men far

---

[1] Professor Skeat has pointed out the looseness of the narrative
here. According to the *Annales Scotiæ*, John Maupas was the
slayer of Edward Bruce, and was himself found afterwards dead
upon his body, while Edward II.'s campaign in Scotland did not
occur till some four years later, in August 1322.

and near till he had so many about him, and
coming to join him, that he felt assured he should
do well. He caused all the cattle of Lothian to
be withdrawn, and sent them into fastnesses, and
appointed men for their defence. With his whole
host he lay in hiding at Culross, for his plan was
to weaken his foes by fasting and long watching,
and after he had enfeebled their strength, to
give them battle.

While this was his plan the English host with
much greater strength than his came into Lothian,
and soon reached Edinburgh, where they dwelt
three days. The English ships at sea had all the
time contrary winds, and could by no means bring
the victual they carried into the firth to relieve
the king. When provision failed the host, and
they saw they could get no victual by sea,
they sent forth a great company to forage
throughout Lothian. But they found no cattle,
except a lame cow that they came upon in
a cornfield at Tranent; her they brought to
the host. And when the Earl of Warenne saw
that cow coming thus solitary, he asked if they
had got no more, and they told him no. "Certes
then," said he, "I declare this is the dearest beef
I ever yet beheld, for of a certainty it has cost
a thousand pounds, and more!"

And when the king and his council saw that
they could get no cattle for their host to eat,

and that the host suffered greatly from the fasting, they turned homewards again towards England. They meant to lie at Melrose, and sent forward a company of nigh three hundred armed men. But the Lord Douglas, who was then near at hand in the Forest, knew of their coming, and what they were, and with his company he lay in wait privily in ambush in Melrose. He sent a right sturdy friar outside the gate to watch their coming, and bade him keep himself hidden till he saw them come to the corner of the wall, and then cry aloud, "Douglas! Douglas!"

The friar set forth. He was daring, stout, and bold; his great hood covered wholly the armour he wore; he rode a strong horse, and in his hand he carried a spear. Thus he waited till he saw the English coming nigh, and when the foremost were past the corner he shouted "Douglas! Douglas!" and made a charge at them, and deftly bore one down. Then with a shout Douglas and his company sallied forth. And when the English saw so great a force come so suddenly upon them they were right greatly daunted, and fled at once. The Scots rode among them, and slew all they could overtake, and made a great martyrdom there.

Those of the English who escaped unslain returned to their main body, and told the manner of welcome Douglas had given them at their

meeting, convoying them roughly back, and deny-
ing them open quarters. Then the King of England
and his men, seeing their harbingers come back
repulsed, were greatly troubled, and deemed it
would be great folly to quarter in the Forest.
They camped therefore in the open ground beside
Dryburgh, and afterwards held their way home-
wards to England.

And when King Robert heard that they were
turned home again, and how their harbingers
had been slain, he gathered his host quickly, and
went south over the Scottish Sea, and marched
towards England. When his host was all got
together, he had eighty thousand men and more,
and of these he made eight battles, with ten
thousand in each battle. Then he passed into
England, and with his whole army followed fast
upon the English king, till at last he drew near to
him, where he lay at Byland with his men. King
Robert had knowledge that he lay there in great
force, and one night surprised him by a forced
march, so that on the morrow, before it was day,
the Scots were come into the open field but a
little space from Byland.

Between them and Byland there was a rocky
hill stretching a long way, with a great pass
going up. By no other way could the Abbey of
Byland be reached, unless they went a great way
round about. And when the vast English host

heard King Robert was so near, the greater part of them went to the pass, and seized the hill, thinking to make their defence there. On that ground they displayed their banners and their battles in broad array, and felt assured of defending the place.

When King Robert perceived that they meant to defend themselves there, he sent for his council, and asked what were best to be done. The Lord Douglas answered and said, "Sir, I will undertake in a short time either openly to win yonder place, or else to cause all yonder company to come down to you here in this plain."

"Do so then," said the king, "and God speed thee!"

Douglas therefore went forth, and taking the greater part of the host with him, marched towards the place.

The stout Earl of Moray left his battle, and in great haste, with but three men in his company, came to the Lord Douglas's rout, and before he entered upon the ground took a place in front of them all; for he desired that men should see him. And when Sir James of Douglas beheld him come thus, he prized him greatly for it, and welcomed him right humbly, and took the field beside him.

The English, seeing them do this, alighted and marched against them. Two knights doughty

of deed, Sir Thomas Arthin and Sir Ralph of
Cobham, came down before all their host. They
were both of right great valour, and met their
foes right manfully; but they were grievously
beset. There some were to be seen making
strong attack, and others making stout battle in
defence. The arrows flew in great abundance,
and the English above rolled down stones from
the height. But the Scots set both will and
strength to win the pass, and pressed their
enemies so that Sir Ralph retired speedily to
his host. Sir Thomas was left manfully and
with great strength defending the place, till at
last he was taken unawares, and made captive
by hard fighting. Because of this defence he
was afterwards, to his last day, renowned as
the knight of stoutest hand in all England. For
this same Sir Ralph of Cobham had the name
throughout all England of being the best knight
in the country, and because Sir Thomas remained
fighting where Sir Ralph withdrew he was prized
above him.

As they thus fought, and King Robert, who
was wise and prudent in action, saw his men
continue so doughtily to ascend the pass against
their foes, and saw the enemy thus well defend
themselves, he caused all the Erse of Argyll and
the Isles who were in his host to speed forthwith
up the hill. He bade them leave the pass

altogether, and climb up the crags at hand, and
make the greatest haste to seize the high ground.
This they did forthwith, climbing always up to
the height, and heeding no whit the strength of
their foes. They bore themselves so that despite
the enemy they got to the top of the hill. There
they could be seen fighting fiercely, and sturdily
driving back their foes. At the same time those
who had gone to the pass, notwithstanding the
efforts of the English, seized the high ground,
and there laid on with all their might, and were
to be seen doing dire battle.

A perilous combat took place there; for a
knight named Sir John of Bretagne chanced to
be at the top of the hill with his men, and made
great defence. But the Scots made such assault,
and did battle with them so fiercely, that they
were brought to dismay, and those of them that
could flee made off. Sir John of Bretagne was
taken there, and right many of his folk were
slain. Two knights of France were taken, the
Lord of Sully and the Marshal Bretagne, who was
a right great lord at home.[1] Of the others, some
were dead, and some taken, and the rest every
one fled.

And when the King of England, who was still
lying at Byland, saw his men wholly discomfited,

[1] John of Bretagne was Earl of Richmond, and Henry de Sully
Grand Butler of France.—*Tytler*, i. 145.

he made off with the greatest haste, and fled
southward with all his might. The Scots, I
promise, chased him hard, and took many in the
pursuit, though King Edward got away clear with
the greater part of his host. Walter Stewart,
who ever set his heart upon high deeds of
chivalry, gave chase, with five hundred in his
company, to the gates of York. There he slew
some of the English, and tarried till near night
to see if any would come forth to battle. And
when he saw none sought to come out, he turned
again with all his company, and hastened to the
Scottish host.

The Scots had quartered in the Abbey of Byland,
and at Rievaulx near by. They dealt among them
the King of England's gear that he had left in
Byland; they caused it all to be brought out and
counted through their hands, and all made glad
and merry over it.

When King Robert had taken up his quarters
they brought to him the prisoners all unarmed
as it behoved. And when he saw Sir John of
Bretagne he looked at him with the greatest
displeasure, for he was wont to speak haughtily
and despitefully at home, and he bade them carry
him off at once, and see that he be straitly kept,
and said, "Were it not that he were such a
caitiff he should pay dearly for his despiteful
words."

Sir John meekly begged his mercy, but they led him forth without more ado, and guarded him well till they were come home to their own country. I have heard say he was ransomed long afterwards for twenty thousand pounds.

When the king had spoken thus the French knights who had been taken were brought before him, and he gave them fair welcome, and said, " Right well I know that because of your great worth and valour ye came here to see the fighting. Seeing ye were in the country your strength, your stoutness, and your valour would not suffer you to eschew the fight, and since by that cause ye were led to it, and neither by wrath nor ill-will, ye shall be received as friends here, where ye are ever welcome."

They knelt and thanked him greatly for the grace that of a truth he showed them, and he caused them to be courteously treated, and kept them long with him, and did them high honour. And when they longed for their own country, he sent them free, without ransom, as a present to the King of France, and gave them great gifts. In this fashion he received his friends with courtesy and kindness, and vigorously confounded his foes.

He lay at Byland all that night, and all the host were glad because of their victory. On the morrow they marched southward, and made their way, burning, slaying, and destroying, and damaging the enemy with all their might, till they came to the Wolds. There they turned northward towards home, and on their way back wholly destroyed the Vale Beauvoir.[1] Then with prisoners and cattle, with riches and many a fair jewel, they marched home to Scotland, blithe and glad, joyful and gay. And each man went to his dwelling praising God that so fair fortune had befallen them as, by valour and strength and their lord's great nobleness, to discomfit the King of England in his own country.

[1] Beverley and the Valley of the Hull. The clergy and inhabitants of Beverley purchased their own safety by a payment of four hundred pounds, equal to six thousand pounds of modern money.—*Tytler*, i. 145.

BOOK XIX

THE ENGLISH PEACE

THUS was the land at peace for a time. But envy, that never ceases from setting men upon evil deeds to win power to themselves, caused lords of full great renown to make a fell conspiracy against the doughty King Robert. They thought to make an end of him, and after his death to enjoy the kingdom and reign in his stead. The greatest infamy in that attempt pertained to Sir William, Lord Soulis, for he was chief of it both by assent and ruthlessness. He had caused several to join him, Gilbert Malherbe and John of Logie, knights, and Richard Brown, a squire. Stout Sir David the Brechin also was charged with the crime, as I shall describe later.[1]

But ere these men could compass their end they were every one discovered. This was done,

[1] The house of Soulis claimed the throne in right of the daughter of King Alexander II. Had her legitimacy been proved their claim would have excluded both Bruce and Baliol. Both Soulis and Brechin had long been traitors in English pay.—*Tytler*, i. 142.

I have heard, through a lady.[1] She told the king
their whole intent and plot, how he was to be
slain, and Soulis reign in his stead, and she gave
him a sure token that the attempt was a settled
matter.

When the king knew this was so, he made his
plans so subtly that he caused the traitors every
one to be captured. At the place where the
Lord Soulis was seized he had in his company
at the time three hundred and sixty squires,
besides certain gay knights. He was taken at
Berwick. Then all his following was to be seen
going heavy and sad; for the king let them
all go their way, and kept those he had proof
against.

Soon afterwards the Lord Soulis made open
confession of the whole plot. A parliament there-
fore was called, and this company was brought
before it. There in open parliament the Lord
Soulis confessed the crime, and soon afterwards
for punishment was sent to Dunbarton, where
he died in the stone castle. Sir Gilbert Malherbe,

[1] According to the *Annales Scotiæ* the lady was the Countess
of Strathern. She was herself engaged in the plot, and for her
share in it was condemned to perpetual imprisonment. Seventy
years ago, when the monument to Sir David Baird was being
erected on Tom-a-chaistle, near Crieff, the workmen broke into
a vault under the ancient stronghold, and certain bones, gold
ornaments, and household articles which they found were believed
to be the relics of the imprisoned countess.

and Sir John of Logie,[1] and Richard Brown, these three were openly condemned by the assize; therefore they were each one drawn, hanged, and beheaded according to the sentence.

Good Sir David the Brechin also they afterwards caused to be right straitly charged, and he confessed that discovery of the plot had been made to him, but he gave no consent to it. And because he hid their plot, and did not discover it to the king, from whom he held his whole estate, and to whom he had done fealty, he was sentenced to be hanged and drawn.

And as they carried him to be hanged the people thronged wondrous fast to behold him and his evil case, which was right sad to see. Sir Ingram de Umphraville was there as a Scotsman with the king. When he saw that great mischance he said, "Sirs, to what intent press ye to see the evil fate of a knight who was so valiant and so doughty? I have seen more folk crowd to see him for his right sovereign nobleness than now crowd to see him here." And when these words were spoken he kept silence with sorry countenance till men had done their will upon Sir David; then with the king's leave he brought him honourably to burial.

---

[1] John de Logie's son was first husband of Margaret, daughter of Sir Malcolm Drummond, who as "Margaret Logy" became second queen of David II.—*Story of the Stewarts*, p. 115.

And afterwards he said to the king, "One thing I pray you grant me; that is, that ye give me leave to do my pleasure with all my land that lies in Scotland."

The king answered him, "I will indeed grant thee this; but tell me what vexes thee."

"Grant me leave," he answered, "and I shall tell you openly. I have no heart to remain longer with you in this country; therefore, except it inconvenience you, I pray you from my heart to let me take leave. For where a knight so right worthy and chivalrous and doughty, so renowned for valour, and so full of all that may become a man, as brave Sir David the Brechin, has been put to so cruel a death, of a truth my heart will on no account suffer me to dwell."

"Since thou wilt have it so," said the king, "whenever it is thy pleasure thou mayest go, and to that intent thou shalt have full leave to do thy liking with thy land."

Sir Ingram thanked him greatly, and right speedily disposed of his land as he thought best; then, before all that were there, he took his leave for evermore of the right gracious king, and went to England to King Edward. The English king gave him right fair welcome, and asked him the tidings of the North, and he told him everything truly; how those knights were destroyed, and all that I have recounted, and the courtesy of the king, who had graciously given him leave to do his pleasure with his land.

At that time messengers were sent from the King of Scotland to treat of peace, if they could get it. To this intent they had ofttimes before been sent, but had not been able to attain their end. For the good King Robert desired, since God had sent him such fair fortune as to win all his kingdom by force of arms, to make peace in his land, and establish the country, so that, if men kept their loyalty, his heir after him should live in quietness.

It was at this time that Umphraville, as I have told, came to the King of England. At the English court he found the Scottish messengers seeking to treat of peace and rest. The king knew Sir Ingram was wise, and asked his counsel in the matter, what he would advise him to do; "For," said he, "it seemed hard to him to make peace with King Robert the Bruce, his enemy, before he was avenged upon him."

Sir Ingram made answer to him and said, "He dealt so courteously with me, that in no wise should I give counsel to his hurt."

"It behoves thee of necessity," said the king, "to declare thy counsel in this matter."

"Sir," said he "since your will is that I speak, know ye assuredly that, for all your great might of arms, ye have no strength to deal with him.

His men have all become so doughty with long
experience of war, and they have been so trained
in these matters, that each active yeoman is
worth a knight. But if ye seek to bring your
war to your intent and good pleasure, ye shall
make with him a long truce. Then shall most
of his following, who are but a peaceful yeomanry,
be constrained all in common to make their
living by their labour. Some of them must needs
take to plough and harrow and other various crafts
to earn their bread. Thus their weapons shall
wax old, and shall be rotten, sold, or destroyed,
and during the long truce many who now are
cunning in war shall die, and in their stead shall
rise others who know little of such matters.
And when they are thus grown unused to war ye
may move against them, and shall right easily,
I believe, bring your purpose to fair conclusion."

To this every one assented, and soon afterwards
a truce was agreed upon between the two kings,
to last for thirteen years,[1] and proclamation of it
was made on the marches.

The Scots kept the truce loyally; but the
English, with great iniquity, destroyed at sea
merchant ships sailing from Scotland to Flanders,
slaying the men every one, and taking the goods
to their own uses. King Robert sent often to
ask redress, but no redress was made, and he was

[1] From March 30, 1323, to June 12, 1336.

left all the time asking. On his part he caused
the truce to be upheld steadfastly on the marches,
and caused his men to keep it loyally.

At this time, while the truce lasted on the
Borders, the valiant Walter Stewart was seized
at Bathgate with a great sickness. His illness
waxed ever more and more, till men saw by his
look that he must needs pay the debt that no
man can escape. Shriven and fully repentant,
and with all things done that a Christian needs
to do, like a good Christian he gave up the ghost.[1]
Then were weeping and crying to be heard among
the common folk, and many a knight and lady
were to be seen openly making right evil cheer.
Thus all men mourned him together, for of his
age he was a valiant knight. After they had for
a long time made their moan they bore the body
to Paisley, and there with great solemnity and
lamentation he was interred.[2] May God, of his

---

[1] April 9, 1326. "Walter the Stewart was thrice married: 1st
to Alice, daughter of Sir John Erskine of Erskine, of which
marriage there was one daughter, Jean, married to Hugh, Earl
of Ross; 2nd to the Princess Marjory Bruce, who survived her
marriage less than a year, leaving an only son, afterwards King
Robert II.; and 3rd to Isabel, sister of Sir John Graham of
Abercorn, by whom he had two sons, Sir John Stewart and Sir
Andrew Stewart, and a daughter, Lady Egidia Stewart. This
branch of the Stewarts is designated ' of Railston.'"—*The Story
of the Stewarts*, p. 84.

[2] Paisley Abbey was founded by the Steward of Scotland in
1163. There Walter Stewart's wife, the Princess Marjory, was

might, bring his soul to that place where joy is everlasting! Amen!

After his death, when two years and a half had gone by of the truce that was to have lasted thirteen years, King Robert saw that no redress was to be got for the ships that were seized and the men in them who were slain, and that the English continued their evil-doing whenever they met a Scottish ship at sea. He sent and fully freed himself, and openly gave up the truce, and to avenge these trespasses caused the stout Thomas, Earl of Moray, and Donald, Earl of Mar, with James of Douglas, and James Stewart, who was leader in the field of all the people of his house after the death of his valiant brother, to make ready in their best fashion to enter England with a great host, to burn and slay.

They set forth soon into England, a host ten thousand strong, and, as they went, burnt and slew and diligently destroyed their foes.[1] After this fashion they marched till they were come to Weardale. At that time Edward of Carnarvon, the English King, was dead, and laid in stone,[2] and the young Edward his son, surnamed of

already buried, and there afterwards the body of their son, King Robert II., was to be interred.

[1] This raid was made in June 1327.

[2] Edward II. was deposed on Jan. 2 of that year, but his murder did not take place till Sept. 21.

Windsor, was crowned king in England. He had been formerly in France with his mother, Dame Isabel, and was wedded, I have heard say, to a fair young lady, daughter of the Earl of Hainault.[1] He brought with him out of that country knights of great valour. Sir John of Hainault was their leader, a man right sage and doughty in war.

At the time when the Scots were at Weardale, the new-made king lay at York, and heard of the destruction they made in his country. He gathered to him a great host, well-nigh fifty thousand strong. Then he marched northward with that following in battle order. At that time he was eighteen years of age.[2]

The Scots had harried all Cockdale from end to end, and had ridden again to Weardale. Their scouts having had sight of the coming of the English, told it to their lords. Then the Lord Douglas rode straight forth to see their advance, and he beheld them in seven battles, riding in brave array.

When he had seen that host, and returned to his men, the Earl asked if he had beheld the English.

"Aye, sir," he said, "without a doubt."

[1] Edward's marriage did not take place till January of the following year.

[2] He was born at Windsor, Nov. 13, 1312, and was not yet 15 years old. The Scottish raid took place in August, 1327.

"What number are they?"

"Sir, many men."

The Earl then swore his oath, and said, "We shall fight with them though they were as many again."

"Sir, God be praised," said Douglas, "that we have a captain who dare venture so great a thing. But, by Saint Bride, battle shall not be thus ventured if my counsel be taken; and on no account shall we fight except it be at our advantage, for methinks it were no disgrace for a small host fighting against a greater to take advantage when it can."

As they were speaking thus they saw one broad battle with many banners displayed riding straight towards them over a high ridge, and another coming close behind. In this same fashion the enemy came till seven broad battles had passed across that high ridge. The Scots were then lying on the north side of the Wear, nearer Scotland. The valley was long, and on either side was a rising ground, somewhat steep towards the water.

The Scots stood ready in brave array, each man in his best guise, on the strong ground they had taken up, well-nigh a quarter of a mile from the Wear. There they stood waiting battle, and the English on the further side came riding down till they were near the river. There they made pause, and sent out a thousand archers, with hoods off and bows in hand.[1] They made them drink well of wine, and bade them go in loose order and skirmish with the Scottish host, and see if they could strike them down. For could they cause the Scots to break array they believed they should have them at their will. They sent men-at-arms down with the archers to defend them at the water side.

The Lord Douglas saw that movement, and he caused a great company, well horsed and armed, to lie in wait behind the Scottish battle for the enemy's coming. When he made a sign to this company they were to come spurring fast, and with their spears slay all they could overtake. Donald of Mar was the chief of this company, and with him was Archibald of Douglas.

The Lord Douglas rode towards the English archers wearing a gown over his armour, and kept riding to and fro as he came back, to entice them near his battle. And they, having drunk of the wine, kept ever coming upwards in a straight line, till they drew so near the Scottish host that many arrows fell among them.

Robert of Ogle, a brave squire, at that came spurring on a courser, and called to the archers,

---

[1] Hume of Godscroft (*History of the Houses of Douglas and Angus*) describes the soldiers of this English army as " clothed in coats and hoods, embroidered with flowers and branches," regarding which vanities the Scots made a derisive rhyme.

"Ye know not who it is that thus entices you! it is the Lord Douglas, and he will play some of his tricks upon you!"

And when they heard the name of Douglas the boldest was dismayed, and all of them turned back.

At this, Douglas quickly made sign to the host he had in hiding, and that company pricked so stoutly on the English archers that they slew full three hundred of them, and pursued the rest back to the water side.

Sir William of Erskine, who was newly that day made a knight, and was well horsed and in brave array, gave chase with others so far in advance that his horse carried him into the throng of the English, and he was by force taken captive. Very soon, however, he was exchanged for other prisoners taken by the Scots.[1]

After these English archers were slain, the Scottish pursuers rode back to their host, and the Lord Douglas did the same. And when he was returned, they could see among their enemies tents being set up. By this they perceived that the English meant to encamp, and do no more that night, therefore the Scots also encamped, and quickly set up their pavilions; they also made tents and huts, and set all in order.

[1] The barony of Erskine lies on the left bank of the Clyde below Renfrew. It gave name to the noble family of Mar.

Two new things the Scots that day beheld, which never before that time had been known in Scotland. One of these was crests for helmets, which seemed to them a very beautiful and marvellous sight. The other was cannon, which they had never heard before. They marvelled at these two things. That night the Scots kept stout watch, most of them lying in arms till the morning.

The English took thought by what means they could cause the Scots to leave their vantage ground; for it seemed to them foolish and absurd to march up and attack them at their fastness in open battle. Therefore they sent a thousand stout horsemen, armed from head to foot, to lie in ambush in a valley behind the Scottish host, and they made ready their battles as if they meant to advance to the fighting. For they deemed Scotsmen so headstrong that they could not hold themselves from coming to the attack. They believed that because of their courage they would leave their strong vantage ground, and meet them in the plain field; then the English ambush in their rear should spur headlong upon them, and thus they thought they should make the Scots repent them of their game.

They sent forth the thousand men, and these privily ambushed themselves. And on the morrow early they caused the trumpets to sound in their

host, and set their battle in broad array, and
ordered themselves all for the fight, and made
straight towards the river.

The Scots, seeing them do this, made ready in
their best fashion, and, arrayed in plain battle,
with banners displayed to the wind, left their
strong ground, and all openly and boldly came
down, in the bravest manner, to meet them, as
their foes had expected.

But the Lord Douglas always set out watches
here and there, and he got knowledge of the
ambush, and forthwith at great speed he came in
front of the battles, and stoutly bade each man
turn about where he stood, so that no opening
be made in the ranks, and march back to the
strong ground. They did as he bade, and went
back to their place of strength, and then turned
in full force, and stood ready to give battle if
the enemy should attack them.

When the English saw them thus again go up
towards their strong ground, they cried aloud,
"The Scots are fled!" But Sir John of Hainault
said, "I' faith, yonder fleeing is right well feigned.
I see their armed men and their banners behind,
so that they need but turn as they stand, and
they will be arrayed for the fight if any force
come upon them. They have seen our ambush,
and are gone again to their place of strength.
Yonder folk are wisely commanded, and he that

leads them were worthy by his prudence, valour, and wisdom to govern the Empire of Rome."

Thus that day spoke this worthy knight; and the ambush, when they saw they were discovered, fared again towards their host. When the English battles saw that they had failed of their purpose, they returned and quartered in their camp. On the other side the Scots did the same; they fought no more that day.

When the day was past, and as soon as night was fallen, they made fires in great number. Now the good Lord of Douglas had spied a place two miles away where the Scottish host might quarter more securely, and defend itself better than anywhere else in that region. It was a park[1] wholly surrounded with a wall, and well-nigh full of trees, but set in a great plain. Thither the Lord Douglas determined to bring the host by night. Therefore without more delay they fed their fires and made them greater, and all together marched forth, and came without hurt to the park, and took quarters close to the river, as near it as they were before.

And at daybreak on the morrow the English host missed the Scots, and wondered, and sent scouts spurring in haste to see where they were gone. And by their fires they saw that they had quartered their whole host in the park at

[1] Stanhope Park, in Weardale.

Weardale. At that the English forthwith made
ready and rode right opposite to them, and on
the other side of the water of Wear set up their
pavilions as near as they were pitched before.

Thus on both sides they lay for eight days, the
English not daring to attack the Scots in open
battle because of the strength of the ground
they had taken up. Each day there was warlike
jousting and skirmishing. Men were taken on
either side, and those that were taken on one
day were exchanged on another; but no other
deeds greatly worth remembering were done till
the ninth day.

Then it befell that the Lord Douglas espied a
way by which he might ride round the English
host, and come upon their further side. And at
night he prepared and took with him a good
following of five hundred right hardy horsemen.
All secretly, without noise, he rode so far as
nearly to go round their host, and on the further
side he rode cautiously towards them. Half the
men with him he bade carry their swords bare
in hand, and ordered them to cut in two the
ropes of the tents, so that these might fall on
the men inside; then the others, as they went
forward, should thrust down sturdily with their
spears. And when they heard his horn they
were to hasten down to the river.

When these orders were given they rode fast

towards the enemy, who had no watches on that side. And as they drew near, an Englishman who lay basking by a fire, said to his comrade, "I know not what may chance to us here, but a right great shuddering has seized me. I dread sore the Black Douglas." And he that heard him said, "I' faith, thou shalt have cause if I can give it thee!" With that he and all his company dashed boldly upon them, and bore down the proud pavilions, and with sharp-cutting spears relentlessly stabbed the men.

Right soon arose uproar and outcry. The Scots stabbed, thrust, and slew, and threw down many tents. A dire slaughter they made there, for the men were lying unarmed, and had no power to make defence, and they slew them without pity. They made them know how great a folly it was to lie near their foes without secure guard.

The Scots kept slaying their enemies in this fashion till the alarm rose throughout all the great host, and lord and yeomen were astir. And when the Douglas knew they were all everywhere arming themselves, he blew his horn to rally his men, and bade them make their way towards the river. This they did, and he waited hindmost to see that none of his men should be left.

And as he thus tarried, going to and fro, one with a club came and dealt him such a great

blow that, had it not been for his mighty
strength and his right sovereign manhood, he
had been slain on the spot. But he, at no time
dismayed, though he was right oft hard assailed,
by his great strength and manhood brought his
assailant to death.

His men, who were riding in loose order down
to the water, missed their lord when they came
there. Then were they in sore fear for him.
Each asked tidings at the other, but they could
hear nothing of him. Then they took counsel
together, meaning to go back to seek him. But
as they stood thus dismayed, they heard a blast
of his horn, and knowing it quickly, they were
wondrous blithe, and at his coming asked him
of his tarrying; and he told how a churl had met
him stoutly on the way, and dealt him with his
club a right fierce blow, "and had not fortune
helped the more, I had been in great peril there."

Speaking thus they held on their way till they
came to the Scottish host, which, armed and on
foot, was waiting to help them at need. And so
soon as the Lord Douglas met the Earl of Moray,
the Earl asked tidings at him how he had fared
in his sally.

"Sir," said he, "we have drawn blood."

The Earl, who was of great courage, said, "And
had we all gone thither we had discomfited them
everyone."

"It might have fallen out well," said Douglas, "but of a truth we were enough to put in venture yonder; for had they put discomfiture upon us it would have dismayed all here."

"Since so it is," said the Earl, "that we cannot attack the might of our fierce enemies with stratagem, we shall do it in open battle."

"By Saint Bride," said Lord Douglas, "it were great folly for us at this time to fight with yonder host, for every day it grows in strength, and it has withal plenty of provender. We are here, too, in their country, where no succours can come to us. It is hard here for us to protect ourselves, nor can we forage to get meat, and must eat such as we have with us. Let us therefore do with our foes that are lying before us here, as I heard tell in time past a fox did with a fisherman."

"What did the fox?" said the Earl.

"A fisherman, once upon a time," answered Douglas, "lay beside a river to draw the nets that he had set there. He had made himself a little hut, and within it he had a bed, and also a little fire. There was a door too, and that was all. One night he rose to see his nets, and tarried long beside them. And when he had done his work, he went again towards his hut. And by the light of the little fire that was burning clear in the hut, he saw, inside, a fox devouring a salmon. He went quickly to the door, and nimbly drew a sword, and said, 'Traitor, thou must here die!'

"The fox, being in right great fear, looked about to see some hole; but no way of escape could he see, except where the man stood sturdily. Beside him, lying upon the bed, he saw a cloth mantle, and with his teeth he drew it across the fire; and when the man saw his mantle lie there burning, he ran hastily to save it. The fox then sprang out at full speed, and fled to his place of safety. The fisher thought himself sore beguiled, seeing he had lost his salmon, and had his mantle burned as well, and the fox got scathless away.

"This example I may apply to yonder host and ourselves here. We are the fox, and they the fisherman that stops the way out. They suppose we cannot get away except only where they lie. Pardie, it shall not be altogether as they think; for I have caused a way to be espied for us. Although it be somewhat wet, we shall not lose a page of our host. The enemy, because of this small surprise, suppose we shall so greatly pride ourselves that we shall undertake to give them open battle; but this once their belief shall fail them. Here all day to-morrow we shall make as merry as we can, and prepare us against the night. Then we shall make our fires up brightly, and blow our horns, and make ado as though all

the world were our own, till the night be well
fallen. Then with all our armour we shall march
in haste homeward. We shall carry ourselves in
all readiness till we be out of the danger that
lies about us here. Then shall we be all at our
pleasure, and the enemy shall hinder themselves,
sore deceived, till they know well that we are
away."

To this they altogether agreed, and they made
good cheer all that night, till daylight on the
morrow.

On the morrow all privily they packed up
armour, and made ready, so that before evening
they were all prepared. Their enemies, who lay
over against them, caused their men who had
been slain to be borne in carts to a holy place.
All that day with carts they were carrying slain
men. It could be well seen these were many,
since they took so long in the bearing away.

Both of the hosts were all that day at peace,
and when night drew near, the Scots, who were
lying in the Park, made feast and revelry, and
blew horns, and made fires, and caused them to
burn both bright and broad, so that their blaze
that night was greater than at any time before.
And when the night was well fallen, with all
their armour every whit, they rode right secretly
away.

They soon entered upon a moss a full mile in

breadth. Across that moss they went on foot, leading their horses in their hand. It was a right troublesome road, nevertheless all who were there came the whole way across safe and sound. They lost but little of their gear, except it might be some sumpter-horse that was left lying in the bog.

When all, as I have related, were come over that broad moss, they were filled with a great gladness, and rode forth on their homeward way.

And on the morrow when it was day the English saw the quarters where the Scots were wont to lie all empty. At this they marvelled greatly, and sent forth sundry of their men to spy where they were gone. And at last they found their trace leading to the great moss. This was so hideous to wade that none of them dared adventure it. Then the scouts returned to their host, and told how the Scots had passed where never man passed before.

When the English heard this they took hasty counsel, and determined to follow no more. There and then they dispersed their host, and each man rode to his own dwelling.

Meanwhile King Robert, having learned that his men lay in the Park, and were in such peril, speedily gathered a host of twenty thousand right hardy men. This he sent forth with two Earls, of March and Angus, to succour the host in Weardale. If they could so far succeed as to join forces with it, their plan was to attack the enemy. Thus it fell out that on the same day when the moss was crossed, as I have told, the scouts riding in front of either host got sight of each other. And they, being valiant and active, set spears for encounter of battle. They shouted aloud their battle-cries, and by these perceived that they were friends and of one fealty.

Then were they glad and blithe, and speedily told their lords. And the hosts met together, and there was right homely welcoming made among the great lords there. They were right joyful at the meeting.

The Earl Patrick and his host had with them victual in great abundance, and therewith they succoured their friends well. To tell the truth, while these were lying in Weardale they had lack of food, but now they were relieved with great plenty. They went towards Scotland with games and merriment, and reached home safely, and scattered presently, every man his own way.

The lords went to the king, and he made them right fair welcome; for of their coming he was most glad, and because they had escaped without loss out of such difficulty they all made merry and were blithe.

BOOK XX

THE DEATH OF THE BRUCE

SOON after the Earl Thomas had thus returned from Weardale the king gathered all his strength, leaving out none able to fight. He assembled a great host, and divided it into three parts. One part went without hindrance to Norham, and set a strait siege there, and kept the garrison close within their wall. The second division went to Alnwick, and set a siege there. And while these two divisions lay besieging the castles they made bold assaults, and many a fair and gallant feat of arms was right doughtily achieved.

The king left his people lying at these castles, and held his way with a third host from park to park, to amuse himself at the hunting, as if the whole land were his own. To those who were with him there he gave in fee and heritage the lands of Northumberland lying next the Scottish Border, and they paid the fee for their seals.

In this wise he rode destroying, till the King

of England, by advice of the Mortimer and his
mother, who, because of his youth, were at that
time his governors, sent messengers to treat of
peace, and they so sped that it was agreed to
make a perpetual peace on these terms. A
marriage was to be made between King Robert's
son, David, at that time scarcely five years old,
and Dame Joan of the Tower, who was after-
wards of right great worth. She was sister to
the young King of England, and at that time
seven years old. By that treaty were given up
many muniments and letters which the English
then had, that bore against Scotland, as well as
all the claim to Scotland they could in any way
have. And King Robert, for the many injuries
that he had done the English by the strong hand
in his wars, was to pay twenty thousand pounds
of good silver money.[1]

When these things had been agreed upon, and
security given, with seals and oaths of friendship,
and of peace that never by any hap was to come
to an end, they appointed the marriage to be at
Berwick, and set the day when it should take
place; then each man went to his country.

---

[1] The full terms of the truce are to be found in Rymer's *Foedera*,
iv. 337, and the treaty itself is printed in Ker's *History of Bruce*,
ii. 526, from the original duplicate in the Register House, Edinburgh.
These documents recognized in the amplest manner the entire inde-
pendence of Scotland.

Thus was peace made where there was war before, and presently the sieges of Norham and Alnwick were raised. King Robert gave orders that the money be paid, and he made great arrangements for the feast against the day when his son David should be married. The Earl Thomas and the good Lord of Douglas he afterwards appointed to be stewards of that feast in his stead, for so sore a sickness seized him that he could by no means be there.

His disease began with a benumbing; for his sore trouble came upon him by reason of his lying out in the cold in his time of misfortune.

During all that time he lay at Cardross, and when the day was come nigh that was appointed for the wedding, the Earl and the Lord Douglas came with much pomp to Berwick, and brought the young David thither with them. On the other side the queen and Mortimer came with great ceremony and royal state, and they brought thither with rich display the young and beautiful princess. They made the marriage at Berwick with great feasting and solemnity. There was great mirth and gladness, for they made right great festivity, and the English and the Scots came together in joy and comfort, and no fierce word passed between them.

They kept the feast a very long time, and when they made ready to depart the queen left her daughter there with great riches and royal state. I trow that for many a year no lady was so richly brought home. The Earl and the Lord Douglas received her with honour, as, of a surety, was her due, for she was afterwards the best lady and the fairest to be seen.

After this great and solemn occasion, when both sides had taken their leave, the queen passed home to England, and the Mortimer with her. The Earl and those that were left, when they had conveyed her a space, rode again to Berwick, and afterwards, with all their company, went forthwith to the king, carrying with them the young David and Dame Joan, the young princess.

The king gave them fair welcome, and afterwards, without long delay, he caused a parliament to be called, and went thither with many knights. It was his plan in his own lifetime to crown his young son and his wife, and he did this at that parliament.

There, with great pomp and solemnity, King David was crowned, and all the lords who were there, and those of the commonalty as well, yielded him manrent and fealty. And before they were crowned, King Robert caused an ordinance to be passed that, should it happen that his son David died without heir-male of his body, Robert Stewart, whom his daughter Marjory had borne, should be king and enjoy the kingdom.

z

In order that this succession should be loyally
kept, all the lords made oath, and confirmed it
with their seals.[1]

And if it should happen that, while the princes
were young, King Robert should pass to God,
Thomas, the good Earl of Moray, and the Lord of
Douglas were to be their governors till they had
wisdom to manage affairs and take upon them
to rule. To this the two made oath, and all the
lords who were there sware their oaths to these
two wardens, to obey them loyally if they chanced
to have the wardenship.

When all this matter had been thus dealt with,
and securely confirmed, the king went to Cardross,[2]
and was there seized so cruelly with his sickness,
and was so sore oppressed, that he knew the
time had come for him to make the common end
of all this life, and to prepare for death when
God should send it. Therefore presently he sent
letters to the lords of his country, and they
came as he bade them. Then before these lords
and prelates he made his testament, and to many
religious bodies he gave money in great quantity

[1] The Act which settled the crown upon the Stewarts was passed
at a parliament held at Cambuskenneth in December, 1318.

[2] In what was then part of the parish of Cardross, a little to the
west of Dunbarton, on a farm still known as the Castle Hill,
tradition points out the site of the stronghold to which
Bruce retired in his last days, and in which the last pathetic
scene of his life took place.

for the saving of his soul. He provided right well for his soul, and when this was all done, he said, "Sirs, so far is the day gone with me that there is only one thing left, that is, without fear to meet death, as every man must needs do. I thank God that He has given me space to repent in this life, for through me and my wars there has been great spilling of blood, and many an innocent man has been slain. Therefore I take this sickness and this pain as a reward for my trespass.

"My heart was firmly fixed, for the saving of my sins, to make a crusade against God's enemies when I should come to prosperity. And since He now takes me to Him, so that the body cannot fulfil the device of the heart, I would that the heart, wherein that resolve was conceived, were sent thither. Therefore I pray you, every one, that among you ye choose me one who is honest, wise, and doughty, and a noble knight of his hand, to carry my heart against the enemies of God, when my soul and body shall be parted. I would that it were brought there worthily, since God will not that I have strength to go thither."

Then were their hearts all so sorrowful that none could keep from weeping. He bade them leave their sorrowing, "For this," said he, " could bring no relief, and must greatly afflict themselves." He prayed them to see forthwith to the matter with which they were charged.

At that they went forth heavily, and among them deemed it good that the worthy Lord Douglas, in whom was both wisdom and valour, should take this journey in hand. To this they all agreed; then they went to the king, and told him that they deemed of a truth the doughty Lord Douglas best fitted for that journey.

And when the king heard they had thus ordained to carry his heart the man whom he most desired should have it, he said, "As God Himself shall save me, I am right well pleased that ye have chosen him, for, ever since I thought to do this thing, his nobleness and valour set me yearning that he should carry it; and since ye are all agreed, it is the more to my liking. Let us see now what he says to it."

And when the good Lord of Douglas knew that the king had spoken thus, he came and knelt to him, and in this wise gave him thanks. "I thank you greatly, my master," said he, "for the many free and great benefits ye have ofttimes done me since first I came to your service; but above all I give you thanks that ye give me so noble and worthy a charge as to take in my keeping your heart, that was illustrious with all nobleness and valour. For you, sir, will I gladly make this journey, if God give me time and space."

The king thanked him tenderly, and there was none in that company but wept for pity; their cheer was grievous to see.

When the Lord Douglas had thus undertaken the high enterprise of bearing the good king's heart to the war against God's enemies, he was praised for his undertaking. And the king's infirmity waxed greater and greater, till at last the sad hour of death drew very near. And when he had caused to be done to him all that behoves a good Christian, with true repentance he gave up the ghost, and God took him to heaven, to be among His chosen people in joy, pleasure, and angel song.

And when his people knew that King Robert was dead, the sound of sorrow went from place to place. Men were to be seen tearing their hair, and seemly knights right sorely weeping, and wringing their hands, and rending their clothes like men who were mad, grieving for his valiant nobleness, his wisdom, strength, and honesty, and, above all, the great companionship that of his courtesy he often made them.

"Alas," they said, "all our defence, with him that was our comfort, our wisdom, and our leadership, is here brought to an end. His valour and his great strength made all doughty who were with him, and they could never be dismayed while they saw him before them. Alas! what shall we do or say? Ever while he lived we were feared by all our foes, and the renown of our valour ran through many a far country. All this was due to him alone!"

With such words they made their moan. And of a surety it was no marvel; for in no country could a better ruler be found. I wot that none living could describe the lamentation that these people made for their lord.

And when they had long sorrowed in this fashion, and he had been disembowelled, and richly embalmed, and the valiant Lord Douglas, as was before agreed, had with great honour received his heart, they bore him with much pomp and solemnity to Dunfermline, and solemnly buried him in a splendid tomb in the choir. Bishops and prelates absolved him there, and the service was performed as they could best devise. Then, on the next day, they went their way sad and sorrowful.[1]

---

[1] In the early years of the nineteenth century, when the Abbey Church of Dunfermline was being restored, the workmen came upon the remains of a splendid tomb in the spot which tradition assigned to the grave of Bruce. Within, amid fragments of cloth of gold, lay the skeleton of a tall man, and the fact that the breastbone had been sawn through confirmed the poet's account of the removal of the king's heart. Sir Walter Scott, who was present at the re-interment, describes the incident in his *Tales of a Grandfather*. See also the Report by Sir Henry Jardine in the Transactions of the Society of Antiquaries of Scotland.

When the good king was buried, Sir Thomas the Earl of Moray took the government of the whole country, and all obeyed his commands. And the good Lord of Douglas had a case made of fine silver exquisitely enamelled. In it he placed the king's heart, and bore it ever about his neck, and diligently made ready for his voyage. He made his testament, and ordained how his land should be governed by friends till his return. This and all things else that in any way pertained to him he arranged with such good and wise foresight before his going forth, that nothing could have been amended.

And when he had taken his leave, he took ship at Berwick, and with a noble company of knights and squires, put to sea, and sailed a long way to the south. He sailed between Cornwall and Brittany, and left the mainland of Spain to the north, and held his way, till he came to the great city of Seville. Though his men and he were greatly troubled with tempests at sea, they landed whole and sound.

They arrived at Grand Seville, and a little afterwards brought their horses every one ashore, and took quarters in the town. Douglas carried himself right richly, for he had a noble company, and gold enough to spend.

The King of Spain immediately sent for him, and received him right well, and proffered in

great abundance gold and treasure, horses and
armour. He would, however, take none of these,
" for," he said, " he took that journey upon pilgrim-
age against God's enemies, that his toil might
afterwards be for the saving of his soul. But
since he knew the king was at war with the
Saracens, he would remain there and help him
loyally with all his strength."

The king thanked him courteously, and com-
mitted to him good men who knew well the wars
of that country, and the manner of them. Then
Douglas went to his inn, and when the king had
left him, he made a right great sojourn there.
Knights of distant countries came in great crowds
to see him, and right hugely honoured him. And
above all men, the English knights who were
there most sovereignly honoured and bore him
company.

Among them was a stranger knight who was
held to be so wondrous doughty that he was
esteemed one of the best in all Christendom. So
much had his face been wounded that it was
nearly all covered with scars. Before he saw
the Lord Douglas he had supposed his face
must be scarred, but in it he had never a hurt.
When the knight saw it without scars, he said
he marvelled greatly that a knight so worthy,
and renowned for such great valour, should be
unscarred in the face. To this Douglas answered

quietly, and said, "God be praised, I had ever hands to shield my head."

Whoever gives heed to this answer may see in it an under-meaning, that if he that put the question had had hands to guard, mayhap his face which, in default of fence, was so broken in many places, should have been left whole and sound. The good knights standing by praised the answer greatly, for it was made with quiet speech, and bore right pregnant meaning.

In this manner they lay quiet till the rumour ran through the country that the haughty king of Belmarine, with many a proud Saracen, had entered Spain to waste the whole country. The King of Spain on the other side quickly gathered his host, and divided it into three battles. And to the Lord Douglas he gave the vanguard to lead and direct. He had all the foreign knights with him. The second battle the king committed to the Grand Master of Santiago, and the rearguard he took himself. Thus disposed, they fared forth to meet the enemy, who came against them right sturdily in battle order, ready to attack.

The valiant Douglas exhorted his host to fight well, and have no fear of death, since the bliss of heaven should be their reward if they died in God's service. Then, with these brave and veteran warriors, he stoutly joined the battle. Fierce was the fighting to be seen there, for all on the Christian side were bold and doughty men.

But ere they joined battle, I shall tell you what Douglas did. The Bruce's heart, which was hanging on his breast, he threw into the field a stone-cast or more, and said, " Now pass thou forth in front as thou wast wont to do in battle, and I shall follow, or else die." This he did without ceasing; he fought till he came to it, and took it up with great honour. Ever thus he fought in the field.[1]

So hard they fought, with all their might, that many of the Saracens were slain. Nevertheless, with their fell falchions they struck down many a Christian there. At last the Lord Douglas and the great host with him pressed the Saracens so hard that they altogether turned their backs. The Christian knights pursued with all their strength, and slew many in the chase. So far did the Lord Douglas with a few followers carry the pursuit that he was past all the knights joining in it. He had not with him above ten of all his company. When he saw that all the pursuit had stopped, he turned towards his host. And as he turned he saw that all the Saracens turned again,

---

[1] On account of the rhymes used, the contents of this paragraph, which are found only in Hart's edition of the poems, are considered, both by Professor Skeat and Mr. J. T. T. Brown, to have been added by a later hand than Barbour's.

and rallied in great strength. Then he saw, close beside him, Sir William de St. Clair surrounded with a great host. At that he was distressed, and said, " Yonder worthy knight will soon be slain unless he have help from us. God bids us speed to help him, since we are so near at hand, and God knows well our resolve is to live and die in his service. His will in all things shall we do, and shall spare no peril till yonder knight be brought out of his danger, or we be all slain with him."

With that they struck spurs into their steeds, and forthwith rode among the Saracens. There they made room about them, and dealt blows fast with all their might; and slew many. Never was greater defence made by so few against so many as was made by these knights while they could stand to give battle. But no valour could avail them there, and every one was slain. The Saracens were nigh twenty for their one. The good Lord Douglas was slain, and Sir William St. Clair as well, with two other valiant knights, Sir Robert and Sir Walter Logan. Our Lord, for His greatness' sake, receive their souls to the bliss of heaven!

Thus was the good Lord Douglas slain. As for the Saracens, they tarried no more in that place, but made off, leaving their knights dead on the field. Some of the Lord Douglas's men found their

lord dead, and went wellnigh mad for sorrow and
despair. They mourned long over him, and with
great lamentation bore him home. They found
the king's heart on the spot, and took that home
with them, and went towards their quarters with
weeping and evil cheer. Their sorrowing was
grievous to hear.

Good Sir William of Keith had been all that
day at home; for, by his great misfortune, because
of a broken arm, he came not that day to the
battle. When he saw the people make such sorrow-
ing he asked quickly what it was, and they told
him frankly how their doughty lord had been
slain by the Saracens when they rallied. And
when he knew how it was, he was most sorrowful
of all, and made such wondrous evil cheer that
all who were by him marvelled.

But it were grievous and to little purpose to
tell of their sorrowing. It can be well understood
without being told, how grievous, sorrowful, and
dire a thing it was to his host to lose such a
lord as Douglas; for he was sweet and debonair,
and dealt well and fairly by his friends, and by
his great feats of arms right fiercely dismayed his
foes. Pomp he loved little, but above all things
he loved loyalty. Treason he detested so greatly
that no traitor could come near him, to his
knowledge, without being well punished for his
crime.

I trow the loyal Fabricius, who was sent with a great host from Rome to war against Pyrrhus, hated treason no more than he. When this Pyrrhus had made dreadful discomfiture of him and his host, from which he escaped by chance while many of his men were slain, and when Fabricius gathered a host again, a great master of medicine, who had Pyrrhus' health in his keeping, made offer to Fabricius to slay Pyrrhus by treason, by giving him deadly poison in his first draught. Fabricius marvelled that he made him such an offer, and said, "Certes, Rome is well able, by strength of arms, to overcome her foes in battle, but by no means does she stoop to treason. And since thou wouldst do this treachery, thou shalt, for thy reward, go tell Pyrrhus, and let him do to thee whatever seems good to him." Then he sent the physician to Pyrrhus, and made him tell the whole tale openly from end to end.

When Pyrrhus had heard it all, he said, "Never was there a man who bore himself so loyally to his enemy as Fabricius does to me. It is as difficult to turn him from the path of right, or to make him consent to treachery, as at mid-day to turn back the sun while he openly runs his race."

Thus Pyrrhus spoke of Fabricius, who afterwards vanquished him by hard fighting in open battle. The honest loyalty of Fabricius caused me to bring him in here as an example, for he had sovereign renown for his loyalty. This, too, had the Lord Douglas, who was honest, loyal, and valiant. For his death all, stranger and friend, made lamentation.

When his men had long mourned him, they disembowelled him, and caused him to be seethed, that the flesh might be taken wholly from the bones. The flesh they buried there in holy ground with right great reverence; the bones they took with them, and went to their ships.

They took leave of the Spanish king, who sorrowed for their grief; then they went to sea, and with a fair wind shaped their course for England. There they arrived in safety, and afterwards made their way towards Scotland, where they arrived full soon. The bones were right honourably buried with great care and sorrow in the Kirk of Douglas, and Sir Archibald, the good Lord Douglas's son,[1] afterwards caused a tomb to be set up of rich alabaster, fine and fair, such as behoved so valiant a knight.[2]

[1] The Good Lord James of Douglas was unmarried. His natural son was Sir William Douglas, afterwards variously known as the Knight of Liddesdale and the Flower of Chivalry. The Archibald Douglas mentioned by Barbour was, according to the family historian, the Good Lord's third brother, "Lord of Galloway and Governor of Scotland."

[2] A generation ago, when the Earl of Home, descendant of the Douglases, and holder of their estates, restored the choir of St.

When Sir William of Keith had in this fashion
brought home the bones of Douglas and the heart
of the good king, and the bones had been buried
with rich and splendid pomp, the Earl of Moray,
who at that time had the whole care of Scotland,
caused the king's heart to be buried with great
reverence at the Abbey of Melrose. There prayer
is constantly made that he and his may dwell in
Paradise.[1]

After this was done the good Earl governed
the land, protecting well the poor, and upholding
the law so well, and keeping the country so in
peace that never since his day has it been
governed so ably. Thus have I heard old men
say. But alas! he was afterwards poisoned; his
death was a grievous sight.[2]

Thus died these lords. May the supreme Lord
of all bring them to His great bliss, and grant of
His grace that their offspring govern well the

Bride's Kirk at Douglas, the tomb of the Good Lord James was
discovered, and at the present day his heart, in a silver case,
along with the heart of a later head of the house of Douglas,
Archibald Bell-the-Cat, rests within a stone combing in the
choir floor.

[1] Bruce had restored Melrose Abbey, and the resting-place of
his heart is pointed out under the great eastern window of the
choir there. The spot and circumstance receive full honour in a
famous passage of "The Lay of the Last Minstrel."

[2] Moray died at Musselburgh July 20, 1332. Scott believed the
pathetic ballad of "Lord Randal" to refer to this death.

land, and give heed to follow through all their
life their noble forefathers' great excellence!

The Triune God bring us to the high bliss of
heaven, where everlasting happiness is found!
Amen.

THE END.

GLASGOW : PRINTED AT THE UNIVERSITY PRESS BY ROBERT MACLEHOSE AND CO. LTD